LIVING DOLL

Published by Metro Publishing Ltd, 3 Bramber Court,
2 Bramber Road, London W14 9PB, England

First published in hardback in 2002

ISBN 1 84358 049 7

British Library Cataloguing-in-Publication Data: A catalogue record for this book is available from the British Library.

Design by ENVY

Printed and bound in Great Britain by CPD (Wales)

1 3 5 7 9 10 8 6 4 2

Papers used by Metro Publishing Ltd are natural, recyclable products made from wood grown in sustainable forests. The manufacturing processes conform to the environmental regulations of the country of origin.

CINDY JACKSON

LIVING DOLL

Cindy Jackson x

For S.H.A.C.

Contents

Prologue

I first went public with my cosmetic surgery back in 1989. As a result, I inadvertently became famous for having had a lot of operations, which is something I never expected. Since then a good deal of misinformation about me has found its way into the public domain. I have long been uncomfortable with this and that's one reason I decided to write my autobiography. Whether the facts were distorted in my favour or against me is immaterial. From my point of view, attempts to sensationalise my story have been disappointing because the truth is much more incredible than anything that has been invented so far.

There has also been speculation about my family and background. Some of the things that have been said and written about them are so wide of the mark that I felt duty-bound to set the record straight for the sake of my loved ones. This is also *their* story. And – as is the case with anyone who writes with honesty and candour about their families – I had to open some closets and give a few skeletons a good rattle to do so. I am grateful to all of my relatives for giving their blessing for this book to go ahead, especially my sister Gloria. She preserved memories and photographs that would have otherwise been lost forever – as well as the Barbie doll I was given in 1961 that became my talisman.

I also wish to thank my friend Jackie Holland for getting me started, my editors, Adam Parfitt and Isabelle Almeida, for their kindness, the boys at Envy design, and my publisher John Blake and his lovely deputy Rosie, for giving me the opportunity to tell my story.

My sanity and motivations for transforming my face and body to such an extreme extent have been hotly debated in classrooms and on thousands of Internet sites. I am in textbooks and have even been the subject of several university theses. Certain sectors of the art world have declared me a 'performance artist'. Barbie doll aficionados either dismiss me outright or regard me as the ultimate collector. Frankly, I find a good deal of this attention – and the level of emotion attached to it – rather spurious since no one could have known the whole story until now.

Over the years I've been sent hundreds of thousands of letters and case histories from my fellow cosmetic surgery patients. They asked how I managed to deal with the medical establishment and get the results I wanted while so many others, both in and out of the public eye, have failed. This book is also for them.

My other book, *Cindy Jackson's Image and Cosmetic Surgery Secrets including the Ultimate Guide to Cosmetic Surgery,* is available from www.cindyjackson.com for prospective patients.

Finally, the question that I am most often asked: 'Why on earth would anyone have so *much* cosmetic surgery?' is answered within these pages.

In order to fully explain all of the above it was necessary to go back to the very beginning and share the genetic and environmental influences that shaped me just as profoundly as did the surgeon's scalpel. For the very first time, here is my extraordinary *true* life story. Because, as John Keats so famously said, 'Beauty is truth, truth beauty...'

Chapter One

Rag Doll

It was 1961. John F Kennedy was inaugurated as US President and 400 combat troops were dispatched to South Vietnam. Chubby Checker invented The Twist, Ernest Hemingway committed suicide and Alan Shepherd became the first American to venture into space. That same year, I took the controls of my father's rickety old airplane and soared above the fields of Ohio. Not exactly a giant leap for mankind you may think, but no small feat considering I was only six years old.

Dad's passion was flying. His 1947 Stinson had dark-blue cloth skin stretched over an aluminium frame, a single propeller and four cracked, grainy leather seats.

The Midwest goes on forever and, as we were a family of hicks living in the middle of a vast, flat farming community, that noisy little plane provided a diversion and a way of getting to Indiana, home of our relatives. We lived just outside Fremont, a one-horse town with one main thoroughfare. Front Street boasted a few shops, such as Woolworth's, JC Penny and Joseph's Department Store, but getting there was a very long walk.

My older sister Gloria and I were often strapped into the cramped space at the back of that plane, our knees crammed up towards our faces because the rear seats were hammock style without firm support underneath. This made them easy to remove for extra cargo space. I couldn't see out of the window because I was too small. All I could feel, apart from fear and the obvious discomfort, was the sensation of the plane rising steeply on take-off and roller-coasting into the clouds, as Dad had his fun doing lazy eights and stalls.

I dreaded getting into that plane. My father knew flying scared me, so he teased me mercilessly. As he taxied for take-off, he turned around with a wicked grin and made remarks like: 'Did I ever tell you about the time the back seats fell out?' It was his idea of a joke, but being too young to understand, I believed every word he said.

'Why don't you like flying?' he suddenly asked me one day. It was beyond his comprehension that his jaunty trips into the skies should not be enjoyable.

'B-b-b-ecause I c-c-can't see out of the w-w-window,' I replied, with the chronic stammer I suffered until I reached my teens. For some reason my mouth didn't quite work and I found it difficult to form words. Losing my speech impediment was to be the first of many steps I would later take to completely transform my life.

Next flight, he fetched a pile of thick telephone books, placed them in a heap on the co-pilot's seat, lifted me up and sat me on top of them, and fastened my seat belt. My feet didn't touch the floor, but at least I could see what was happening outside. I didn't like it. The ground disappeared below and the trees became smaller and smaller. From the air the trees looked like bunches of broccoli, the fields like one of grandma's patchwork quilts.

Dad then barked instructions as to how the plane worked. I suppose he was trying to ease my fear of flying but it didn't really help.

'Look out of your side. Keep the wing parallel with the horizon.'

I didn't understand what the horizon was.

'When you see where the sky meets the earth, that's the horizon. Keep your wing parallel with it.'

I didn't know what parallel meant.

Pointing to one of the dials, he hollered above the engine noise, 'Hold the altitude steady at 1,500 feet. If you start to dive, pull back on the control. If you start to climb, push it forward.' He suddenly let go of the controls, sat back and crossed his arms in a rigid act of authority.

'OK, now you fly the plane.'

The lesson was obviously over. What happened next is a blur. All I could hear was shouting from Dad, and all I could see was a sea of dials on the control panel. I don't remember how we got back to the ground. From that day, the fear of flying gripped me with a vengeance. For many years I suffered with recurring nightmares involving plane crashes and endless runways.

My father, born in 1914, was an only child who grew up in Indiana during the Depression, on an isolated farm. Perhaps it's understandable that he had a communication problem with children, adults or any other form of life. Instead of being a fighter pilot during the Second World War, like some of his friends, Dad was assigned to work in a factory making aircraft brake linings.

My mother was the second of six children born to a poor but hard-working Kentucky coal miner in 1921. She married my father, who was seven years her senior, when she was 24. They both worked in another factory, Delco Remy, Dad as an engineer, Mom on the assembly line. Shortly after their marriage they left Indiana and settled in Ohio.

Dad was 38 when my sister Gloria was born. I arrived by mistake three years later. Dad made no secret of the fact he had desperately wanted a son. So he did his best to overlook the fact that he had two daughters, bragging that he treated his girls just like boys. In other words he expected us to pull our weight from a very early age. This included, but was by no means limited to, shovelling snow and chopping firewood in the winter, and mowing the grass and looking after the vegetable gardens in the summer.

Mom was very beautiful but terribly introverted. She was completely overshadowed by Dad. He didn't want to mix with other people. Mom was his constant companion because he worked at home. Dad was not a touchy-feely type and never demonstrated any kind of affection. He watched Mom like a hawk and became jealous if anyone outside the family talked to her. Dad was always shouting at her. He made sure everyone knew he was the boss, and yelling was his mode of communication.

Although he made a lot of noise, he didn't really talk. His shouting scared me, so I hid whenever he started one of his verbal tirades. If I couldn't get away from him, I'd just tune him out.

I can't remember ever having a conversation of any merit with Dad. Even when we were very small, he never spoke to my sister or me as if we were children. Instead, he barked orders at us using complicated technical terms peppered with liberal doses of obscenity. There was never any reward or encouragement for our efforts; only criticism and punishment for things we didn't do perfectly.

All of my life I've been told that I'm overly sensitive to criticism. Physical pain has always been easier for me to endure than psychological pain. I was born in the summer of 1955, so my star sign is Cancer and in Chinese astrology I'm a Goat. Both interpretations note the extreme sensitivity of people born at this time. Whether or not it's due to my birth sign, I definitely fit that particular description. Comments that others would just laugh off wounded me deeply.

We lived in a farmhouse out in the country. It wasn't a working farm as such, and we didn't keep livestock. We grew our own tomatoes, potatoes, corn, peas, radishes, watermelons and pumpkins. Tools were kept in the chicken coop instead of chickens.

Never destined to be conventional, Dad considered himself to be an inventor. Although he had no interest in boating and we were miles from the lake, he converted our barn into a small factory where he spent hour after hour making boat anchors. From the ages of seven and four respectively, Gloria and I were forced to work as unpaid labourers, doing men's jobs in his makeshift factory. Surprisingly, he turned anchor manufacturing into a viable business and managed to sell his creations to marine supply companies in California and Florida, and even to the US Navy. Enormous freight-hauling trucks arrived at the house to collect them.

Dad stored a lot of boat anchor parts and machinery outdoors behind the chicken coop and the barn. To keep the rain and snow off them, he made Gloria and I cover them with crumbling sheets of asbestos from the supply he kept in the barn.

Being a loner, Dad was compelled to work for himself. He claimed that during the time he worked for a company in Indiana called Wayne Pump he developed an idea that would have made him a fortune – but it was stolen from him. Dad said he invented the device used at filling stations that cuts off the supply from the gasoline pump as soon as the car's tank is full. But, he complained bitterly, the company kept the patent because he was an employee. This was why he never worked for anyone else again, apart from himself, that is.

Dad was the ultimate gadget freak, always busy customising bits of machinery. He was forever writing letters to various component manufacturers to point out their design faults and put forward his recommendation for corrective modifications.

No project was too daunting. Dad even built his own hi-fi system, housed in a white-and-gold-flecked cabinet on legs, on which he played 78rpm vinyl albums of Roaring Twenties music. When Dad wasn't around, Gloria and I put his albums on and danced the Charleston. Sometimes Mom, who had taught us the moves, would join in. He also had a sound effects record, which I hated because he played it full blast so it sounded just like a freight train was tearing through the house.

Dad had a series of cars and trucks that he perpetually took apart and put back together again. There were always spare parts scattered around the yard, the barn and throughout the house. We often had to eat off our laps because parts from the current project would be all over the dining table.

Since the barn had been converted into a factory there was no room for Dad's vehicles. His solution was to build an aircraft hangar for them. He obtained the corrugated aluminium steel panels – direct from the manufacturer – and erected them in the yard. He attached one end to the barn so he would need fewer panels, using the side of the barn as a common wall. The result was a bizarre structure consisting of a traditional-looking wooden barn with a colossal soaring silver carbuncle bolted on to its left side. Dad was thrilled with the results of his handiwork, but aesthetics were never his number one priority. (By contrast, I'd been born obsessed with them.)

The first car I remember him having was a dark blue Chevy with a grey interior and running boards, the type you often see in gangster movies. The only vacations we went on were to visit our relatives in Indiana. Dad drove the car in the same way he piloted the plane – like a maniac. He tore along like a bat out of hell and cursed and shouted at other drivers. Hot ash from the pipe he smoked blew all over Gloria and me in the back seat, and burned tiny holes in our matching dresses.

One summer Dad drove us all the way to New York because he wanted to see the new inventions exhibited at the World's Fair. Being accident-prone as he was, Dad had lost part of the index and middle fingers on his right hand in a meat grinder, making hamburgers when he was a teenager back on his parents' farm. On the way to the Big Apple, we had a minor crash in Philadelphia when Dad rear-ended another car, but not too much damage was done and no one was hurt. (Before I was born Dad had a light blue Cadillac that he wrote off in a more serious accident.)

When we finally got to New York City, the first thing I noticed was the air. It was heavy and smelled like exhaust fumes compared to the fresh country air I was used to breathing. And I wondered why everyone in New York City was in a bad mood, especially the taxi drivers. They were almost as mad at everyone else on the road as my Dad was. We stayed in the cheapest roadside motel Dad could find in nearby New Jersey, all sharing the same room to save money.

The World's Fair was fascinating. There were all kinds of amazing exhibitions, including a 'House of the Future', which had a kitchen full of labour-saving appliances for housewives of the future. One display had a television, and when you got right in front of it to see what was on, you were actually on TV. When I went to look and unexpectedly saw my own face on the screen, it was a tremendous shock. I got away from it as quickly as I could, blushing furiously.

Of all the exhibitions, the one I liked best was a live river otter in a muddy glass tank. It was the cutest thing I had ever seen. I was so disappointed when Dad dragged me away muttering that we hadn't come all the way to New York City to look at 'varmits'.

We got back safely to Fremont with a new blender Dad had seen demonstrated at the House of the Future. To him it was amazing, the best invention ever. He blended everything, and we had liquid meals for months afterwards ('Until the new wore off,' as Mom observed) and every drink was a milkshake.

Mom and Dad possessed that hillbilly clannishness which meant they didn't trust strangers, so they had few friends. One family we were allowed to be friendly with were the Dresslers, who ran the small local airport where Dad kept his plane. They had five kids, including a boy my age named Donny. When I was a toddler, my parents used to put me into his playpen to keep me occupied while the adults talked about airplanes and flying.

Dad also used to hang out with Ernie, who ran his own

plumbing and sewage repair business. His clothes had a wet, dirty look, but Dad didn't seem to notice, and they swapped tools and repair ideas. That was about the extent of his social life.

We also took a couple of trips to Grosse-Point, a classy suburb of Detroit. Dad had a friend who lived there. They had been neighbours back in Indiana when they were young, and then this guy made it big and moved away. Grosse-Point was *the* place to live in Michigan. The day I walked into his antique-filled mansion changed my life. Suddenly I realised exactly what I was missing.

Dad's friend showed us around the neighbourhood. As we strolled along the tree-lined avenue, a stylish woman with long blonde hair glided past me with two longhaired Afghan hounds in tow. Her hair was flowing; the dogs' hair was flowing. Her name, I later discovered, was Charlotte Ford. She was married to the man who ran Ford Motors and she was Dad's friend's neighbour.

I couldn't wait to grow up to be exactly like Charlotte Ford. I hated my own life. From my very first day of school, at the age of four, I got a sinking feeling whenever the school bus picked me up. My heart sank even more when it dropped me off in the evening, because I had to be a labourer in my father's noisy factory. Every single day the driver would make us sing: 'I've been workin' on the railroad, all the livelong day, I've been workin' on the railroad, just to pass the time away ...' I thought he was cool, and singing along cheered me up, but unfortunately he only knew one song. To this day, I can still sing it from beginning to end.

All of us children were told to bring a blanket from home for our afternoon nap. Other kids had nice fluffy, normal blankets. I was given a tatty bathroom rug to take 'in case something happened to it'. Not that I ever got any sleep at school anyway. I could never relax enough. Instead, I lay down and pretended to be asleep for the allotted time, watching the other children through half-closed eyes as they drooled and snored. I didn't feel like one of them. I felt like an alien.

The isolated existence my father insisted on had left me lagging far behind in social skills. What's more, it was impossible to identify with other kids because their lives were so different from mine. Where they went home after school to watch TV, I went home to work in a factory. While playing came naturally to them, at break I watched from the sidelines, wanting to join in but not knowing how. They would gleefully look forward to celebrating Christmas. My father, being the ultimate killjoy, declared it 'just another day' at our house. Halloween was the only holiday I enjoyed. I liked getting dressed up and wearing a mask – a pre-echo of things to come. Hiding behind another identity allowed me to be less of an introvert.

Even my birthday had to be different. Other children celebrated theirs openly, bringing treats for everyone and having 'Happy Birthday' sung to them by the rest of the class. Mine fell during summer vacation so nobody knew I even had one. That's also the reason why I started school at only four. My parents were given the option of putting me in a year early, and they took it.

Being the smallest and least popular, I was always the last one to be chosen by team captains to be on their side for volleyball and baseball games. I suppose being clumsy didn't help either. On the rare occasions the ball was passed to me, I would invariably drop it, much to the dismay of my fellow players. That's why I avoided team sports whenever I could. By the time I reached high school, I'd managed to obtain a doctor's note permanently excusing me automatically from gym class. My clumsiness, of course, automatically ruled out a great number of career options, ranging from professional athelete to brain surgeon.

At lunch I had to sit with the other misfits because there were separate lines for children who bought the school lunch and those who only purchased milk to go with their packed lunch. You could never miss which lunch was mine. My crumpled, grease-spotted brown paper bag stood out among the crisp new paper bags and colourful lunchboxes decorated with the latest cartoon characters carried by other children. Mom was under strict instructions to pack school lunches, because it was cheaper than paying for my lunch. I was under strict instructions to bring the bag home for re-use.

Although I excelled at reading and writing, I found arithmetic – and later mathematics – a complete mystery. To me, each number stood alone, and the mental process that required it to change into another number by interacting with yet another left me dazed and confused. My solution was to memorise the images of the tables and exercises in the textbook, like taking a picture. That came easily to me and, as long as I'd seen the equations, I got perfect grades. (My photographic memory also means that I never forget a face.)

The difficult part came when we were asked to add, subtract, divide or multiply number combinations I'd never seen before. I went from getting A+ in arithmetic to getting D-. No one could understand it. (The fact that Gloria's superior abilities in the subject meant she was put into the Advanced Maths Class did little to enhance my self-esteem.) In addition, I suffer from a form of numeric dyslexia where more than three numbers in a row begin to transpose. There was clearly no future for me as an accountant or air traffic controller either.

My severe lack of physical co-ordination extended to my inability to hold a pencil like everyone else. It was yet another thing that set me apart. So did my handwriting. I had trouble with joined-up writing, so I used to print as neatly as I could. At the height of my obsession with printing, my homework looked like it had been typewritten. Despite being corrected incessantly, to this day I cannot hold a writing instrument 'normally'. And my handwriting has deteriorated to the point where it resembles chicken scratching – a drunk chicken at that.

Although I loved reading, I hated the material we were assigned to read. The characters in our schoolbooks were called Dick and Jane, and I couldn't have cared less about them. They sounded silly and childish. I preferred a book I had at home entitled *The Enchanted Egg*. It was about a gigantic egg in the middle of a forest. This beautiful white and gold egg had a window and inside you could glimpse a magical paradise. How I wished I could go and live in that egg.

Instead, there was dirt under my fingernails from dragging anchors around, and my clothes were no better than rags. Some of the other girls had pretty dresses, shiny shoes and satin ribbons in their hair. I wondered what it was like to be them, instead of the tomboy Dad forced me to be.

My mother must have also secretly yearned for a more glamorous life. She subscribed to *Harper's Bazaar* magazine. I used to flip through the pages and gaze in awe at pictures of gorgeous models in fancy clothes, longing to be one of the beautiful people. But when I looked into the mirror, I was confronted by the truth. The way I looked betrayed what I felt inside. Fate had dealt me the wrong face, the wrong body. What's more, I had been born in the wrong place to the wrong people. I was odd, different, strange.

Others noticed, too. When Mom went to parents' night at the grade school, she reported that my teacher, Mrs Harmon, told her, 'Cindy lives in a dream world.' It was many years later that I found out that Mrs Harmon also told my mother she thought I was mildly autistic. Back then, there was still a huge stigma attached to such things, so Mom played it down. She didn't want Dad to know what my teacher had really said. I guess she didn't want to give him any more ammunition.

I retreated further and further into a world of my own. And that world existed in the future tense – I was never in the here and now. That would have been too painful. I lived for the day that things would be different. And somehow I knew they would be. That certainty was the only thing that kept me going.

Mom used to say I had delusions of grandeur. At least my so-called 'delusions' were a vast improvement on reality. Far from being swathed in elegant designer outfits like the grown-up models of my fantasies, I wore nothing but worn-out hand-me-downs, having been assigned Gloria's old cast-offs. But she was very feminine and girly, wearing things like flower-print dresses with puffed sleeves decorated with big bows in the back. None of Gloria's clothes suited me. They didn't even fit. She was bigger and taller than I was. Being small and painfully skinny, I swam in her twist skirt decorated with a poodle motif. It looked more like a dog in a dress than a girl with a dog on her dress.

My insignificance was reinforced at every turn. When I was finally taken shopping for my 'own' clothes, Mom would let Gloria choose an outfit and then just buy an identical one for me in a smaller size. Furthermore, my family would amuse themselves by endlessly repeating the story of how three-year-old Gloria, on being introduced to me as a baby for the first time, begged my parents to take me back to the hospital. (Nowadays the joke is that I won't stop going back to the hospital.)

Gloria reminded me of the blonde daughter Marilyn in *The Munsters* TV show. She was the only normal person in our family, which meant she stuck out like a sore thumb. She was pretty and graceful, while I was gawky and unco-ordinated with knobby knees and a big nose. Mom had thick, luxurious auburn hair and didn't understand the dynamics of fine fair hair like mine. She periodically permed our hair with a Toni home-curl kit. Whereas Gloria's turned out bubbly and cute, mine ended up as fuzzy as candyfloss.

Every summer we went barefoot, and by autumn the soles of our feet would be tough as shoe leather. Then when it was time to get new shoes for school, we ordered them from the catalogue. Mom drew around our feet with a pencil then sent the tracing off to Montgomery Ward – or 'Monkey Ward' as it was known in our house. I was 16 years old the first time I experienced the luxury of going into a store and trying on a pair of shoes before buying them.

I was not a particularly healthy child. When I was three years old I had severe tonsillitis and my tonsils had to be removed. I got the chickenpox, measles and mumps when they were going around. Every winter I suffered a non-stop marathon of colds and flu. I had a weak stomach and threw up a lot. Mom was invariably kindly and sympathetic but we were rarely taken to see the doctor. Her standard remedy for whatever ailed us was always Coca-Cola and dry Saltine crackers.

Mom also cut our hair. I didn't go to a professional hairdresser until I was 20. She cut my fringe half an inch long and I looked like Buster Brown. Added to this, the water supply to our house was pumped from a well. The water was rich in iron and even though Mom washed our hair with green Prell Shampoo, it still turned orange.

When Dad read a report about skin cancer and decided the sun was bad for us, Mom smeared us with Vaseline, thinking it would protect us. And I, of course, being pale with white eyelashes and eyebrows, ended up bright red and blistered, while Gloria remained pristinely beautiful. Gloria was popular and had lots of friends. Gloria was a straight A student. She seemed perfect in every single way. I noticed that other people, including my parents, often deferred to her.

I admired Gloria's perfection and self-confidence. Next to her I felt awkward and ugly. I didn't look anything like her or anyone else I knew, which convinced me that I didn't belong to my family. My father had a makeshift office in the house, in which there was a filing cabinet and a small safe where he kept all his papers. Whenever Mom and Dad were out working in the yard or taking a trip into town, I sneaked in and rifled through them. I found insurance documents, the deeds to the house ... and Gloria's birth certificate. Mine was nowhere to be found. Now all I needed to do was to find my adoption papers. I searched and searched, but I never did find them.

Over the years, I have come to realise that I take after my father, and not only in looks. I inherited his sense of adventure, which one day would take me all over the world. We also share a love of music – during his youth, he played trumpet in a Glenn Miller-style big band – and I would eventually become the lead singer in a rock band. Most of all, I inherited his inventiveness. But whereas Dad invented ridiculous gadgets, I was to completely reinvent myself. And like my own plan, Dad's schemes were often hatched as a determined effort to triumph over Mother Nature.

Northern Ohio is flat, very windy and we often had tornadoes. When we got our first colour TV so we could watch Dad's favourite programme, *Bonanza,* in colour, the outside aerial became very important. It kept blowing off the roof of our two-storey farmhouse, leaving us staring at a static-filled screen. Dad would be forever climbing up a ladder to fix it. He had guy wires all over the house trying to hold the aerial in place but it still kept blowing down. One day he had finally had enough. He came up with the bright idea of driving huge scaffolding poles into the ground beside the house. Then he bolted on a series of horizontal metal bars that linked the scaffolding to the aerial, starting at ground level and reaching up as high as the eye could see. It looked like the Eiffel Tower. The aerial never blew off again. He was a determined man, and I inherited that determination.

I'm grateful to Dad for the positive traits he passed on to me, but I didn't inherit his relentless obsession with saving money. He had lived through the Great Depression and he always believed there was another one around the corner. Nevertheless, the prospect of making easy money by playing the stockmarket was more than he could resist, so he invested in a few stocks and shares and kept a watchful eye on their progress. He was always grumbling about the economy and making pronouncements as he watched the news or read the paper. He automatically assumed that his opinions were all of our opinions. There was never any debate.

Not only had slave labour not been abolished in our house, but also the democratic process was not recognised. Instead, we lived in a dictatorship, redneck-style. When he and my mother went to vote, Dad bullied her into casting her ballot the same way as he did. He reasoned there was no point in going to the polls at all if they were just going to cancel out each other's vote. My grandmothers could remember not being allowed the freedom to vote. And – despite the fact that American women had been granted that constitutional right in 1920 – so could my Mom.

Dad never paid the full price for anything if he could help it. When we went to the grocery store, he always made a beeline for day-old bread and doughnuts or dented cans of baked beans and spaghetti in tomato sauce ('Spaghetti al dent' as we now call it) at marked down prices. We cringed with embarrassment while he insisted that all produce sold by weight be placed on the scale loose and only put into the small paper bag *after* it had been weighed and priced. 'I'm not paying for the damned bag,' he bellowed loud enough for the whole store to hear. He would go to the cash register with fistfuls of money-saving coupons that he'd painstakingly clipped out of the local newspaper. If any had expired, he steadfastly refused to take no for an answer, insisting the store honour them anyway, ignoring the growing line of impatient shoppers who glared at the backs of our heads.

When we got home we always had to go through the ritual of checking off all the grocery items in the bags against the receipt, to make sure Dad hadn't been overcharged for anything and that nothing was missing. New bottles of aspirin and vitamin pills were emptied on to a page from the evening paper spread out on the dining room table. Each tablet was carefully counted and the totals checked against the content stated on the bottle. The brown paper grocery sacks were neatly folded and placed next to the fireplace where they would be used to carry cinders and ashes to the front porch.

To save on heating bills, Dad hacked down trees with a chainsaw for firewood. All flammable waste and junk was regarded as fuel and burned in the fireplace. He counted how many squares of toilet paper we used, and regularly drove to another town to save half a cent on a tank of gas. Dad was more than a little paranoid about being ripped off. His worst nightmare would be to buy something and then see it cheaper somewhere else. On those occasions, the item, no matter how much it had been used, would be polished up and reunited with its original receipt, always kept on file, and Gloria or I would be sent back into the store to obtain a refund. Then Dad would buy the item elsewhere at the cheaper price.

I can remember him being generous to me only once when I was small. It was Sunday lunchtime and Mom had served tinned fruit cocktail for dessert. As I looked around the table, I noticed that everyone had a juicy maraschino cherry on top of their fruit cocktail except me, which was just typical of my luck. I burst into tears at the injustice of it all and, to my amazement, Dad actually gave me the cherry off his. But I'm sure he only did it because Mom's family was visiting – he always acted differently in front of other people. Not that it mattered to me at the time. It just felt good to be given that cherry by Dad.

Retail outlets and the economy weren't the only threats to Dad's resources. He couldn't bear the thought that nature might deliver him a raw deal. He covered the potatoes and corn growing in our vegetable garden with a noxious concoction and was constantly checking them for bugs. If there was so much as a bite out of a leaf on one of his plants he flew into a rage, mixed up more DDT and sprayed it all over them again. Between Dad's enthusiasm for pesticides and the 'crop dusters' – the airplanes that swooped down on the fields surrounding our house dumping poison on to the crops and turning the air brown with toxins – the local bugs didn't stand a chance.

We had to inspect the tomato plants for tomato worms, which are bright green, about half an inch thick and around five inches long. If you touch them, they stand up on their haunches as if spoiling for a fight. I was afraid of them. Gloria and I were ordered to flick them off with a stick into a can of used motor oil. Dad was the drill sergeant and he forced us to be his troops in his eternal battle against nature. I hated having to kill anything, even the horrible tomato worms.

It would also infuriate my father if birds dared to peck at the fruit on our apple, pear and cherry trees. As a treat, my mother bought Lemon Chiffon Pies (five for a dollar) which came in tin foil pans. So Dad invented his own bird repellent. He sent Gloria and me up a 25-foot rickety wooden ladder to tie these pie pans all over the trees. They frightened the birds when they rattled in the breeze. The method worked, but our trees looked ridiculous.

I didn't inherit Dad's cruelty to animals either. Like most farmers, Dad owned an assortment of guns. He had rifles, shotguns and various pistols that were kept in a cabinet behind the kitchen door. At the end of our back yard there were woods where rabbits, ground hogs, raccoons and chipmunks frolicked and the occasional deer ambled by. Dad used these defenceless creatures for target practise on the ground and blew birds right out of the sky. He ordered me to gather up the rabbits he had shot and bring them to him so he could cut off their heads and skin them for supper. Later I would watch him at the table picking the buckshot out of his rabbit stew, while all I could do was stare at mine, unable to take so much as a single bite. Most of the other animals Dad shot were deemed inedible and tossed unceremoniously into the gully. (These days I'm a committed vegetarian and dedicated animal rights supporter.)

I loved animals and my father knew it. He was well aware that watching him kill them devastated me. That's one of the reasons he did it, and the sole reason he made me collect the bodies. He thought repeated exposure to the broken and bloodied bodies of the animals I loved would 'toughen me up', like he believed that forcing me to fly his airplane would cure my fear of flying. He could not have been more wrong in either case. Instead, these experiences taught me to disguise who I really am in order to protect myself and the things I love.

Dad would ruthlessly exploit any form of weakness you showed. If I didn't behave – like being too young to know my left from my right – he threatened to shoot my kittens. Once, when one of them became sick, he actually did blow its head off with his shotgun. He didn't want the expense of taking it to the vet and took great pride in the economy of his solution, bragging to his friends in front of me for weeks afterwards, knowing the subject was guaranteed to produce a flood of tears from me. Maybe he thought if I cried enough I would run out of tears and stop crying – another way of toughening me up. Or maybe he just liked hearing me cry. I'll never know. Either way, I still can't tell my left from my right. No joke, I really can't.

When I was six, not long after my flying lessons, Dad tried to teach me how to shoot. He lined up some beer bottles on the fence post and handed me his enormous rifle. Then he got down on his knees and showed me how to look through the sights at the target and how to fire the gun, but neglected to mention how powerful the weapon was. When I pulled the trigger, the impact sent me flying backwards, much to his amusement. Later, when we were older and my parents went away overnight, Dad always placed a handgun in the top drawer of our chest of drawers, with firm instructions to 'shoot to kill' anyone who tried to break in. Fortunately, we never had to confront a burglar, which is just as well, because I could never have shot anybody.

It's little wonder that I had few friends. Once the school principal, Mr Woodland, had to drive me home after I fell off the merry-go-round in the playground. I cringed in agony – not because of my injuries, but because I was terrified of what he would think about my house. I nearly died of embarrassment. The Eiffel Tower. The aircraft hangar. Dozens of pie pans tied to the trees. Spare parts all over the yard. Dad taking pot shots at animals. Yet the irony is that because of Dad's eccentricity and cheapskate ways, I was eventually to find someone who would have a profound influence on my life.

My lack of human friends drove me to form deep emotional bonds with our family pets, especially the cats. I marvelled at their grace and dignity, traits that I sorely lacked. (I agree with Leonardo da Vinci that, 'The smallest feline is a masterpiece.') In them I found unjudgemental, devoted companions who didn't care what I looked like. And, joy of joys, my cats loved me back. (Having to work for my father, I did envy my tabby cats' leisure time. After all, sitting around with an 'M' on your forehead all day is hardly a full time occupation.)

Luckily for me, before we had cats, we had mice, so Dad could justify keeping them in the house. Even so, he still resented paying for their Purina dry cat food. He thought they should live on whatever they could catch. Little did he know I ran a secret First Aid station in a cardboard box lined with leaves and grass at the side of the house for the casualties my cats presented to me that were still alive. There I treated wounded mice and chipmunks with remedies from our medicine cabinet. In the winter, my cats had litter trays in the basement, consisting of cardboard boxes containing topsoil from the garden, which I regularly had to empty back on to the garden 'for fertiliser'. My father *invented* recycling.

When the tabby cat with white paws named Sweet Alice ran into the road and got run over by a truck I was inconsolable. 'I didn't know she meant that much to you,' Dad said to me incredulously, since Sweet Alice was not even my cat, but belonged to our neighbour. Ever since we moved to that house I had fed and looked after Sweet Alice. I considered her my cat, and eventually so did the neighbour she belonged to, since Sweet Alice was always at our house. It was the first time anything that I loved died and I thought the pain would never end.

But Dad was preoccupied by a new Bargain Barn that had opened down the road, which sold all sorts of tools, clothes, food and supplies at big discount prices. To stop my wailing and pick up some cheap goods, he decided we'd all go and take a look.

Chapter Two

Pretty Woman

It was there in the Bargain Barn that I found her. The most beautiful thing I had ever seen. The teenage fashion model whose world was her catwalk. The high school prom queen that I would never be. The ultimate fecund female with a 38 DD cup. She had a mane of golden blonde hair, a come-hither sidelong glance and legs that stretched higher than the Eiffel Tower (the Paris one). Her name was Barbie – and I simply had to have that doll.

'No, too expensive,' barked Dad when he saw the $3 price tag. He dragged me home in tears. First, there was no Sweet Alice to play with and now I wasn't allowed to have the Barbie doll – the only toy I had ever asked him to buy for me. The tragedy was impossible to bear. I cried so much over the next few days that he finally relented and took me back to buy the non-biodegradable plastic object of my dreams. Just to shut me up.

Now I had something on to which I could project my fantasies. In my mind, I would dress Barbie up to go out with her boyfriend Ken. She wore stunning outfits because she was going to fabulous parties and mixing with rich and famous people. Ken was always on his way to pick her up, so I had to make sure she was ready. I never actually wanted to own the Ken doll. Ken was there in my imagination, and that's exactly where he stayed. Nobody was going to control my Barbie doll except me.

Instead, Ken was going to come and get her, take her somewhere wonderful and bring her home again. I spent a lot of time thinking where Barbie was going to go and what she was going to do. I thought, What a fabulous life this doll has. I really want to have a life like that when I grow up.

But then I looked at my own clothes and the threadbare rug on the floor. All Gloria wanted in life was to get married, have a little girl and live in the suburbs of a bigger town. It was her dream and it ended there. It was also achievable, whereas my dream of being like Barbie seemed preposterous. Still, it didn't stop me imagining that one day I would wear clothes like Barbie's and travel the world like her. When I got to high school, the first thing I did was to sign up for French classes because one day I hoped to go to Paris. I thought it was the kind of place that Ken would take Barbie.

Whenever we went back to the Bargain Barn, I'd see what new outfits I could get for her. But I was allowed pitifully few. I desperately wanted the Solo in the Spotlight Dress, a strapless black sequinned gown with a frill fanned at the ankles. (I still have that magpie-like penchant for anything that glitters.) It came packaged with a rose and a miniature microphone, essential items for Barbie when she sang at swanky nightclubs. But, however much I lusted after it, I wasn't allowed to have it. It was always too expensive. 'And, anyway, it's far too racy for a little girl to be playing with,' added Dad with redneck, narrow-minded predictability.

Gloria, meanwhile, acquired a Midge doll – Barbie's sidekick.

She had brown hair in a flip and freckles painted across her nose. Not being allowed to buy new outfits for Midge never bothered Gloria. When she wanted more clothes for her doll, she decided to sew tiny gingham dresses and corduroy suits for her. I suppose Gloria was expressing her conventionality through Midge, where I was expressing something else altogether.

I never wanted boring homemade outfits for my Barbie. I wanted store-bought ones – something I never had myself. And certainly not the practical daywear that Midge wore. I wanted shimmering evening gowns and the highest heels for Barbie. I wanted extravagant, impractical haute couture creations that were as far removed from my dull and lonely existence as possible. Most of all, I wanted fuel for my escapist fantasies. When Christmas came I always asked for more Barbie outfits. But they never did get me that Solo in the Spotlight dress.

I had a baby doll as well as Barbie. Her name was Shirley Temple. Playing with dolls like her was meant to serve as training for little girls' future roles as mothers. But when I noticed that her clothes were just about the right size for a six-week-old kitten, I used her wardrobe (unlike Barbie, she came fully equipped) to dress my kittens, leaving poor Shirley Temple abandoned and naked in the toy box.

Upstairs in the attic, I had already found all the baby clothes that Gloria – and then I – had once worn. They were perfect for the mother cat. I put an embroidered pink dress with puffed sleeves and a big bow that tied in the back on her and thought she looked marvellous. I took it very seriously, deciding what outfits went best with tabby fur, what suited the black and white kitten and agonising over what the grey one was going to wear. Even if my own clothes were tatty, at least Barbie and the cats looked their best.

I also put wigs on the dog. We always had an interchangeable dachshund. When one died, we simply got another one. If Mom didn't like the way one of them looked, she's say it had the 'double uglies'.

In the house, there was a laundry chute where we had to open a small door in the wall and drop in our dirty clothes. They would then slide down to the basement where the washing machine was. Mom named this the 'scuttle hole' and we used it as a communications device. When we were upstairs and wanted to talk to Mom, we opened the door and hollered down the chute: 'Come to the scuttle hole, I wanna tell you something.' Walkie-talkies were all the rage at the time, and we had to make do.

A good deal of our laundry came back in various shades of blue, some quite pleasing and others rather disappointing. Mom used to add a substance called 'bluing' to the wash that was supposed to make whites look whiter. She would lob some of it into the washing machine with every load without bothering to measure.

Mom never failed to get a kick out of giving a spoonful of Skippy Peanut Butter to the dog. She employed a particular wrist action that deposited the sticky lump straight on to the roof of its mouth. We all enjoyed watching him frantically try to lick it off its long dachshund palate. She figured they used this peanut butter trick to make Mr Ed, the horse on television, appear to talk.

Mom also lived in another world. She called me Baby Tenderlove and rubbed waxed paper on our slide so that we could slip down it quicker. Like most of her relatives, she had a slapstick sense of humour and, while tinkering was Dad's life, she spent much of hers inventing a whole new language.

For instance, Gloria and I had an odd piece of furniture in the room we shared when we were young. It had a section to hang things, some small drawers and a single large drawer at the bottom. Mom said it was a 'shifferobe'. Anything unpleasant was 'nastness'. Litters of puppies were 'doglets'. Ginger, one of our dachshunds, got an allergic reaction every spring and came home puffed up and covered in lumps. Mom called this ailment 'the gleeps'. It wasn't until I was older that I realised that there were no such words.

She had also taken French in high school so when I was a teenager Mom and I spoke French to each other when we didn't want anyone else to understand what we were talking about.

Mom did not like to cook. It showed. During my childhood, I rarely had a piece of toast that didn't have to be scraped. Whenever she baked cupcakes (always from a mix) she'd burn them, so we had to turn them upside down and cut at least a quarter of an inch off the bottom. She had a habit of leaving the kitchen drawers open while she cooked, so crumbs and bits of food fell in. When the debris had accumulated to a certain level, she would vacuum the drawers out and start again.

To illustrate Mom's culinary skills, here are a few examples of what she used to fix for supper:

CORNPONE:

Prepare corn bread mix leaving plenty of lumps. Grease skillet. Pour in batter. Put in oven until completely black. Place on top of stove. Wait until someone touches and burns hand. Rinse hand under cold water. Serve.

LUMPY GRAVY:

Burn toast to a cinder. Scrape thoroughly. Spread on margarine straight from fridge, tearing what's left of toast to shreds. Meanwhile mix flour and water into fat in a pan. Add pack of cured, shredded dried beef. Ignore until thoroughly lumpy. Serve on toast as main dish.

SOP GRAVY:

Fry Jimmy Dean brand sausages in lard until good and black. Remove from pan and leave to cool. Add a cup of milk to the grease in pan, boil for two minutes or until skin forms on top. Transfer to large Pyrex measuring cup. Place slice of Wonder Bread on each plate. Pour over sop gravy until bread is wet and mushy. Eat with fork. Tip up plate to drink remaining gravy. Dab at any gravy dribbles on shirt with paper napkin provided. Take off shirt before going to bed and stick it down scuttle hole to get washed.

CANDIED SWEET POTATOES:
Boil sweet potatoes until mushy. Place in ovenproof dish. Dot top with butter and brown sugar. Completely cover with marshmallows. Place in very hot oven until marshmallows are black. Serve.

FRIED GREEN TOMATOES:
Pick tomatoes early in season while green and hard. Rinse crust of dried pesticides off under tap. Slice thinly. Dip into beaten egg. Smash Saltine crackers with rolling pin. Coat tomatoes with cracker crumbs. Fry in corn oil until charred and crispy. Serve with Smuckers grape jelly.

STUFFED DATES:
Fill pitted dates with peanut butter. Roll in granulated sugar. Serve.

THANKSGIVING TURKEY STUFFING:
Remove gibberskizzards (Mom's word for giblets) from turkey and give to cat. To make stuffing, soak stale bread in sour milk. Add two eggs, a plastic tub of rubbery oysters and three sticks of chopped celery. Mix together. Stuff mixture into turkey before putting into oven. Cook forever.

MOM'S MOONSHINE:
Pick grapes from back yard. Squeeze in old wooden

winepress. Transfer to wine barrel. Add lots and lots of sugar. Leave to ferment in basement for approx. one year. When mature, should taste like 80 proof sherry. Serve to brother-in-law Carl (no one else will touch it).

COLD POP TO DRINK:
Place bottle of Pepsi Cola in deep freeze. Develop amnesia and forget it's there for several hours. Regain memory and retrieve. Frozen liquid should by now have burst out of the bottle and coated inside of freezer. Spend hours picking at ice, extract any broken glass and suck until it melts. (Drive-through Burger King today in the US, and pick up the newest drink – frozen Coke. It's served like a slushy drink with a straw and tastes just like our freezer accidents.)

Our breakfast orange juice was prepared from frozen concentrate. Nothing unusual there, except that Mom's mode of preparation consisted of hacking off a slice with her butcher knife and dropping the frozen round into a glass that was then held under the tap to get topped up with our rusty well water.

Not to be outdone, every summer my father would get in on the act:

DAD'S BARBECUE:
Strip car engine and clean parts thoroughly in gasoline. Pour dirty black gasoline into empty plastic domestic bleach bottles. Pour this solution over charcoal in grill. Ignite. Stand well back and admire spectacular black smoke. Step forward. Place steaks or burgers on grill above noxious fumes. Cook to Dad's taste (cremated on the outside, raw in the middle). Pour on more gas if coals seem to be burning out. Extinguish flames with

large bucket of water. Carefully dry coals out for use next time while food gets cold. Serve burgers with lots of ketchup, mustard and dill pickle to mask the flavour of engine oil.

Funnily enough, I can't remember anyone ever complaining about our crazy meals. Although I didn't have much to compare them to, I somehow knew they weren't quite right, and surreptitiously slipped a good deal of the contents of my plate to a grateful dachshund waiting under the table. That's one of the reasons I was so skinny as a child.

I inherited my klutziness from Mom. We had a big electric stove and Mom always had burns on her hands and wrists but she never seemed to notice. She was also usually bruised from walking into things and tripping up, and was nonchalant about that, too. Whatever she ate landed on her shirt. I think this was a family trait, a genetic blip because, on one occasion when her whole family came to dinner, I looked around the table and everyone had food items dripping down their shirts, myself included. We call them 'chest disasters'. When we say, 'Dinner's on us', we mean it literally.

Mom had no social life apart from entertaining relatives or going to visit them. I don't know why she thought it was necessary but on such occasions she always made a cake (from a mix, of course) and iced it and, because of my father's bad driving, this confection took place of priority on the back seat. Gloria and I had to hold it steady and we never knew if it would make it there or not.

Mom also had a unique hobby. She regularly put gold gilt on household items. I remember how she painted our mahogany piano white, put gold gilt all over it and then did the same to the piano stool. (Nobody in our house played, by the way.) Next she took her paintbrush to the basement, painted everything baby blue, then systematically gilded the workbench, the brick walls and finally the rickety wooden staircase. She emerged triumphant, gold gilt glistening in her hair. Many other things in the house were oddly gilded, including the windowsills. Mom also cut pictures out of magazines, pasted them on to pieces of furniture and coated them with varnish. She did that to decorate an old commode, her sewing box and a number of other things that weren't gildable.

So there I was sporting an orange Afro hairdo communicating in French with my mom, who was busy gold-gilding the place, as my father built an aircraft hangar in the yard. Looking back, I suppose we were rather a surreal family.

Mom loved practical jokes. Once she roasted a chicken and left it on top of the stove to cool. I carefully removed the skin, took off all the meat, put it on a plate and stuck it in the refrigerator. Then I draped the skin back over the skeleton and left it on top of the stove. You should have seen the look on her face. She thought it had dissolved in the oven. I also covered myself with tomato ketchup and told her that the bogeyman had stabbed me. The split second of terror in her eyes meant it was always worth repeating the prank

The bogeyman, according to Mom, lived in the woods. She invented him to stop us venturing there because it was frequented by hunters and she was afraid we might be hit by stray bullets. But the bogeyman wasn't my biggest fear. There was an imaginary Red Indian who lived under my bed at night. He had a tomahawk and I kept completely covered up because I believed that if I so much as poked a toe out he would chop it off.

According to Mom, I had a Guardian Angel. This divine being, she said, was there looking over me, watching my every move. Being painfully shy, I felt this was an invasion of my privacy, especially when I went to the bathroom. I would shut the door firmly, hoping that my Guardian Angel wouldn't watch me on the pot. No wonder I was a nervous wreck.

Bogeyman or not, nothing could keep me out of the woods. It

was as if a mystical lure beckoned to me. I disappeared for hours, following the narrow, winding path that led to the river. In the springtime, the air was fragrant with budding wild flowers and the ground was covered with tender shoots of grass and clover. Occasionally a rabbit and I would startle each other.

Sometimes I took along one of Dad's old fishing rods and brought back tiny fish for my cats. Sitting barefoot on the riverbanks in my cut-off jeans and chequered shirt, I used to watch the jet airliners fly over, daydreaming about the people who were on board and the glamorous places they were going. Those woods were my personal wonderland, a place to be alone with my thoughts and drink in the beauty of nature. The odd bullet that whistled past my head and ricocheted off the trees did little to disturb my reverie. I loved the smell of the earth so much that I used to eat chalk and plaster to the point where my baby teeth were worn down in the front, which worried my mother and grossed Gloria out.

Before Ohio became a State, the land had belonged to Indians. I often found arrowheads and other artefacts on the ground, which I collected and kept upstairs in my room. Many years later I learned about the brutal mass slaughter of the American Indian nation. Remembering my arrowhead treasures brought the chilling realisation that I must have grown up on the very land where some of it took place. Yet we were taught that Indians were savages, hence the scary one under my bed.

My home life revolved around Barbie, my kittens and television. TV was my window to the rest of the world. I could see endless possibilities out there. Dad was a channel surfer before we got a remote control. He reclined in his green vinyl, multi-speed-vibrating easy chair and Gloria and I had to change channels for him on demand. If any of us ever dared to walk in front of the TV when he was watching it, he yelled at us – if we wanted to cross the room, we had to crawl on all fours.

When remote controls were eventually available, he rushed

out to invest in a new TV that came with one. He was in hog heaven and we were off the hook. Dad surfed like a bandit, watching five or six channels at once. I loved the snippets of *Doctor Ben Casey* I spotted. I persuaded Mom to send away for the official Ben Casey operating smock and I wore it all the time. But I could never understand why no one else noticed that there were two different Darrens in *Bewitched* or why the cameraman wouldn't help poor Lassie when she was lost and limping down the road in the rain.

I cried when the Flying Monkeys came and took Toto the dog away in *The Wizard of Oz*. Every Christmas I watched that movie hoping the next time I saw it someone would prevent those Flying Monkeys doing such a horrible thing. But of course no one ever did. 'Run, Toto, Run!' I would silently entreat, afraid my father would notice my interest and use it against me. Why doesn't somebody stop them? I wondered, year after year, tears streaming down my face. Hearing me crying, my father yelled, 'Shut up, Cindy! It's only a TV show, damn it! It's not real!'

Every year we all gathered around the TV set with bowls of buttered popcorn to watch the *Miss America Beauty Pageant*. Each of us had our favourite, and hoped she'd be chosen. Women's physical beauty was something to be made into a commanding spectacle and paraded, weighed up, compared and judged. That scrutiny is something the beautiful have to accept. Burden or blessing, it goes with the territory. But so does power over men.

When the winning contestants were announced in reverse order, third runner-up, second runner-up then first-runner-up, those girls burst into tears. The announcer always said they were tears of happiness because they had been chosen, but it was obvious to me that they were crying because they had got so close, but did not win the title. Every year there were 49 losers. I felt sorry for them, although we were all pleased for the winner.

On the *Dick Van Dyke Show*, I watched transfixed as Dick Van

Dyke and Mary Tyler Moore went shopping for shoes. The assistant brought out dozens of boxes and they tried on every pair in the shop. I didn't like my own world much. I preferred theirs.

There were also lighter moments. Having inherited a love of comedy from my mother's side, I always looked forward to seeing stand-up comedians on TV. One of my favourites was another ugly duckling from Ohio. Just when every other woman on television was trying to look beautiful and be the perfect housewife, here was one that told jokes about her homely face and odd clothes – and even made fun of her bad housekeeping. And, although I wished I could be Barbie, I found myself identifying more with this woman, whose name was Phyllis Diller. Maybe seeing the funny side of my misfortune was the answer.

The first thing I remember of anything going really wrong in the outside world was in 1963. I was eight years old when John F Kennedy was assassinated in Dallas. Although I was used to Dad shooting animals, I couldn't grasp the fact that anyone could shoot a president. I watched all the documentaries and listened to all the conspiracy theories. Dad, believing the lone gunman theory, said, 'Oswald should be tortured for the rest of his life.' He had a lot of political opinions, a good number of them the opinions of people on TV, rather than his own. Therefore Dad assumed that because Lee Harvey Oswald had been arrested for the murder, he must have been guilty of the crime.

More than three decades would pass before I made a pilgrimage to Dealey Plaza where JFK was shot. I walked along the grassy knoll, then looked out of the very window of the former Texas School Book Depository building where Lee Harvey Oswald allegedly fired the fatal bullets. He must have been a very good shot.

The year after JFK's death, the Beatles made their US television début on the *Ed Sullivan Show*, and I began a lifelong love affair with pop music. 'I Wanna Hold Your Hand' was the number one song, and I became a Beatles fanatic, buying bubble gum with Beatles cards inside each pack and begging to get their albums. I had to have every one, and they were quite cheap at the Bargain Barn, so Dad let me have them, even though he thought they were undesirable. One album had a smiling picture of my heroes on the cover: 'They've all got crooked teeth and they need haircuts,' Dad barked.

When I grew up I would go and live in England, I decided. That's where I dreamed I would meet and fall in love with a nice young man with a fab suit and long floppy hair like one of the Beatles.

I had no desire to hang out with local farm boys. Then again, I had no other choice.

The first boy I ever took interest in was named Ronald. We were both ten and in the same grade. He was tall and cute and had a chipped front tooth. I have no idea what he saw in me.

We never kissed but he gave me a ring, which was far too big, so I wound yellow angora yarn around the silver band until it became a snug fit. In the winter, we went ice-skating together on the Sandusky River. We would fall over again and again, bruising our backsides, but that was all part of the fun. He told me he loved me but dropped me like a hot potato when a new girl named Beth came on the scene. She was prettier than me, lived in town, and wore nice clothes. However her real claim to fame was that she was the very first in our class to wear a bra. Maybe having breasts was the answer.

Before too long, she was wearing the silver ring that had been mine. Rejection and humiliation became a pattern that would be repeated until I changed my looks and my life.

Beth was the first girl in my class to get pregnant and *have* to get married in high school – but not to Ronald. She's still happily married to the same man. As for Ronald, well, he went on to marry some other girl. One day they had a terrible argument. She got a gun and shot him dead.

Chapter Three

Purple Haze

When I was 13, I got my first kiss from a local boy named Chuck. He had red hair and freckles, and was a popular, studious boy – one of the in-crowd at school. Chuck stared into my eyes, took my hand and led me into a cornfield. This was a good place to make out, because the corn was over eight feet high – no one could see what we were up to.

I got The Kiss when my father let me have a few kids over for the first and last party I ever had at home. We decked out some trees at the edge of the woods with lights, and my guests – all the school misfits (Chuck excluded) – drank soda pop. Dad found a place where you could buy it in bulk, dirt-cheap. It tasted awful and had foreign objects floating around in it. We never did figure out what they were.

Dad set up a sound system so that we could sit around the bonfire he built and listen to records. A couple of years earlier John Lennon had stated that the Beatles were more popular than Jesus.

They were still pretty popular – and now the Rolling Stones were, too. My *Magical Mystery Tour* and *Jumpin' Jack Flash* albums were played over and over. But 'Everlasting Love' by Love Affair was blaring when Chuck led me into the cornfield.

The Kiss lasted a good 20 minutes and I was trembling with nerves the whole time. He stuck his tongue in my mouth. Nobody ever explained what you were supposed to do with the spit that kept building up, so I swallowed it every few minutes. Even though the experience was pretty unpleasant, I was very proud of myself because I finally had a boyfriend, and he was from the in-crowd to boot. Chuck already had a girlfriend named Diane, a straight-A student who was the niece of Dad's plumber friend Ernie. I thought that, because of The Kiss, it must be me he really liked now. I naively believed he would ask me to go steady, and that I too would be in with the in-crowd at last. But Chuck never spoke to me again.

First Ronald and now Chuck. Although rejection was something that would blight my life, perhaps in this case, it was a godsend. Chuck went on to marry Diane – demure, delicate, doe-eyed Diane. Chuck became a factory worker and they still live in Fremont – whereas I was going to embark on a spectacular adventure that would take me all over the world. (Eventually I would come to understand that Chuck's actions weren't personal. Instead, it was a prime example of the 'matching hypothesis' theory at work, which essentially means that people seek to be with those whom they perceive to be on their own level of attractiveness. Our encounter in the cornfield was his biological equivalent of 'slumming.')

Thank God I didn't let him put his hand down my shirt. I was wearing my first bra and it was stuffed with Kleenexes to bring the appearance of my chest in line with the girls in my class. It was size 28AAA and I had the embarrassing ordeal of having to order it by telephone from the mail order catalogue. While women all over the country were seen burning their bras on the six o'clock news,

I was plunging mine up and down in the bathroom sink. Instead of putting it down the scuttle hole with my underpants and shirts, I hand washed my white, one-hundred-per-cent-cotton starter bra and hung it to dry on my bedroom radiator. I was too ashamed for it to go in the washer with other laundry; I didn't want my own family to see it, let alone anyone else.

It was always stiff from the heat and had radiator grooves embossed on it, but it was better than displaying it on the back yard clothesline. I hated puberty and spent the whole time trying to avoid embarrassment. Being agonisingly self-conscious, I would almost die if boys at school tried to 'skunk' me. 'Skunking' was the art of craftily running your hand down a girl's back to feel if she was wearing a bra.

I tried to put on weight by drinking cans of Nutriment in a futile attempt to find a way of being like other girls in my class, who were for the most part one year older than me. Being one crucial year further into puberty, they were more developed. When they formed cliques at school to talk about their boyfriends I was never invited to be in one. Just like at home, I was the youngest at school and so furthest down the pecking order, forever destined to be the unwanted little sister trailing along behind the older girls. People made fun of me and I felt it was my fault. Apart from being skinny and dressed in old clothes, I sprayed my hair with Sun-In and it turned an even more glorious shade of orange.

When I told Mom I wanted to wear perfume, she gave me a bottle of vanilla extract to dab behind my ears. I smelled like an ice-cream cone. And then there was my face. Gloria had a good-looking boyfriend named Mark Little, who used to bring her flowers and write her love notes. One day, when he was at our house, he suddenly said to me – and I'll never forget this in my life – 'When you smile, your nose and chin almost meet.' I was devastated. While he put Gloria on a pedestal, he thought I looked like the Wicked Witch of the West. I already knew my nose was too big and my lips were thin. My legs weren't long like Gloria's, and now to top it all off I was told I had a large chin. When I studied myself in profile smiling into one mirror in front and holding another to the side, I saw the awful truth. And if Mark noticed it, I reasoned, so did everyone else. I became even more self-conscious. I immediately stopped wearing my hair in a ponytail, which I thought emphasised the problem. (Mark's younger brother Tony, who was my age, took up the ponytail wearing instead. He went on to become the famous fitness expert and king of the infomercial Tony Little.)

Nobody saw me for the person I was inside. They were too busy passing judgement on my clothes, my hair, my face and now my stupid chin. I set about changing my image. Since I couldn't change my face, I started with my clothes. Taking a leaf out of Gloria's book, I learned how to use Mom's sewing machine and visited Joesph's, which was Fremont's only department store, to look through the Butterick pattern books. I didn't want Gloria's frilly cotton dresses any more – I wanted to be different. One of the first outfits I made was a suit from mock snakeskin upholstery fabric. I thought it was really cool. Dad wouldn't allow me to wear mini skirts halfway up my thighs like Twiggy so I rolled my handmade skirts up at the waist after I got on the bus. Then everything had to be black, like the cocktail dress immortalised by Audrey Hepburn in the 1961 movie *Breakfast at Tiffany's*.

And, whereas Hepburn accessorised her look with sunglasses and a Martini, I used jingle bells for jacket buttons, and decorated outfits with the plastic eyeballs usually used for stuffed toys. Instead of being sleek and sophisticated, I looked even weirder. Mom, meanwhile, took a more conventional approach. She made me little jumpers, but she wasn't a very good seamstress. It would take her forever to complete a garment. One plaid wool jacket she started making for me never got finished. She didn't know how to make a lining so I wore it just as it was. I liked the fabric and I couldn't wait any longer.

Domestic pursuits bored us both and our minds would wander.

Periodically, Mom and I ran over our fingers with the sewing machine as we fed the fabric into the path of the needle. The next thing we knew the machine was brought to a sudden halt by the needle entering a fingernail and breaking off deep inside one of our fingers. We always took it pretty much in our stride – we dug out the embedded thread and broken needle with a rusty old pair of eyebrow tweezers and applied pressure to stem the flow of blood. This annoyed Gloria no end. She often had sewing projects under way, and there was never a spare sewing machine needle in the house. They were sold individually and were meant to last for years. Dad was not one to allow us to stock up on such items.

Walking to town was a two-mile hike down a long country road and the chances were that a truck might mow you down. We weren't allowed to have bicycles because Dad said they weren't safe. In fact, it was just another way of keeping us within his sight and under his control. Mom didn't drive. She would have liked to, but by Dad's rules that would have given her far too much freedom. He even hated her wearing make-up and always thought her clothes were too revealing, although she dressed like a Quaker. She liked to wear lipstick but he always tried to get her to tone the colour down. He was extremely controlling. I have since learned that a lot of men are like that.

If we wanted to go shopping downtown, Dad dropped us at Joseph's department store and waited outside in the car for us so we didn't go astray. One day Mom, Gloria and I went to look around Richard's, the women's clothing shop. As we came out of the store, I fell in love at first sight ... with an amazing silver car parked outside. I thought it looked like a spaceship. We went to the front of the car and bent down to read the badge on the grill. It said Mercedes Benz. I had never seen anything like it. Its sleek curves were in striking contrast to the dusty pickup trucks and boxy functionality of the family station wagons parked nearby. Just like me, it was glaringly out of place in Fremont, but for very different reasons.

I became Mercedes Benz obsessed. Having seen the car of my

dreams, I went home to do some research and found out that it was of German manufacture. 'Do I really have to go to Germany to get that car?' I asked Mom. She had no idea whatsoever and comforted me with a mayonnaise sandwich (Miracle Whip spread on Wonder Bread), which had become my favourite snack. Then Janis Joplin came out with that song, 'Oh Lord Won't You Buy Me A Mercedes Benz.' Oh Lord, I had to have one. It's the car I drive today.

My father, after much bargaining, bought himself a flatbed pickup truck. Now we had a car and a pickup truck and, depending on how many of us would be travelling and the distance involved, he used whichever vehicle gave most miles to the gallon. He systematically worked out weight and drag and calculated the gas consumption for each journey.

Dad's mathematical formulae went into overdrive in 1968 as he planned a trip for us to visit his parents in Daleville, Indiana. They were very old and the house was immaculate. Nothing was out of place. When we got there Gloria and I would sit still as statues so nothing would get broken, messed up or suffer a fingerprint for which we would get the blame. This was in complete contrast to my mother's side of the family, who would *thank* children for accidentally breaking things – just so they wouldn't feel bad. ('Honey, I hated that glass so much, thank you for breaking it, sweetheart, now let me get you some more iced tea.') Mom's hillbilly relatives made sure you never cried about something so insignificant. They never put material things above people.

In contrast to the unbreakable melamine dishes we ate off at home that we got, one by one, for free by collecting coupons at the grocery store, my father's mother had a set of real china dishes with delicate flowered teacups. The furniture in their house was adorned with the same plastic packaging it came in. Dozens of lacy doilies smothered all the chairs and side tables. Grandpa had a little workbench in his garage where he tinkered for hours on end. Like Dad, he was always making things. He kept a series of interchangeable miniature pinschers, which, because of their name, I was afraid might pinch me. They were yappy little horrors that snapped at your ankles. And they stank. Our dogs never smelled doggy because they ran around in the fresh air, but these were kept inside to sweat in a polyester-lined basket.

Gloria and I always dreaded receiving presents from our paternal grandparents. Grandma would give us strange things that we figured someone had given to her that she didn't want – I once got a pink, size-16 quilted bed jacket. Grandpa's presents were even worse. He had worked for the Indiana Highway Department and over the years had hoarded a garage full of junk he'd picked up from the side of the road that people had thrown out of their cars. For Christmas and birthdays he would wrap up these items and give them as gifts. Writing thank you letters to my grandparents were early – and excruciating – lessons in diplomacy. If it was really the thought that counted, they obviously didn't think much of us.

Grandma wouldn't have been a bad cook except for her habit of using way too much granulated white sugar. She put it in everything, including vegetable dishes. Her ancestors were English, and I now recognise a lot of intrinsically British dishes she used to make. Dinner was always a long, drawn-out affair. When we had meals at home in Ohio, everything got stuck on the table in one hit and then you went ahead and ate it. Here we had a starter, a main course and a dessert. At home, Gloria and I could leave the table as soon as we finished, but at my grandparents' we had to sit through all these courses and then have a cup of Bigelow's Constant Comment tea. This ritual made a lasting impression; I still feel like I'm putting on airs when I order a first course in a restaurant today.

I don't know if Grandma's cooking was to blame, but Grandpa suffered from 'sugar diabetes'. He was insulin dependent and ate different things from the rest of us. Grandma prepared his meals separately, weighing it all up on kitchen scales to make sure he didn't get too much. Meanwhile, Grandpa sat in his chair and did the crossword puzzle in the daily newspaper while chewing tobacco, which he spat noisily into a makeshift spittoon he'd made from an empty quart milk carton that he'd cut the top off of.

They had a teenage neighbour named Kathy Jackson. 'She's got a feller,' Grandma whispered as though she was revealing a state secret. The feller picked up Kathy and took her on a date. I wished I had a feller to take me somewhere else – like Kathy had hers and like Barbie had Ken.

During our visit, Martin Luther King was murdered and racial violence erupted across the country. Even though we were deep in redneck country and these were still very ignorant times, I vividly remember the family being genuinely upset about the shooting. The publication of the Kerner Commission Report on civil disorders that year concluded: 'Our nation is moving toward two societies – one white, one black – separate and unequal.' At school, my best friend Rachel was from one of the few black families in the county. She had an upbeat personality like a ray of sunshine, and an outrageous sense of humour. We laughed all the time. The other white girls didn't seem judgemental but some of the blacks taunted her and scrawled 'whitey lover' all over her school locker because of her friendship with me.

'All these black people go on protest marches but they're still black when they get home and look in the mirror,' Grandpa observed. He genuinely believed they were protesting about being black, not about the injustice they suffered. It was around that time I learned another shameful chapter of American history at school. Not long after the genocide of the Indian nation, black Africans were captured and shipped across the ocean in chains. The ones who survived the treacherous journey were taken to markets and sold into a life of slavery. It was barely 100 years since President Lincoln freed the slaves in 1863.

When I was small, I asked my mother why some people were white while others were black. 'God paints them black when he runs out of white paint,' she said. For ages, I believed that God was up there painting folk. When he wasn't going bowling, that is.

Mom would reassure me during Ohio's ear-splitting thunderstorms that the noise was only the sound of God bowling with the angels.

Whenever I asked my mother where I came from, to avoid any discussion about the birds and the bees, her answer was always 'Cincinnati,' which is the town where I was born. If something was upsetting me, like being teased by my big sister, she dismissively told me 'not to come unglued,' At an early age I took the hint that it was up to me to find my own answers. It wasn't really learning to become independent, more like realising that I was on my own in life.

Race was not the only issue causing tension. Vietnam became the longest war in the nation's history, the US troop strength reaching a peak of 542,000. Robert F Kennedy was shot dead. Andy Warhol survived an assassination attempt. But the Beatles' *White Album* and the Rolling Stones' *Beggars Banquet* hit the charts and offered a pleasant diversion. Simon and Garfunkel sang 'Coo coo ca choo' to Mrs Robinson as the movie *The Graduate* caused widespread moral outrage.

In 1969, while the carnage escalated in Vietnam, the beautiful actress Sharon Tate and six of her friends were brutally murdered by Charles Manson and his 'family' in the Hollywood Hills; James Earl Ray pleaded guilty to the murder of Martin Luther King Jr.

Gloria, being the older sister, had control of our transistor radio. We listened to music late at night under the covers. But she liked romantic songs by all-American whitebread bands like the Lettermen that the Toledo station played, where I preferred rock'n'roll and soul music played by the Detroit 'Motown' station (or 'damn jungle music' as my father called it). On hot summer nights these musical power struggles took place against the backdrop of our own disco-style light show, the flashing lights in our bedroom emanating from a mayonnaise jar containing lightning bugs we had caught earlier in the evening. Not as cruel as it sounds – we punched holes in the lid so they could breathe and we always let them go in the morning.

Around that time, the Motown label signed a group called the

Jackson Five, whose lead singer was only a little boy. Normally I found child singers excruciating, like having to read those Dick and Jane books back in grade school. But Michael Jackson was different. Unlike Wayne Newton, he didn't sing cutesy kid songs only your grandparents would like.

Instead he sang adult songs with grown-up lyrics, despite being only a child. I was an instant fan. At last there was someone in the charts close to my own age. Furthermore, at a time when so many pop stars were British, he came from a place I knew well – Indiana. So, like most of my relatives, Michael Jackson was a Hoosier. I never dreamed that one day I would laugh with him about that.

Sometimes Gloria's friends came over to listen to records, which I found incredible considering our weird home life. But she remained straight laced and, being level headed, managed to rise above everything. She always had boys calling her up but was very choosy, as is the privilege of pretty girls, and had just a couple of boyfriends before getting married.

I made the mistake of trying out for cheerleader when I was 14. Other girls did the splits and turned graceful cartwheels, but I was useless at those things. Because I had no co-ordination naturally, I was turned down. When I tried to practise turning cartwheels in our front yard, I accidentally kicked Gloria in the mouth, knocking out one of her front teeth. There was blood everywhere; she was very upset and I felt awful about it. It seemed I couldn't do anything right.

I was never invited to high school dances and if any decent boy asked me out, it wouldn't be long before he dumped me. Obviously, I wasn't much of a prize.

My first real date was with Luke Roberts when I was 15. He was a popular 16-year-old and I couldn't believe my luck when he asked me out between classes at high school. He picked me up in his Dad's gold Chevrolet Nova and took me to a party. Not much was happening so we left and headed downtown to the cinema to see *Son of Flubber* starring Fred MacMurray.

I didn't tell my father about the date, in case he stopped me from going. If I asked permission to do anything, he always said no. I knew it was easier to seek forgiveness than to obtain permission anyway. Besides, Luke was a polite, decent boy and I couldn't see any reason why Dad should object to him. When he dropped me off, I got brave and invited Luke in. He wasn't the type who would make fun of my home life, he was far too kind for that.

But Dad went absolutely mad.

'Get in the house!' he yelled at me. 'And you, boy, get out!' he ordered Luke.

I wanted the ground to swallow me up. Why couldn't Dad realise that this was my one shot at getting a really good guy? Why wasn't he impressed? The answer was simple: he didn't want anyone in his family to be out of his control.

Luke never asked me out again. He eventually left town and became a preacher. Who knows, I could have been his wife.

A few months later Dad almost killed himself when he decided to clean his truck's carburettor by spraying it with gasoline while the engine was running. When the inevitable flames erupted he became a human torch. Because his clothes were soaked with gas due to the blowback of airborne gasoline, he was unable to extinguish the flames by rolling on the ground. Gloria had to put him out with the garden hose. She drove him to the emergency room at Fremont Memorial Hospital, where he was treated for second and third degree burns on his hands, chest, arms and back. He came home bandaged up like Tutankhamen and was laid up for weeks.

Meanwhile, Dad's unreasonable behaviour threw me off the rails. In an effort to hide from the world and keep a low profile, I grew my hair and kept my fringe long enough to cover my eyes, but it probably had the opposite effect. Gloria said I looked like Cousin It from the *Addams Family*.

No one decent was allowed to be my friend, so I began to hang out with the local misfits, or 'hoods' as they were called, being short for hoodlums. It was not just as an act of defiance – we were all misfits together, so we had a common bond. The gang I started mixing with were all different ages and from different towns – some from Fremont, others from Clyde or Bellevue. Some were still at school, others had had dropped out. A few of them had their own rattletrap cars, the ones who didn't would borrow their dads'. We cruised around playing Led Zeppelin and Black Sabbath on the eight-track car stereo, many of my new friends high on dope.

I had a friend named Miranda and her older brother Bubba often picked me up. Whenever Dad hollered, Bubba simply put his foot hard on the gas and whisked us away in his convertible Corvette. Bubba loved that car, but it was to cost him his life in the most dramatic way. One day it flipped over and he was decapitated. Bubba's death put me in touch with mortality and taught me how precarious life is.

But I still started smoking. Most of my friends did and it was another way of asserting my independence. We thought it made us look cool. We even smoked Kool brand cigarettes. I don't have an addictive personality and it didn't particularly appeal to me, so my smoking career was sporadic and short-lived. (Nowadays I'm very glad it was never a serious habit, because I've seen how it ages people. Smokers have nicotine pallor and are often prematurely wrinkled, especially around the mouth. Surgeons don't like to perform deep face-lifts on smokers because the reduced circulation to the skin compromises the healing process, so I would not have been eligible some of the treatment I went on to have.)

The first time I got drunk was with Bob Stetzel. His father was the Mayor of Fremont and they lived in a big, three-storey house, yet Bob was a real tearaway. His dad's homemade blueberry wine was sweet and, to me, it tasted just like a soft drink. Bob kept plying me with the stuff and I got so plastered that I didn't know what I was doing. My parents thought I was at a girlfriend's house doing homework. It got to be around 10.30pm and I should have been home hours before.

Eventually, Bob had to wake up Mayor Stetzel to drive me home. I don't know how I got away with it but my parents were in bed asleep. The next morning there was all this purple puke in my bed. Before going to school, I stripped the bed and put the sheets into the washing machine and lobbed in plenty of bluing to hide the evidence.

Bob's older brother, Steve, was a tearaway too. We all played pool in Chudzinski's Bar. One weekend, a guy from Toledo called Isaac Mines was in there drinking and he and Steve started arguing. It developed into a brawl and the bartender ordered them to fight outside. When they did so, Isaac drew a gun and shot Steve dead. The court ruled self-defence as Steve was pulling Isaac from his car when he was shot. As Isaac was an ex-con he got five years simply for possessing a gun.

Another classmate was Joe Kindred Jr. His father – Joe Sr. – was the town sheriff. Joe Jr. married his childhood sweetheart straight out of school. One day, they had an argument. He put a gun to her head and held her hostage in the basement of their house. With typical American overkill, the place was soon surrounded by every law enforcement officer in the area, all shouting, 'Give yourself up!' The police opened fire and shot the house to pieces. In the process Joe was shot dead, although some believe he may have taken his own life. When I saw the house afterwards, it was riddled with bullet holes.

Fremont, like the rest of America, was a very violent place to live. One of the gun stores in town even sold machine guns. What anyone there wanted with an M16, I could not imagine. Surely not for rabbit hunting.

In 1970, four student demonstrators were killed and nine wounded by National Guard gunfire at Ohio's Kent State University. Crosby, Stills, Nash and Young later immortalised the tragedy in the song 'Four Dead in Ohio.' Another two students were killed and nine wounded by police gunfire at Jackson State College. President Nixon's Commission on Campus Unrest called the gap between youth culture and established society 'a threat to American stability.' A terrible atmosphere was brewing. There were even student demonstrations at my school, Fremont Ross High.

The same year Jimi Hendrix and Janis Joplin, popular icons of the Sixties drug culture, were both found dead. It didn't stop everyone I knew from doing drugs. The misfits I hung out with got them from pushers in Detroit or Toledo but, as time went on, drug taking became so mainstream that even the popular kids were trying them.

Although I'd watched others inject heroin, I was never tempted to join them. The kids I knew who 'shot smack' were addicted to it, and I didn't like the look it gave them. They were strangely glassy-eyed and had lost all interest in personal hygiene.

I preferred beer. 'Don't give her any drugs, she doesn't need them,' laughed a friend when I was offered some at a party, pointing out that I was off-the-wall enough without them. Like everyone else, I tried smoking marijuana, but I almost coughed my head off and it put me to sleep. Pot was not a temptation for me after that – but I did experiment briefly with LSD. I never actually bought the stuff but, if anyone else was tripping, they'd want to share the experience and offer the tabs around.

The first time had been completely by accident. One summer, just before my 14th birthday, I picked up a glass of purple liquid off the kitchen counter at a friend's house and drank it down, thinking it was grape Kool-Aid. But it was water into which a 'Purple Haze' tab had been dropped, that my friends had mixed up and were planning to share. There was enough in the glass to get an elephant high. It garbled my brain as I sat on my friend's front porch, barefoot and wearing my homemade hippie flares covered in peace-sign patches, tie-dyed T-shirt and love beads. The lawn and flowers all around me danced in formation to 'Strawberry Fields Forever' and 'Sunshine Of Your Love'.

After that, high school took on a whole new meaning. I was high in class on more than one occasion.

I cut class whenever I could by composing excuse notes and imitating Mom's handwriting. Once, when I was 15, I secretly took the day off school and went to New Baltimore, in Ohio, to see Ike and Tina Turner in concert. I'll never forget the spellbinding sight of Tina and her backing singers, the Ikettes, dancing on stage in the strobe lights. (Ike played guitar behind them wearing a bright yellow suit with flared trousers.) Tina was sexy and uninhibited, like a wild animal. Sandra Dee she wasn't. She seemed strong, powerful and totally in control. Reading her autobiography many years later, I learned that she was being beaten up and intimidated by Ike at that time. Yet another example of how some men are compelled to harness and control beautiful women.

Other times, I would skip off just to cruise with my friends, and I got away with it until the school started phoning Mom to check up on me. Mom said she'd cover for me but warned me not to do it again. But I went straight ahead, skipped school and stayed the night at my friend Cathy's place – she was an older girl with her own apartment and was throwing a party. Mom didn't know that I hadn't been to school that day, but she said it was OK for me to stay the night.

'Whatever happens, I have to go to school tomorrow,' I said to Cathy. 'They call my house now and I get into trouble. Please promise you'll make me get up.'

Knowing I had to go to school the next morning, I was reluctant to join the others in dropping acid. But there was a guy there I had a crush on who said, 'Come on, Cindy, it'll wear off in a few hours. We're all going to trip together. Here, just take it.' He handed me an acid tab and his tequila sunrise to wash it down with.

We all got completely out of it. Everyone else passed out, but I was tripping my brains out. For hours I lay on the floor passing my fingers through a candle's flame to make patterns on the ceiling.

The next thing I knew someone was shouting in my ear: 'Time to go to school ...'

I could see patterns and colours everywhere.

'I can't go to school, I'm still tripping, please don't make me go,' I pleaded. I looked around Cathy's living room. It was alive with swarming, dancing textures that rose up out of every surface I focused on. As I gazed out of each of the windows, I saw a different movie playing complete with distinct individual soundtracks. I went into the bathroom and watched in horror as my face melted into a bloody skull grinning menacingly at me from out of the mirror. I became paranoid and started to panic. It was a terrifying experience, especially for a 15-year-old.

'What if I stay like this forever?' I kept asking. The others calmed me down and fed me downers and orange juice. No matter how bad things got, I made them promise not to take me to the hospital because my dad would kill me if I overdosed on drugs. 'Wow, don't worry, man, we won't,' I was assured. 'We don't wanna get busted.'

The effect lasted until about two that afternoon by which time I had been tripping for a good 18 hours. I went home at the usual time as if I'd been to school and, miracle of miracles, the school hadn't called my house. Then I vaguely remembered that one of the other kids had called in sick for me, pretending to be my mother. I was glad I wasn't in trouble, but I was still reeling from that bad acid trip. No punishment my parents could have dreamed up could have possibly compared to the self-inflicted torture I had been through that morning.

Mick Jagger is quoted as saying, 'It's all right letting yourself go, as long as you can get yourself back.' I know just what he means. To say I learned my lesson is the understatement of the century. I never touched drugs again. I hated being controlled by something – or someone – else, and still do.

I also hated being ordered around by my father and I realised that following the crowd was just another way of doing what I was told. Although I had a mind of my own, I often lacked the confidence to trust my own judgement. My father had told me I was stupid ever since I could remember. Even though I got good grades and would eventually qualify for membership of Mensa, which requires an IQ at genius level, deep down I believed he was probably right.

Gloria and I were at our most distant during our teenage years. She was a real goody-two-shoes and didn't approve of my friends. Nor did I, in many ways. But thanks to Dad I didn't have anyone else to hang around with. I was only human, and I yearned to be liked and accepted, even by a bunch of losers. They were better than nothing, or so I thought at the time. At any rate, I simply could not bear to be at home.

Meanwhile, Gloria and I, along with most of northwestern Ohio, were intrigued by a cool mysterious Italian-American guy from a neighbouring town who used to cruise through Fremont on Saturday nights. He drove a bright purple 1957 Chevrolet Biscayne with the words 'The Purple Grape Stomper' and a bunch of grapes painted across the side of the car. No one knew who he was, but we all admired his style. Any sightings of 'The Purple Grape Stomper' were gleefully reported, and the car became an Ohio legend.

During my junior year of high school, I continued to sneak off to rock concerts with my friends whenever I could get away with it. We drove to Toledo to see the latest bands, such as Jethro Tull and Genesis. Peter Gabriel did about ten costume changes during the Genesis set, which I thought showed real dedication, since they were only playing to a few dozen kids at the Toledo University student union. In my hometown of Fremont, new bands like Iggy Pop and Bob Seger played Ole Zim's Wagon Shed, and I went to see them, too.

While America was rife with political unrest, my home life grew weirder and weirder. Just like Luke Roberts and anyone else I tried to befriend, Dad hated my new 'hoodlum friends', as he called them. Because I began to ignore him completely, he shouted at me all the louder and became even more spiteful to animals. He set leg traps around the back yard that would snap their razor-sharp steel jaws shut on any animal that stepped on them, tearing into its leg and clamping down all the way to the bone while it struggled in agony to free itself. At night I heard the terrified screams of the animals caught in his cruel traps and seethed with rage at my own powerlessness to stop him.

In the morning Dad made the rounds with his shotgun and finished off the poor tortured animals at pointblank range then ordered me to collect the bodies and throw them into the gully. Seeing their beautiful fur soaked in blood, bitter tears of pity and frustration streamed down my cheeks as I was forced to carry out the grim task. There was nothing to prevent one of my cats being caught next. I started to sneak out before going to bed and tiptoe around in the dark with a broom handle setting off as many of the traps I could find. I could have lost a foot myself. My Guardian Angel must have been working overtime.

Dad's chemical warfare with animals became even more bizarre. He put pink rat poison on to popcorn and left it outside for raccoons to eat. He decided that every 'coon in the country had to die because he had lost a few ears of corn.

'It'll be dark, so they won't know it's pink,' he reasoned. He erected a wire fence around his crops and plugged it into the mains so it would electrocute everything that touched it.

His world had to be germ and bug free and he fought his corner every chance he got. There were baited mousetraps everywhere, despite the presence of cats. In the house, we all had to breathe air tainted with deadly fly spray that he'd mixed up himself and poured into one of those old-fashioned aerosol dispensers you had to pump by hand. Leaving nothing to chance, Dad also plastered smelly No-Pest pesticide strips all over the house and installed the latest electric bug-zappers. He seemed to find satisfaction in the sound of insects being electrocuted.

His obsessive behaviour meant our dinner plates had to be completely clean before we left the table. He flew into a blue fit if we left the refrigerator door open and he was forever turning off lights because he'd heard that the Queen of England did the same at Buckingham Palace to save electricity.

'You're a load of heathens – why can't you behave like civilised human beings,' he rasped if we accidentally left a door open. 'I'm not paying to heat the whole country outside.'

It also drove him mad that Mom's spectacles were often covered with dabs of pancake mix. He gave her patronising lessons on how to remove them without touching the lenses with her fingers.

Dad came up with yet another innovation. He erected a small plastic swimming pool, suspended on aluminium panels, in the back yard next to the chicken coop. But the water was icy cold, even in the middle of Ohio's long, hot summers. This threw him a challenge. He went out and bought a 100-foot length of black garden hose and arranged it in a spiral on top of the chicken coop's tin roof. Then he put one end in the pool, and siphoned the pool water through the hose, so it would go up to the chicken coop roof and continuously circulate through the length of black hose where the sun was beating down. By the time the water returned and poured out the other end of the hose back into the pool, it was warm.

Next Dad decided to strip down and completely restore the Stinson, so fragments of airplane joined the assortment of car and truck parts in the yard. At one point it looked like the aftermath of some freak accident – there was a wheel here, a wing there, a carburettor lying in the grass beside a propeller, a fuselage propped up on breezeblocks in the driveway ...

Dad underestimated the enormity of taking apart a whole airplane and eventually ran out of places to leave freshly painted parts to dry. I came home from school one day to see the 30-foot clothesline in our back yard loaded to capacity with airplane parts flapping in the breeze. Dad had suspended them from their rivet holes by tiny wires he'd made into 'S' hooks. The other end was wound tightly around the clothesline so they wouldn't slide into each other and scratch the paint. Gloria made up her mind that she was never going to get in that plane again because there were so many parts left over when he put it back together again.

When he'd finished, there was a set to over his handiwork with Jerry Dressler, who ran the local airport.

'You'll have to get a safety certificate from the FAA (Federal Aviation Administration) before I let you take off,' Jerry insisted.

But Dad reckoned his plane had never been in better shape and didn't want anyone else going near it. When eventually the FAA guy was allowed to look it over, it turned out that Dad had tightened the wing bolts so much that the threads had been stripped. He was told that both wings would have dropped off the very first time he took it up.

And that wasn't the only brush with disaster Dad had with his airplane. One clear summer day when he went flying with Mom they noticed strange liquid splattering all over the windshield, and it certainly wasn't raining. Dad saw that the oil pressure was falling so he made an emergency landing in a field. Before take-off he'd checked the oil and forgotten to put the cap back on. Oil was draining out of the engine and being blown on to the windshield by the propeller. He was pretty shaken as he paced back and forth assessing the situation. That's when he hit his head on the wing support, almost knocking himself out.

Luckily he carried a spare can of oil, which he poured into the engine. In true redneck fashion, he stuffed an old rag into the tank opening in lieu of a cap. He came home swearing and shouting, with a bleeding gash and a goose egg on his head. Dad could out-curse anyone.

Another time I went along with Dad and Mom when they flew to Cleveland to visit a boat show where Dad could talk to others in the marine business about marketing his anchors. Gloria, of course, stuck to her earlier resolution and stayed at home. Cleveland is famous for its fog, and this day it was a real pea-souper. He was in a hurry to get home before dark and in a filthy temper because the control tower at Burke Lakefront airport wanted him to wait a while for the fog to clear.

After a flaming row, he was given clearance for take-off but couldn't see a thing. Suddenly he yelled, 'Oh, shit!' as he saw something straight ahead rising out of what we all thought was a cloud. But it was a church steeple coming out of a fog patch instead. Not only were we at a dangerously low altitude, but we were supposed to be flying out across Lake Erie, not over land. Dad had no idea where he was. He was flying in a blind panic with zero visibility.

Then he couldn't find his maps and he kept yelling at Mom because she didn't know where he put them. The air was blue and he wasn't thinking straight. Suddenly everything seemed unreal and I thought, This is it. We're going to die. When death seems inevitable, it's strange how easily you accept it and just wait for the final moment. It really was nothing less than a miracle that he eventually managed to get back on track and follow his flight plan. My Guardian Angel must have steered the plane back on course because Dad sure didn't know what he was doing. I never went up in that airplane with him again.

Dad was becoming a real danger to himself and others – like the time he taxied into an airport runway light and damaged his propeller in Michigan. 'Damned stupid place to put a runway light,' was Dad's defence. He straightened the propeller by jerking at it in a rage with his bare hands – but propellers are precision instruments that are set on an exacting balance. Dad got the plane back in the air but was in for a serious rollicking from Jerry when he hit the ground again. Dad managed to talk his way out of it. Everything was always someone else's fault. He was forever doing crazy things, such as putting a black hood over his head so he couldn't see out, while pretending to be on automatic pilot.

Thankfully, Dad didn't teach me to drive. If his flying lessons were anything to go by, I had a lucky escape. Officially, I learned to drive in Drivers' Education class at school, although the truth is they only taught me the rules of the road. I had been driving illegally for years. When I decided drugs were not for me, instead of being rejected by my reject friends, I gained unexpected popularity and a unique position of importance in the gang. The term 'designated driver' hadn't yet been coined but that is exactly what I was.

I enjoyed driving. It was something I was good at during a time when women drivers were being constantly derided. Mom cited it as yet another example of my 'mechanical mindedness', referring to my natural ability to master modern technology. Never were any terms that implied femininity used to describe me. (Who could have predicted just how useful that ability would be with the advent of personal computers and the Internet? These days I'm glad to be the local nerd.)

There can be no doubt that I am my father's daughter. Within weeks of getting my driving licence I got arrested for doing 60 in a 35mph zone in Dad's car – a canary yellow 1967 Oldsmobile Cutlass Supreme. It looked like a banana on wheels. I was cruising down Rawson Avenue with 'Fun Fun Fun' by the Beach Boys blaring. I didn't realise there was a police car behind me. The officer put his flasher on and pointed to the side of the road for me to pull over.

'D'you know how fast you were going there, young lady? I'm gonna have to give ya a ticket. Your dad sure is gonna be mad at you,' he said.

My father was livid, but only because I had been caught. He couldn't complain about my fast driving because he was reckless too. I had to go to the courthouse and appear before Judge Riley. The burly, redneck judge gave me a brusque ticking off, took my licence away for 10 days and fined me $25. His daughter Rebecca went to school locally and his wife, a teacher, was a real sourpuss. Judge Riley eventually had a sex-change operation and went to live in another town and practise law as a female lawyer. I couldn't believe that such a macho man could turn himself into a woman.

Although I was no stranger to the local constabulary, I never did anything serious. I was conspicuous because of the gang I hung out with. One day Dad found a 'speed' pill called a Black Beauty on the driveway after a car full of my stoned misfit friends came to pick me up. They had sent 'the straightest-looking one in the car', who happened to be a drug dealer, to the door. I'd never even met him before. He had so many pills on him that they were falling out of his pockets and he accidentally dropped one.

Dad didn't know what was in the capsule, but he sniffed it, poked it and eyed it with suspicion. 'The sheriff's coming to pick it up first thing tomorrow,' he finally announced and placed it on the kitchen shelf. He didn't even question how it came to be lying on the driveway. I had no idea what he would do if he found out it contained illegal amphetamines. He'd often threatened to have me put into the local juvenile detention centre, and this could have been his golden opportunity.

But I wasn't going to let him have it. I tiptoed down to the kitchen in the middle of the night, pulled the capsule apart, emptied it down the sink, filled it up with a mixture of crushed aspirin and Aunt Jemima pancake mix, and stuck it back together. The police analysis said it contained 'aspirin and caffeine'. Although I was a little surprised about the caffeine part, I was relieved to be off the hook.

Chapter Four

Up Around The Bend

In the middle of a particularly icy winter's night in 1970, Ginger the dachshund woke Gloria up to let her know that the house was on fire. She in turn alerted the rest of the family. We all coughed and groped our way downstairs through the thick black smoke that would have choked us all to death had the dog not raised the alarm.

The fire engines came and we stood outside in the freezing cold watching our home burn down. Although he blamed it on 'the electrics', I was convinced Dad had had something to do with starting the fire. We'll never know the truth. Besides being so accident prone, he always insisted on cleaning out the fireplace before we went to bed, then putting the smouldering ashes into a brown paper grocery sack from the A&P and placing them outside the front door – on to the wooden front porch. That's where the fire originated.

As I stood shivering in my nightgown watching the flames grow higher and higher, I suddenly realised that I had left my cat Cilla (named after Cilla Black) shut in my bedroom. 'Mom, I've got to go back in to get her,' I pleaded. But Mom wouldn't let me. She grabbed a wet towel from the kitchen – the flames hadn't hit there yet – and climbed the stairs with it wrapped around her head, breathing through the wet fabric to filter the smoke. A few minutes later she emerged clutching my terrified cat.

There's no doubt she saved Cilla's life at great risk to her own. The whole house was charred and the stench afterwards was so bad that I can still remember the smell to this day. (Thirty years later I was reminded of that same acrid burning smell - I was in New York City on September 11th, 2001). We had to stay in a motel while builders repaired all the damage, which was covered by the household insurance claim Dad filed.

The whole experience pushed me over the edge. Everything was always going wrong and, if my father's incompetence wasn't going to kill me, I would end up killing myself.

I waited until summer to make my move. Two weeks before my 16th birthday I ran away from home. My father probably wouldn't have minded too much, but I took my mother with me.

'I'm going, Mom. There's nothing for me here any more. I hate high school. I hate this town. I hate my whole life. I'm going to quit school and get a job,' I told her.

'Where will you go?' she asked.

'I don't know but I'm going and I'm not coming back.'

Mom started crying. 'Well, if you've made your mind up, I'm coming too,' she decided.

We packed our bags. Mom bought the tickets and we took a Greyhound bus to her father's house in Leesburg, Florida. My maternal grandfather was a good man. After he retired from the Kentucky coal mines, he became a local lay preacher and respected pillar of the community. Like the rest of Mom's family, he also had a wacky sense of humour, always telling jokes and making up silly songs.

At Grandpa's house we were well looked after and had a

wonderful time. We shopped, lunched in restaurants, gossiped with neighbours and went to church. I got a great suntan but, more importantly, for the very first time, I got a taste of normal life.

Mom's youngest sister, Aunt Sibby, came down from Arkansas to visit us with her two teenage daughters Susan and Sharon. My overwhelming memory of Aunt Sibby is of her wearing Susan's underpants on her head to keep her hair curlers in place. To this day if you put your knickers on your head and ask 'Who's this?' everybody will know you're taking off Aunt Sibby.

Dad, meanwhile, went crazy. He immediately tracked us down, but 'let' us stay for six weeks. He persuaded Mom to return home but, before I agreed to do the same, I laid down a few conditions.

'If I come back, you have to leave me alone, let me go out, let me see my friends,' I said. He never allowed me to do anything without making a terrible scene. Other parents let their girls go to dances at Roger Young Park on Friday and Saturday nights. The park was across the river at the back of our woods and I listened in envy as 'Wild Thing' by the Troggs and 'Louis Louis' by the Kingsmen drifted across to our yard. Being forbidden to do things other kids took for granted was one of the reasons Dad and I argued. Whereas Mom and Gloria would do anything to keep the peace, I stood up to him. I just wanted to lead my life like any normal teenager.

'And I'm not working in your factory any more.'

He promised to try to change his ways, although he wasn't too happy about it. Mom and I went back home and Dad made an effort to become more careful. He reluctantly allowed me to go places and hang out with my friends. He hired some part-time men to work at minimum wage to take my place in his factory.

Things became easier for me at home. Dad started putting rat poison on Wonder Bread to kill ants and he still took pot shots at woodland creatures, but he pretty much left me alone – apart from the occasional cutting remark.

'You've got enough holes in your head already,' he said when I announced that I was getting my ears pierced. Perhaps he wasn't entirely wrong. The youngest Dressler girl, Sarah, performed my first-ever cosmetic surgery procedure – in the lobby of the local airport, which doubled as their living room. She dabbed my ear lobes with whiskey to disinfect them, used ice cubes as anaesthetic and held an orange behind each ear before plunging the needle in. Blood spurted everywhere.

Then I went to see a jeweller to get some $3 studs. The guy behind the counter must have thought he was some kind of stud himself. The dirty old lecher locked the door behind me and tried to feel me up. I screamed, escaped, went outside and threw up.

It took a while to recover from both traumas and, once my ears stopped bleeding and swelling, I dreamed of owning all kinds of glittering, dangling earrings. I saw Cher on TV singing 'Gypsies Tramps and Thieves', her massive gold hoops swinging as she danced on stage. I wanted some like that. (What's more, she had costumes by Bob Mackie, who also designed special edition outfits for Barbie.) But asking Dad for help was always an excruciating ordeal guaranteed to make you resolve to do without next time. 'What d'you think, money grows on trees?' he was always saying.

During my junior year at Fremont Ross High, at the age of 16, I got a part-time job as a burger slinger on a hamburger stand, working evenings and weekends. Apart from earning a few bucks and being able to buy my own earrings, the work had other advantages: all the free milkshakes and fries I could eat, it got me out of the house, kept me out of trouble and I met lots of people. It was quite a social outlet. I was given the hamburger chain's official white uniform and frilly apron and hat to wear. Putting on that uniform gave me a sense of belonging to something at last.

Although the job was a lot easier than the men's factory and farm work I had been doing at home since the age of four, it took me a long time to get used to receiving a pay-cheque for my efforts at the end of the week. Despite the fact that Dad made us work long hours, none of us – not even my mother – was ever given an allowance. We had to ask for every little thing and justify the expense to my father. On the rare occasions he allowed us to make a purchase, we had to shop around and compare prices, then turn in the receipt along with every penny of the change.

Even though I was only earning the minimum wage, having my own pay-cheque changed my life. It was then that I decided that no man would ever control my finances, as my father had my mother's. Economic independence would be mine. I worked as much overtime as I could and stood in for the other kids when they couldn't work their shift. My hard work and dedication to duty made me my boss's favourite.

Having already worked hard for 12 years without pay, getting a pay-cheque gave me more drive than the others who worked on the burger stand with me. Most of them were used to spending their spare time hanging out and watching TV. Their weekly pay-cheque was probably less than their allowance and clothing budget combined. To those kids working for a living must have been a rude awakening, whereas I saw a world of opportunities opening up before me.

Money may not be everything, but only a fool would deny that it helps. As my friend Rachel used to say, 'Life is like a shit sandwich. The more bread you have the less shit you have to eat.'

Ironically, when I was finally allowed some freedom after getting back from Florida, I began dating probably the only boy in town my father would have approved of: Jerry Dressler's son, Donny.

We didn't have anywhere to go to make out, but Donny knew this great spot on a country road where we could park. 'Nobody ever goes there,' he promised. The windows were getting very steamed up and Van Morrison was on the car radio singing, 'Hey where did we go, days when the rains came, down in the hollow, playing a new game,' to a brown-eyed girl. Suddenly a cop knocked on the window with a flashlight. We quickly rearranged our clothes and Donny rolled down the window.

'Yessir?' he asked anxiously.

'You all right in there, kids ... hey, ain't you Jerry Dressler's boy?' asked the cop.

Donny was scared his dad was going to get to hear about our night of non-passion but the cop was in a generous mood.

'Move on and look after yourselves,' he said as we drove off. Donny took me straight home – we weren't going to make another attempt at consummating our relationship that night.

Although I wish I could say that Donny was my first, unfortunately he wasn't. I have to admit that I lost my virginity under the Ohio Turnpike in a dented maroon Ford Fairlane to one of the hoods I hung out with. He assured me I couldn't get pregnant the first time and, in any case, he promised he would pull out at the crucial moment. He didn't, of course. Like my first kiss, it was not a pleasant experience. I was glad it was over so quickly. And, of course, the jerk never called me again. (*Et tu,* my misfit friend.)

Luckily I didn't get pregnant, unlike a lot of girls I knew. Abortion was illegal in Ohio at that time, so they had to go out of state to backstreet abortionists. One friend of mine did just that. A couple of weeks later she felt terrible pains. Blood started streaming down her legs and she saw something fall out on to the beige carpet. It was a tiny putrefying ribcage. The abortionist had scraped out her womb, tearing up the foetus in the process, but didn't get it all. She promptly fainted. Her mother, who had taken her for the abortion in the first place, rushed her back to have the job redone in the dead of night by the same doctor.

Another friend of mine who got pregnant had a long-term boyfriend who promised to marry her and raise the baby. Then his parents stepped in and insisted he go to college instead. She reluctantly had an abortion. Shortly afterwards, she contracted a raging infection that nearly killed her. She had to have a complete hysterectomy. She was left sterile and menopausal at the age of 17.

Although I adored Donny, he was more like a brother. The problem was that there could never really be any real passion between us. We'd shared a playpen as toddlers. He'd been in my class every year since kindergarten. We were comfortable with each other because we both had peculiar families. Neither of us had to explain anything, we both knew the way things were. We spent hours on end in his room listening to albums like Bob Dylan's *Freewheelin'* and John Denver's *Rocky Mountain High*. Donny was into folk music and could play a mean banjo.

Having been brought up at the airport, Donny had to learn to fly at a young age too. Being the local county airport, it had just one tiny runway and his dad or mom, Lola, manned the control tower. This wasn't as complex as it sounds; if a pilot wanted to land or take off they simply had to make radio contact with the airport and, if it was dark, get someone to flip on the runway lights. If Jerry and Lola were out, one of the kids would bring the planes in.

They lived in some converted hangars built from corrugated structures called Wonderbuildings. Inside one, Jerry built a reception area that doubled as a living room and, in another there were bedrooms.

Jerry had always promised Lola that one day they would get a real house. When that day arrived, he simply erected a Wonderbuilding in the middle of the woods. Walking into their living room was like stepping into a beautiful, sculpted garden. Instead of carpet, grass grew on the floor. There were plants everywhere and the roof had a translucent panel so that the sun could shine in. It also had solar panels for power. One of the chairs was a two-seater swing suspended from the ceiling. The room even had a cute little resident lizard.

Another Dressler boy, Lance, also learned to fly when he was just a kid. In his late teens and early twenties, he delivered planes to missionaries in Africa. Before setting off, he removed the spare seats from two- or four-seater single-engine planes and filled the space with spare barrels of gas. He was effectively a flying bomb.

On one trip, he made headlines in an Irish paper because the plane began to splutter and cough just off the Irish coast. Thinking he was going to ditch in the sea, he radioed a frantic mayday.

Although he had run out of fuel, Lance managed to coast to shore and made an emergency landing in a cabbage patch. He was still trying to bring the plane to a stop when an ancient brick wall loomed in front of him. He had just one chance. If he could make the plane hop over the fence, he might just manage to clear it. Miraculously he did, and Lance became a hero. That night, he went to the local pub and everyone bought him drinks.

Other times, his fuel consumption was so precisely calculated that he was unable to divert when ordered to do so by air traffic control. Often, the shortest route took him over restricted military zones, where he was nearly shot down on a number of occasions. After finishing college, Lance married his high school sweetheart, Rita. He went on to run the airport in a neighbouring town, and he's now pursuing a political career.

Since we were under the legal drinking age, Donny and I developed a cunning plan to get us into bars. Both of us were interested in photography and Donny had a darkroom in his Wonderbuilding bedroom. Driving licences back then were nothing more than a coloured piece of paper on which no pictures were required. I photographed Gloria and Lance's driving licences and we blew them up to the correct size. The developing paper was glossy, so we placed our fake licences in frosted plastic wallets, hoping no one would pull them out for closer inspection. From that day on, in bars all across Ohio we were known as Gloria and Lance.

Donny was my date for the senior prom. I wore a long, black velvet, halter-neck dress split up to the thigh for the occasion. I was the only girl in the class of '73 to wear a dress like that. He flew me to Michigan for dinner at a fancy restaurant called Win Schuler's before we went to the dance. He had a soft, kind face and the warmest smile you have ever seen, but we should never have been anything more than very dear friends. Our relationship was more spiritual than physical.

A few months after graduation, we broke up. I had made up my mind to get out of Fremont and have an interesting life. He wanted to stay where he was, get married and raise a family. The very thought of doing that, even with Donny, left me cold. I said it was best we didn't go on. We were both upset but it was inevitable. Another pattern was forming. In the same way that boys unceremoniously dumped me, being with the ones who cared for me always meant giving up my dreams in order to help them realise theirs.

I've never met anyone else like Donny. I didn't have to explain to him about my father because he'd known him all his life. I was never afraid to fly with him because he was down to earth and reliable. But I could see him slipping into obscurity, a world I was trying to avoid. Still, he was my childhood sweetheart, and nothing can take away the tender feelings I'll always have for him.

Donny eventually became a very religious member of the God squad and married Marianne, who until then was a teacher. They have four beautiful children and live in an Ohio farmhouse.

One by one, most of the other kids paired off, got married and started families of their own. But it wasn't the kind of life I envisaged for myself. I wasn't in with the Fremont in-crowd and if I couldn't win I didn't want to play.

Other kids regarded me as some kind of weirdo. And there were just three teachers who were nice to me: Viola Deppen, my study hall teacher (we cruelly called her VD), who was soon to die of cancer; Mrs Newman, who taught English and died from a brain tumour the year after I graduated; and Jim Burroughs, who taught creative writing. In my senior year there was also a very pleasant new history teacher called Mr Harris. It was his first year of teaching and, as he was just 22, I found him easy to talk to.

Even though I often skipped classes and rarely studied, I found high school courses easy and managed to keep a good grade average. But Dad flatly refused to consider sending me to college. 'It would be a senseless waste of good money,' he reasoned, 'because girls are supposed to get married and raise children.' In other words, it would have involved paying for me to live away from home, out of his control. But if I stayed in Fremont my only alternatives were unskilled jobs that paid minimum wage or working in a factory.

When Graduation Day came, it was a great relief, like being let out of prison. Having been put ahead a year back in kindergarten, I was only seventeen. All of the other graduates were eighteen or nineteen. Some of them were even married. Our school colours were purple and white and I spent a good deal of my time there in a purple haze. But at least I learned one good piece of advice. My senior class motto was: 'A journey of a thousand miles must begin with a single step.'

And now I had to take it.

Chapter Five

Kodakrome

I thought my big break had come at last when a shopping centre opened on State Street. It was a tiny strip mall with a sewing supply shop, a bargain outlet, a drug store, a supermarket and an Olan Mills photography studio.

Being interested in photography, I applied for a job as receptionist. As it was a well-known chain that set up in every hick town, it seemed that everyone across America had their photo taken by Olan Mills. They hired me, and I was duly put in charge of answering the phone and booking appointments.

After a few weeks the photographer handed in his notice. Wanting to jump in and take his place, I asked the studio manager if there was any way I could have his job.

'Look, I don't want to be a receptionist, I really want to be a photographer,' I told her. 'I've already had a picture published in the local paper.' Desperate to get the job, I acted as if I was the next Annie Liebovitz.

I showed her a newspaper cutting with an advertisement for the hamburger stand I'd worked on. There was a picture of my friend Mike Fox flipping burgers in the kitchen, which I'd taken. (Mike had very long hair and, because they didn't want a hairy hippie making burgers, he was forced to wear a short nylon wig to conceal his flowing tresses. As wigs were far from convincing in those days, he looked like a poor man's Burt Reynolds.) Here was proof that I was a published photographer. What more could she ask for? I didn't see the problem.

Because I was just seventeen, the studio owner said I was a bit young for the job, but my enthusiasm must have swayed her. She arranged for a senior photographer from the head office to come to train me. I got a perfect score on the examination and before long I was awarded my photography certificate.

Taking pictures came naturally to me. As well as being an inventor and pilot, Dad was a semi-professional photographer and even had some of his work published in *Life* magazine. Because I'd shown interest in something *he* cared about, he'd allowed me to borrow his camera since I was about twelve. 'Don't lose it,' he warned, 'it's worth more than you are.' I took pictures of anything and everything.

When he decided it was time for me to have a camera of my own, he searched through every mail-order catalogue to find the cheapest 35mm Minolta SRT 101 in the United States. When it arrived, I was thrilled. Until he immediately took it to his workbench and got out his set of jeweller's screwdrivers and completely dismantled it. I was absolutely aghast and thought it would never work again.

Maybe I should have seen that coming. Dad was endlessly fascinated by any object with working parts and had to know exactly how it worked. Anything new in the house was immediately taken apart. After he put things back together again, any left-over parts were kept in jars on shelves at the back of the garage.

My job at the burger joint had also allowed me to purchase other camera equipment. I'd amassed an impressive collection of interchangeable lenses, backdrops and professional lighting gear.

Through photography I finally found an outlet for my stifled creativity. For the first time in my life I could be proactive instead of reacting to the situation around me. According to *Compton's Encyclopedia*: 'As a nonverbal means of communication, photography can surmount the barriers of language and communicate through universal visual symbols.' So I set out to make a statement through my work. Clients wrote flattering letters saying they had never had such creative pictures taken by Olan Mills.

For the next year, I was Fremont's town photographer. I snapped individual portraits, shot family groups and took baby pictures. Infants were the bane of my existence. They kept spitting up on my drop cloths. Then they'd start crying but, as I had to get a smiling picture, I cheered them up by bouncing little fluffy bunnies and teddy bears at them. Weddings were my favourite because there was always plenty of cake. (When I discovered how good food could taste outside of my mother's kitchen, I made up for lost time and began to put on weight.) I bought a man's style tuxedo to wear for photographing weddings, but I took such a liking to it that it became my usual attire.

I was still living at home and desperate to get my own place. There was just one problem: my salary was very low and there was no way I could afford it. Since my work had been praised and I had even won company awards, I thought I deserved a bit more money. But the head office flatly refused to give me a decent raise. Maybe they thought they were on to a good thing having a kid as a photographer and paying her a pittance. I decided to quit the job, further my education and then consider getting out of America and settling in Europe. I never did think small.

It was 1973, the year a formal peace agreement was signed in Paris, ending the Vietnam War hostilities. Combat troops were withdrawn and US prisoners of war were released, but not before 58,148 people were killed at an average age of just 23.11 years old.

I attended art school in the State's capital, Columbus, for a year and a half. At night I worked behind the bar at a campus rock venue, where I got to watch early performances by artists such as Queen and Lou Reed as I served beer and pizza. I lived a typical student life and loved the freedom ... and the food.

Ohio University was in nearby Athens, Ohio, where Donny Dressler's sister Sarah was a student. I hung out with her quite a bit. Dad loaned me his 1967 yellow Cutlass Supreme so we could drive home at weekends. One night we drove up to Cleveland to see my then hero, David Bowie, who was on his *Diamond Dogs* tour. We were right at the front. I was mesmerised by his red hair, matching red suspenders and ballet shoes. You didn't see many guys dressed like that in Ohio back then. I took lots of photographs.

At art school I studied drawing, art history, architecture and interior design. As with photography, I was keenly interested in the visual aspects of things. I became absorbed in classical architecture and learned all the formulae for columns, eventually being able to identify which architect had designed a certain style of woodcarving, such as work by Sir Christopher Wren. (These days I use that ability to identify which surgeon carved what face.)

I also began to understand more about proportion and presentation. As a result, I became acutely aware of how far my face was from the ideal. And now, for the first time, I was able to quantify it.

They say a little knowledge is a dangerous thing. I became fascinated by Leonardo da Vinci's theory of the classically proportioned face, which has been used for centuries by artists to create faces that would be considered beautiful to the observer. More recently it has been employed by reconstructive surgeons who need to apply standardised measurements when attempting to make a disfigured face appear 'normal'. These are by no means random judgements they all use da Vinci's proportions. Otherwise you could end up with your nose in the middle of your forehead or your eyes where your cheeks should be. This theory divides the face into equal sections: from top of the forehead to mid-eyebrow, from mid-brow to base of nose, and from base of nose to the chin. In profile, the upper lip should be in line with the chin.

When I measured my face in the mirror, I discovered that my jaw was too long from the front and too far forward from the side. In other words, the lower third of my face was out of proportion. When my sister's boyfriend said that my nose almost met my chin when I smiled, I know he didn't mean to humiliate me, he was only stating the obvious.

Although I'm sure Mark knew nothing about the rules of classic proportion, he had instinctively noticed that the composition of my face was actually incorrect. (Later my research into physical attraction revealed that human beings compare every face they encounter with a mental template of what an attractive face 'should' look like.) It was a bone structure problem. I was disappointed because I didn't think I could ever do anything about it, and it certainly wasn't going to go away.

Despite all my physical flaws , I had youth on my side and there were times I think I looked OK – if a little masculine.

I enjoyed art school and felt at home with the bohemian types I met there, but I still had no idea how I was going to make a living. Back then I had no way of knowing that I would eventually apply Leonardo's theories to my own cosmetic surgery plan, and then teach other people about the proportions of their features.

I didn't really want to be an interior designer, even though that's what I was being trained for. As one of our end-of-year projects, the teacher gave us the dimensions of an empty room and assigned us to turn it into a galleried one-bedroom studio apartment.

I excitedly drew up a plan using hanging grass wallpaper that transformed the room into a jungle. There was green Astroturf on the floor, and each piece of furniture was upholstered in a different animal print. During the day the ceiling was sky blue, but when it got dark the stars came out. I'd created a twinkling night sky with tiny spotlights set into a glow-in-the-dark overhead mural. I was using the concept of the jungle and bringing it indoors – a bit like taking the Dressler's Wonderbuilding from the woods and transporting it into the bush. The finishing touch was a glittering crystal spiral staircase up to the sleeping area.

I thought it was fabulous, but my teacher was horrified. 'This is impractical. No one could live in this room,' she said. I felt hurt. Anyone could paint a room beige, get a chequered sofa or a flowery settee and lay some carpeting down. 'And the staircase is too dangerous. Someone might fall down it and break their neck,' she added. I thought my ideas were brilliant but obviously no one else did.

The place where I lived was no more acceptable. I'd moved into a one-bedroom apartment on the third floor of a run-down green breeze-block building on King Avenue. It wasn't in the best part of town – most of the tenants in the building had had their apartments broken into at least once – but it was cheap. And no one drove past laughing at airplane parts in the yard or tin pie pans rattling in the cherry trees. I invited friends from college over to my little apartment without fear of embarrassment, which felt like a real luxury. All I was embarrassed about now was my expanding girth.

Meanwhile the Watergate scandal had hit the headlines. Richard Milhous Nixon stepped down in disgrace as US president. Maybe the hippies had been right about not trusting anyone over 30.

One day I came home to find several members of the FBI waiting for me outside my apartment, clutching huge rifles. They seemed to know everything about me, including the time I normally got home. After flashing their badges and ID cards at me, just like they do on television, they asked for the keys to my apartment, which I duly handed over, although I didn't know what they could possibly want with them. I hadn't been expecting visitors, so I tried to remember whether I'd made my bed or not. A few minutes later one of them opened my door and motioned for me to come up and answer the phone. My number was unlisted, but the call was for them. It's amazing what the FBI can find out about you when they want to.

'What's going on?' I asked. They didn't answer. I'd just been to the grocery store and bought a newspaper. There on the front page was a mugshot of Frank, the guy who lived two doors down from me. It said he had robbed a bank. I couldn't believe it. He seemed such a friendly neighbour, a real regular guy. One evening when I had a gas leak he came over to help. Now the FBI were using my apartment to stake him out.

I cowered in my apartment while the FBI crept across the fire escape. When I heard them yell, 'Freeze!' I thought, Oh my God, they're going to kill him. What if they have a shoot-out and I get hit in the crossfire? Luckily there was to be no bloodshed. My bank-robbing neighbour had already left the state. It had been his nephew who answered the door.

Unfortunately when the FBI came back into my apartment to tell me they had been unable to apprehend the suspect and we could all relax, they got a little slipshod and forgot to follow standard procedure. One of them said to me, 'There's a federal agent outside your bedroom window. Go and tell him we have the all clear and to come on up.' I let out a huge sigh of relief. Feeling like I was on an official government mission, which, in fact, I was, I went into my bedroom and leaned out of the window to look for the guy. Suddenly I heard the unmistakable sound of a rifle being cocked. I had found the agent all right. And he had found me. He was looking at me through the sights of an enormous rifle, which was pointed straight at my head. My blood ran cold. I sure didn't see that one coming. 'He's going to shoot me!' I thought. 'That's just typical. What a stupid way to die.'

In the tense few seconds it took us both to assess the situation, I eased myself back inside and dropped to the bedroom floor. Then I yelled to the agents in my living room that they'd better tell their guy to come up themselves, since he had no idea who I was and he was prepared to shoot first and ask questions later.

It emerged that Frank had carried out the armed raid because he needed the money. When I was a little short, I worked two jobs or did some freelance photography. When he needed money, he held up a bank. His nephew later told me that Frank had thrown his gun into the Ohio River on his way to Kentucky and we wouldn't be seeing him again.

Something similar happened later in my life in London when law enforcement authorities again used my apartment to stake out a criminal. I tend to attract weird incidents. Well, they do say like attracts like.

During my time in Columbus I was fairly well behaved, although I loved to drink. We threw 'beer shooting' parties where we stood in the bathtub wearing plastic raincoats. You'd open a can of beer and start to drink it, while another kid stood in the tub with you and pierced the bottom of the can, so it flowed straight down your throat and you'd get drunk quicker. The challenge was to resist the impulse to swallow and just empty the can directly into your stomach. Most kids couldn't do it, hence the bathtub and raincoat.

There was also a drink we called the 'miserable bastard', which we mixed in a clean plastic garbage bin. Someone threw a party, everyone brought a bottle and we just kept emptying the alcohol in. This cocktail ended up being a mixture of beer, gin, cheap white wine, tequila, red wine and whiskey – you name it. The next morning, we were all miserable bastards. That's how it got the name.

The drunkest I ever got was when I was challenged to join in with some friends who were alternating shots of green Chartreuse with Wild Turkey whiskey. Not wanting to look like a bad sport, I accepted. It was a decision I lived to regret. I rounded off the evening with a session of projectile vomiting all the way home, including hitting one guy right down the front of his shirt. The next morning there were herds of wild horses stampeding through my head and my mouth felt like the bottom of a parrot's cage. I had to ring up my friends to help me reconstruct the previous evening's events.

It might sound as if I was wild, but I was crazier back in Fremont during my drug-taking phase. Again, it was all about escapism. What I wanted was to *really* escape, not just pretend I wasn't where I was. But I was living hand to mouth and I needed more money before I could realise that ambition.

For a short time I worked as a receptionist at an exclusive tennis club in a multi-million-dollar Continental-style development in the high-rent district that was frequented by well-heeled professionals and the local glitterati. I loved it there because it was how I pictured Europe. There were even a few real Europeans working in the shops. It was truly unique, especially for Ohio. The money and brains behind it, a guy named Mr Goodier, was evidently a very clever and cultured man who had travelled the world, bringing a corner of the Continent back to Ohio. He was also filthy rich. No expense had been spared. The place had everything, including a cinema, shopping mall, an amazing Continental food hall, all kinds of restaurants, theme bars and nightclubs all surrounded by a fabulous apartment complex. I wished I could have afforded to live there instead of in the green breeze-block carbuncle on King Avenue.

For the first couple of weeks at my new job, I was concerned by the regular presence of a scruffy-looking unshaven middle-aged man who kept coming in to look around. Even though I thought he must have been down on his luck and I felt sorry for him, I wished he would go away. Looking like he did, he stood out like a sore thumb among the trendy rich members who frequented the club. He always smiled humbly and said hello to me, but I never really gave him the time of day, thinking it best not to encourage him.

One day, when he had been hanging around longer than usual, I motioned for a passing tennis coach to come over to my desk. I leaned over and whispered in his ear, finally asking why that tramp kept coming into the club, as he clearly didn't play tennis and never said two words to anyone. The reply left me dumbfounded. 'Oh him. That's Mr Goodier,' the coach informed me with a knowing grin. I was obviously not the first one to mistake the multi-millionaire industrialist for a down-and-out.

Mr Goodier counted the tennis club where I worked as well as the entire Continental development among his property portfolio, apartment complex and all. That 'tramp' was the man I worked for. He was known as quite an eccentric and went around looking like that on purpose. I guess he found it amusing.

It was an experience that left quite an impression on me. I believe it's what is known as a 'defining moment' and I'm eternally grateful to Mr Goodier for giving it to me. In a single unforgettable lesson, he'd demonstrated to me the extraordinary capacity we all have for manipulating other people's perceptions of who we are, simply by projecting a certain physical appearance. In other words, he taught me the power of masquerade. I have been endlessly fascinated by it ever since. It has served me well on the many occasions I have employed it myself. However it would be almost two more decades before I was able to embark on the ultimate masquerade.

While I lived on King Avenue and worked at the tennis club, I continued to do freelance photography on the side, as I do to this day. I got some quite good commissions, which I always enjoyed. Once I even got to go to the Columbus State Capital building to photograph a group of US Senators. You could just smell the power in the room. I was attracted to it. But the men looked right through me as I instructed them on where to stand and posed them for their pictures. They saw me as a photographer there to do a job, not as a woman. Still, I left a few of my business cards on the off chance that one of them might call and ask me out. Of course, none of them did.

At that time women were still fighting for something I had always taken for granted – equality in the workplace. Not only was I in no danger whatsoever of sexual harassment, but no one seemed to even notice that I was a woman. And the fact that, at 5 foot 5 inches, I had ballooned from 110 pounds to 160 pounds didn't help matters much.

After a year and a half of odd jobs and taking art courses, photography still wasn't making me rich or getting me to the places I wanted to go. If I was serious about building up my savings account, I had no choice but to go back and live at home with my parents in Fremont.

I got a job in Joseph's department store on the make-up counter. At least I could experiment with different products to disguise the shape of my face. A touch of clever shading here and there must have done the trick, because my high school teacher, Mr Harris, came into the store and talked to me about what I had been doing since graduation. After a few minutes' conversation, he asked me out on a date. I was convinced I 'd heard him wrong, but he called me that evening to make arrangements.

He took me out to dinner at a place in Port Clinton, about 12 miles north of Fremont. Mom had just two rules for dates, which I have never forgotten: 'Don't order fried chicken or spaghetti.' These were the two foods most likely to end up all over your face or down your front. I ordered the Caesar Salad.

It was 1976 and Bryan Ferry sang 'Love Is the Drug'. I fell madly in love with Adam Harris. He bought me gifts of heart-shaped jewellery – some of which I still wear. Kind, thoughtful and the perfect gentleman, he was also a respected academic and teacher. It ran in the family. His father was my guidance counsellor at high school – the man I gave my forged sick notes to.

Working at Joseph's still wasn't getting me the salary I needed, so I got a summer job at the Heinz factory where they made ketchup and chilli sauce. Ohio grows a lot of tomatoes and Wapakoneta is the tomato capital of the world. By coincidence, another man who, like me, learned to fly at an early age was born in that town. He became a licensed pilot on his 16th birthday and on 20 July, 1969, became the first man to walk on the moon. His name, of course, was Neil Armstrong. Along with Edwin E Aldrin Jr., he spent 21 hours and 37 minutes on the moon collecting soil and rock samples, taking photographs and deploying scientific instruments while millions, including me, watched transfixed on television. He made history and splashed down in the Pacific on 24 July.

Which brings me back to earth. Tomatoes arrived by the truckload and were tipped on to a long conveyor belt at the back of the Heinz factory. They put all newcomers 'on tomatoes' where your job was to stand there and pick out any rotten tomatoes, dead mice, tree branches – anything that wasn't fit for human consumption. We were lined up side by side all the way down both sides of the conveyor belt. At the height of the season the tomatoes came in thick and fast and were piled so high that we couldn't possibly grab every alien item.

Before long I was taken off tomatoes and moved over to bottling. Ketchup bottles came along on a conveyor belt like hundreds of little soldiers all in a row. On their way to the end of the line, one machine would slap their labels on, another would fill them with ketchup, and the last machine screwed the lids on. Part of my job was to keep a look-out for crooked labels and tops that didn't quite fit properly as they went down the line. The machinery wasn't one hundred per cent accurate and occasionally a bottle would topple to the floor. I had to sweep up the broken glass and hose down the spilled ketchup, coaxing the little red river towards a drain behind the bottling machines. Wearing my factory-issue hard hat, industrial goggles, protective gloves and rubber boots, I took on the company identity, fitting in perfectly with the other workers, which was important to me. It was hard work but I quite enjoyed it. Hosing down wayward ketchup can be strangely gratifying.

Next I was moved to chilli sauce. It was poured down a foot-wide white chute that was translucent and brightly lit from behind. I had to remove any wayward black specks with a pen-sized sucking instrument from among the seeds, which were supposed to be in it. This job made me dizzy. After a while all I could see were spots in front of my eyes. It happened to everybody, and that's why we all dreaded being on chilli sauce – and why they never kept anyone on it for very long.

The final move I made at Heinz was to the graveyard shift at the paste farm. Because of the unsociable hours (11pm to 6am) they paid triple time. Heinz was the only factory in the US to make ketchup all year round so tomato paste was made in the height of the season from the abundance of fresh tomatoes. That way they could produce ketchup for the rest of the year using the tomato paste.

This was one of the highest level blue collar jobs in the factory. I was in charge of huge, great boiling towers of simmering tomato paste. All through the night I had to sit and watch the dials and, if the temperature should rise, I had to scale the side of the vat and peek through a porthole for a visual check. It was a great responsibility because, if the paste should boil too far up the tower, the top of the vat could explode. Then there would be gallons of erupting tomato paste and we'd have to run for our lives.

It was hard work but good money. On days off, I had another part-time job pumping gas at the Mobil station on the busy Ohio Turnpike. One car after another would roll up and I had to greet the customer, put the gas in the car, check the oil, wash the front and rear windshield, take the money and try to sell the customer oil. I was always too honest to 'short stick' the customer like some of the guys did. This involved not pushing the dipstick all the way in then showing the driver the 'proof' that he was a quart low.

Both jobs were backbreaking. They were really intended as men's work – and it was beginning to show. The truth hit me one day when I was checking the oil under the hood of a car. A customer came up behind me and said, 'Excuse me, sonny ...' I thought he'd mistaken me for a boy because I was wearing greasy overalls and a cap. But when I turned around he still couldn't tell I was a woman.

Chapter Six

Born To Run

At the end of the tomato season, my spotless employee record meant I was offered a permanent job at Heinz. It was good pay and some of my friends told me I was mad to turn it down. Jobs like that didn't open up every day. But I knew if I accepted it I'd be signing up for a life sentence. A lot of local people spent their entire lives working at that factory, and they were glad for the job. It paid for their houses, their cars and their children's college education. But I didn't have any of those commitments, nor did I plan to take them on. I was by no means work shy, I just wanted something different out of life.

Having studied art, I had taken a journey through European history and it was time to go and see it for myself. Besides, I felt at odds with the throwaway culture in which I'd grown up. There were new fads forever sweeping the country that made you feel that you weren't worthy if you didn't spend money on them. But I had my own ideas and didn't want to wear/have/collect/do the same things everyone else did. What's more, I get attached to things, like my Barbie doll and my Ben Casey shirt, and treasure them for years. That kind of behaviour is unacceptable in a consumerist economy that demands consistently high product turnover. If I stayed and became a cog inside that machine I would never get ahead. *Shop 'til you drop?* That's the whole idea. It's short for: *Work like a dog to make money to put back into the economy then you die.* I knew down deep that I was going to leave and never return.

Only one thing was tugging me back. I hadn't bargained on falling in love with Adam Harris. But we both knew how hard I was working to get out of Fremont and even he couldn't stop me. (Little did I realise it was going to be one of the best relationships I would ever have.) Ever generous and supportive, Adam even found me an extra job to help finance my escape. He lived with two other bachelors in a farmhouse they called The Spa. I became their maid – cleaning, washing dishes, clearing the yard – and they all chipped in to pay me $5 an hour.

I saved up all my nickels and dimes and put away every dollar. And then I saw what I was looking for advertised in *Vogue* magazine: a course at the Inchbald School of Design in London. I applied, got a place and paid the $1,000 in advance. Then I started shopping around for the cheapest air ticket I could find. Adam and his bachelor friends owed me some back salary and handed over a couple of hundred bucks.

Gloria, like me, had financed her own education by working her way through a nearby university, emerging with a Bachelor of Science in Business Administration, Magna Cum Laude, no less. Now a newlywed and beginning a business career with a multinational corporation, she was too preoccupied with her own life to worry about mine. Gloria married the guy who drove the Purple Grape Stomper. He turned out to be a charismatic young man named Carl from nearby Bellevue, Ohio. Typically, she'd netted a top jock. He was a talented athlete who'd gone to college on a football scholarship, earning a Bachelor of Science in Social Welfare.

Mom was excited for me. She thought I'd be back home pretty soon. She may have reacted differently if she'd known I was going forever.

I didn't tell Dad I was going to England and there were no goodbyes. As I was working the midnight shift at the factory plus doing all my other jobs, he rarely saw me the whole tomato season anyway. It wasn't until I had actually gone that he discovered the truth. He went to the post office and the guy behind the counter said, 'Your daughter's over in England now, huh?'

'What do you mean?' asked Dad.

Some of my friends had gone into the post office to find out how much it cost to send a letter to me in London. Few people in town could keep their business secret from the local post office personnel.

Also, after I had left home, someone in town remarked to Mom that she hadn't seen me for a while. 'Cindy's gone to the United Kingdom,' Mom explained.

'Ooh, I am so sorry, I didn't know,' she replied. The poor woman thought I was dead and had gone to the Kingdom of Heaven.

It was left to Mom's brother Uncle Fred to give me a parting pep talk. His remarks were hilarious, although he didn't know it.

'What'll happen if you get in trouble with the law?' he asked.

'Same thing that happens here.'

'What if you get banged up in some foreign jail without representation, being an American citizen in a foreign land?'

'I'm not planning to,' I promised.

He thought that sort of thing always happened abroad. 'I'm not going to live in Beirut. I'm off to London,' I said.

Uncle Fred still lives in New Castle, Indiana, not far from where he grew up. It was unusual for him to even venture to Fremont. Uncle Fred is also known for his dedication to Perry Como's music, which he delights in playing at full volume to a captive audience of passengers in his brown Chrysler minivan.

My beloved cat Cilla had passed away and I had a black cat, Steven (named after Cat Stevens), who needed to be re-homed before I left for London. I had rescued him as a tiny kitten after someone threw him out during a snowstorm. The lady I gave him to lived on a farm that already had cats. She was a fellow animal lover I'd met when I was taking photographs for Olan Mills and she brought in her little boy with a litter of kittens to be pictured together. No one else had ever done that, so I knew she was a dedicated cat person. It about killed me to say goodbye to Steven. I cried for days. Twenty-one years would pass before I could get another cat.

Even being torn from those I loved didn't stop me leaving. Nor did my fear of flying and the thought that I could really end up in the Kingdom of Heaven. The cheapest air ticket I could find was with Icelandic Airways. I had to fly from Cleveland airport to New York and then to Reykjavik, Iceland. I'd never been out of the States before, and suddenly there I was in Iceland. Next the plane stopped off in Luxembourg where I took a British Airways flight to London. It was hardly a direct journey, but it was cheap. I didn't realise at the time that I was taking a leaf out of my father's book – flying a thousand miles out of my way to save 50 cents is exactly what he would have done.

I arrived in London in April of 1977 at the age of 21, with two suitcases and the remaining $600 I had saved. During the ride in the black taxi from Heathrow airport to Fulham in West London, I was surprised that I didn't see Big Ben along the way – I thought it would dominate the skyline. It was dark, I couldn't see very much but, even so, I immediately felt like I was home, in the place I was meant to be. I was going to stay with a family who took in foreign students that had been recommended by the school.

They were easy going, looked after me well and my time with them was fairly uneventful. There were a couple of other female students also staying at the house, who were in London to study English. One was French, the other Lebanese. I was in for a severe culture shock. Having finally managed to put on weight because of all the Nutriment, fries, wedding cake and mayonnaise sandwiches, I overdid it and now weighed well over 160 lb. I felt self-conscious because the other two girls were petite, attractive and ate next to nothing. The French girl wore chic clothes whereas I sported loud polyester blouses and chequered slacks. I thought I looked fairly stylish until I saw how the others dressed.

I had a little trouble remembering which way the traffic was coming from, since the British drive on the opposite side of the road. It wasn't long before I was hit by a truck. Or, as they say in England, 'struck by a semi-articulated lorry'. Luckily the driver saw me almost in time and slammed on the brakes as I stepped out in front of him. I bounced off the front fender and was thrown about ten feet – into the path of an oncoming car, which fortunately came to a screeching halt just in time. The only damage I suffered was a rather spectacular bruise on my hip and a torn skirt. It seemed that my Guardian Angel had followed me to London. I was more careful after that and took time to stop and figure out which way was right and which way was left before I attempted to cross the road.

It was the Queen's Silver Jubilee year so there were street parties and Union Jack flags everywhere. The Sex Pistols' 'God Save The Queen' and David Bowie's 'Sound And Vision' were in the UK charts. The Stranglers had a hit album. (More than 20 years later the band's lead singer Hugh Cornwell would help me name one of my cats.) Blondie was touring the UK and newcomers The Boomtown Rats and Adam & The Ants were attracting media attention. Two glamorous blonde models, Jilly Johnson and Nina Carter, appeared on TV as Blonde On Blonde singing a remake of Led Zeppelin's 'Whole Lotta Love'. It was considered fairly raunchy at the time, and the girls were sent back into the studio to record a toned-down version. (Little did I know that one day Jilly would become one of my best friends.)

I found the art course very easy. When it came to an end I transferred to the Heatherly School of Fine Art in Victoria. My money had run out and, as I didn't have a work permit, I tried to do a little bit of freelance photography to subsidise myself. I didn't have the right connections to make it work so instead I bought a secondhand Polaroid camera, hung around in Regent's Park and took snapshots of tourists which I sold to them for £2 a piece.

Then my luck improved and I found a job working as a cashier in a restaurant that hired foreign students. The Stockpot in Knightsbridge was in a posh part of town although I didn't know it at the time. I was earning enough to move into my own bedsit on Oakley Street, Chelsea, which cost £14 a week. I could just about afford it. Having grown up under my father's regime, I knew exactly how to live on the cheap. Getting by on a shoestring came quite naturally to me. I had, after all, learned from the master.

Adam Harris came over to visit in July. School was out until the first week of September so he stayed with me for six weeks. We went to Paris for a few days and I got to use my high school French for the first time. Adam was my Ken. He seemed impressed with my linguistic skills. 'How come I've got two masters degrees, yet you're smarter than me?' he asked. While we were in Paris the King died. The headlines on the newstands shouted, ELVIS EST MORT! We bought a paper and sat down with it at a café while I translated the best I could.

We stayed at L'Hôtel des Balcones in the bohemian quarter of Paris on the Left Bank. During a night of passion, one of the bed's legs completely snapped in two. The following morning, we went out for the day and, when we returned, it appeared to have been mended. When Adam lifted the bedspread we discovered that the maid had fixed it by propping it up using three bricks. We still laugh about that.

In the room was a bidet but we had never seen one before and didn't know what to do with it. We thought it was a broken toilet because it didn't have a lid. We used it to wash our feet in.

We visited all the tourist spots, including the Eiffel Tower and the Louvre where we saw Leonardo's *Mona Lisa* and the *Venus di Milo*. That's when I realised that my feet were the only perfect part of my anatomy. Gloria had always made fun of them because my second toe is longer than my big toe. At the Louvre I noticed that on the

p left: I was not a pretty baby. This is me at three months with my sister Gloria.

p right: Unable to compete with my older sister, I hit the bottle.

ottom: Dad with his 1947 Stinson. When he put me at the controls in mid-flight I
eveloped a terrible fear of flying – which I put to rest by taking the driving seat in
is helicopter (*inset*).

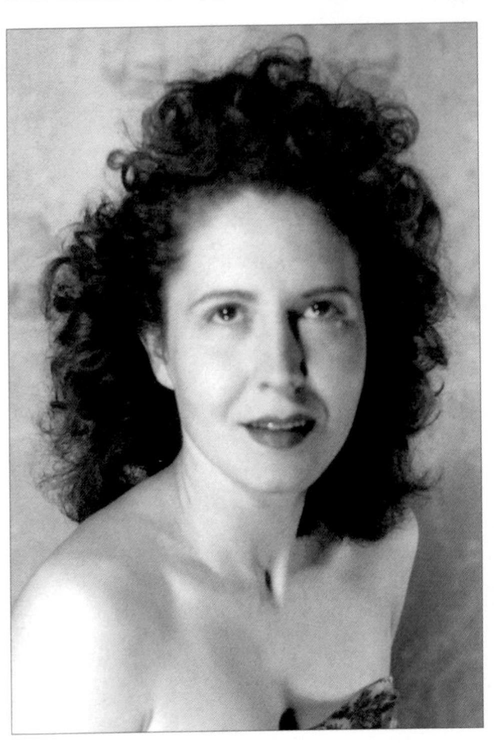

Top: Me aged seven and Gloria aged ten. Even at an early age, I had a thing about dolls!

Bottom left: My mother at the age of twenty-four.

Bottom right: Mum and Dad in 1942.

op left: Aged twelve.

op right: Me at the age of fourteen, and Gloria at the age of seventeen.

ottom left: An attentive student in study hall. Despite my occasional lapse in
oncentration, I went on to become a member of MENSA.

ottom right: Back on the farm aged twenty.

Top: In the days before I even thought about cosmetic surgery.

Bottom: Martyn and me on our wedding day in 1978.

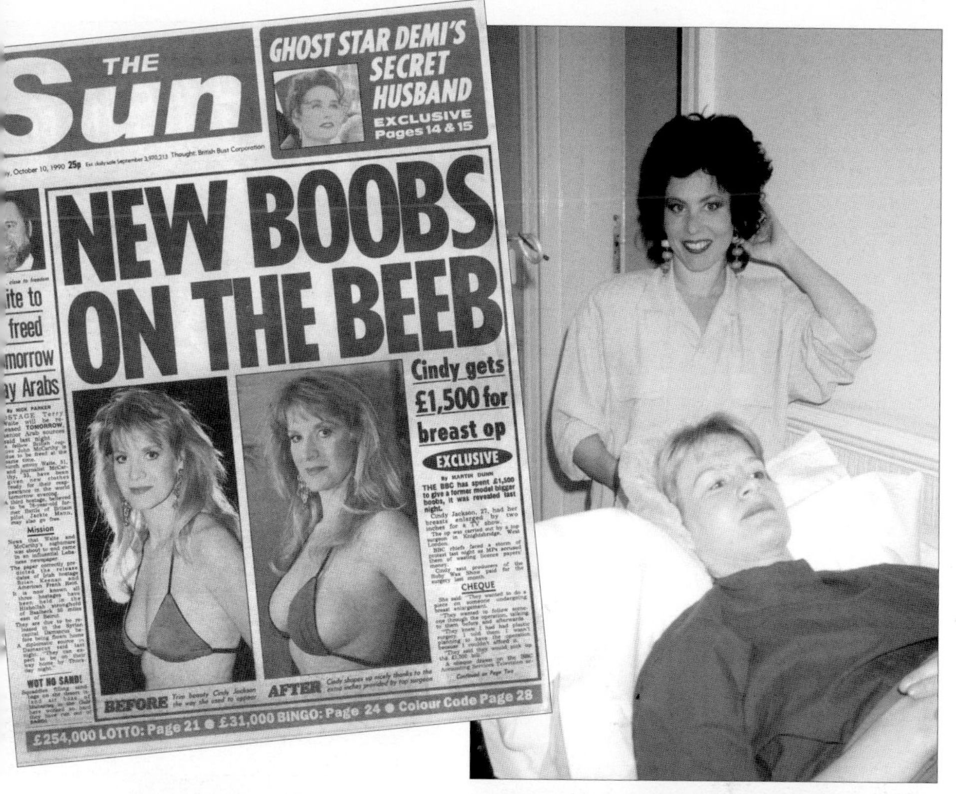

THE Sun

GHOST STAR DEMI'S SECRET HUSBAND

EXCLUSIVE Pages 14 & 15

…y, October 10, 1990 25p Thought: British Bust Corporation

…ite to freed …morrow …y Arabs

By NICK PARKER

…STAGE Terry Waite will be re…leased TOMORROW, …senior Arab sources said last night.

Mission

WOT NO SAND!

NEW BOOBS ON THE BEEB

Cindy gets £1,500 for breast op

EXCLUSIVE

By MARTIN DUNN

THE BBC has spent £1,500 to give a former model bigger boobs, it was revealed last night.

Cindy Jackson, 27, had her breasts enlarged by two inches for a TV show.

The op was carried out by a top surgeon in Knightsbridge, West London.

BBC chiefs faced a storm of protest last night as MPs accused them of wasting licence payers' money.

Cindy said producers of the Ruby Wax Show paid for the surgery last month.

CHEQUE

She said: "They wanted to do a piece on someone undergoing breast enlargement.

"They wanted to follow someone through the operation, talking to them before and afterwards.

"They knew I had had plastic surgery. I told them I wasn't planning to have the operation because I couldn't afford it.

"They said they would pick up the £1,500 bill."

A cheque drawn on the BBC Accounting Services Television ac…

Continued on Page Two

BEFORE Trim beauty Cindy Jackson the way she used to appear

AFTER Cindy shapes up nicely thanks to the extra inches provided by top surgeon

£254,000 LOTTO: Page 21 ● £31,000 BINGO: Page 24 ● Colour Code Page 28

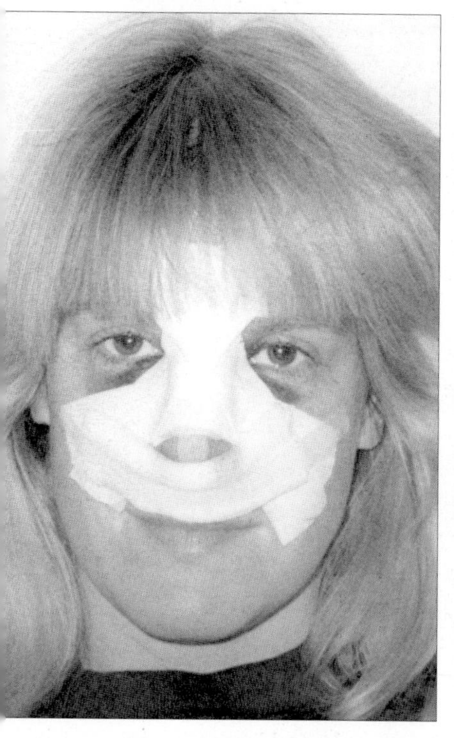

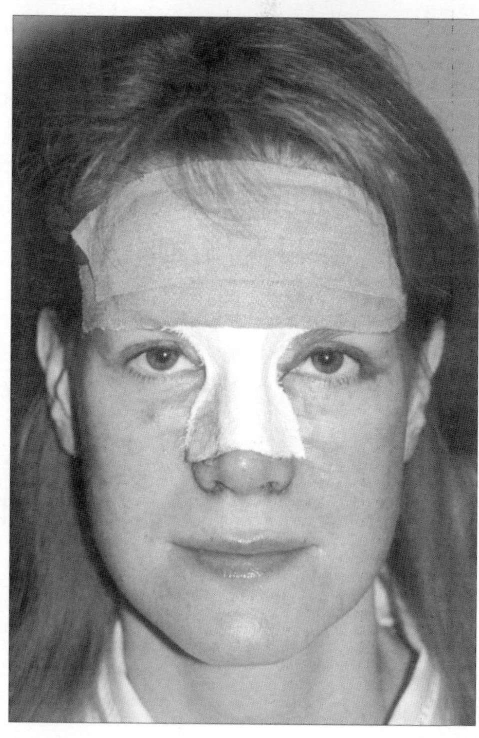

…: My boob job made front-page news – the BBC paid for it when I went on Ruby …x's show – here you can see Ruby wheeling me into theatre.

…ttom: Recovering from two of my nose jobs.

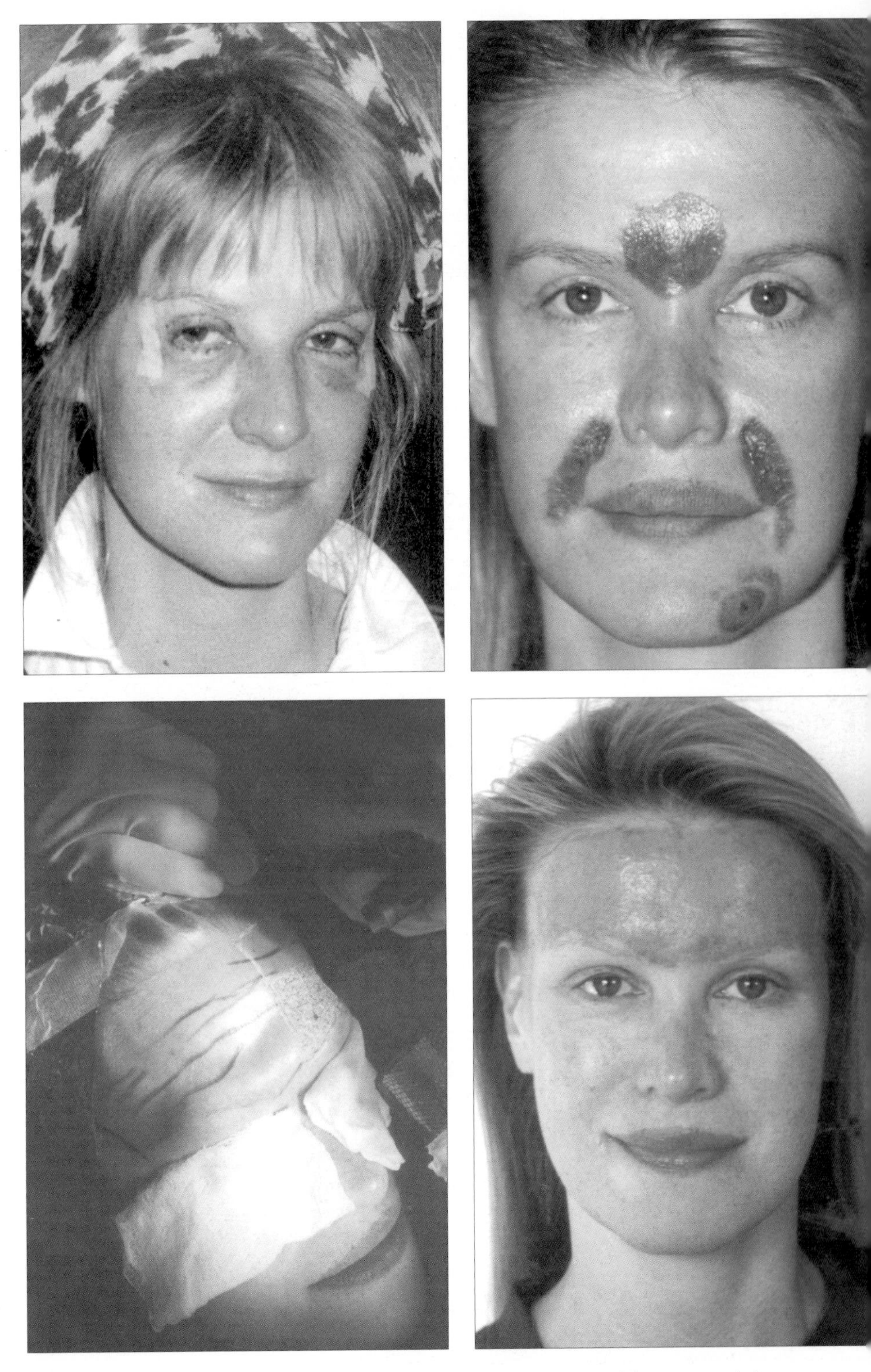

Top left: The eyes have it – the after-effects of my upper and lower eye job.

Top right: This is how I looked immediately after my dermabrasion.

Bottom: Undergoing and recovering from laser resurfacing on my forehead.

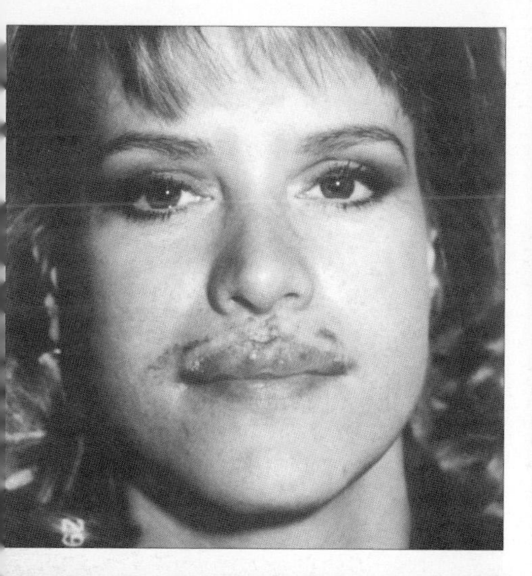

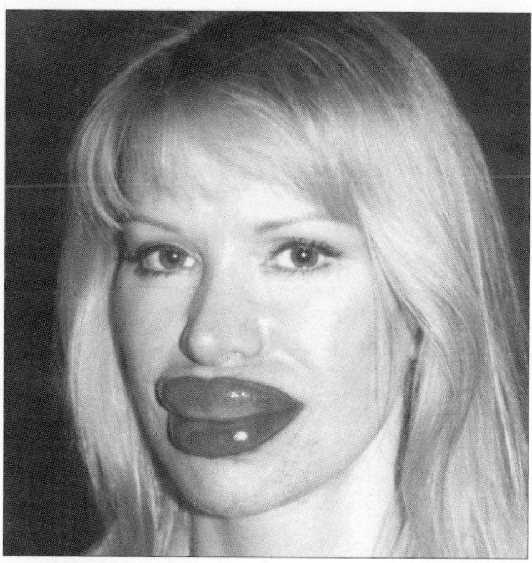

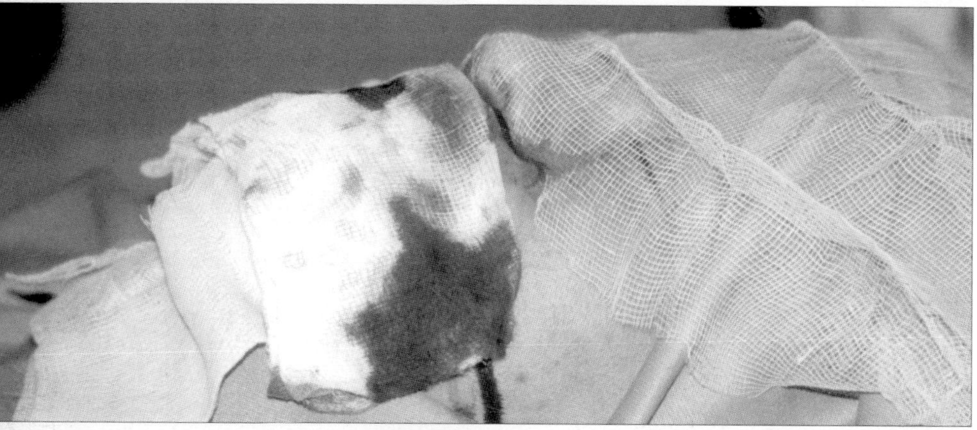

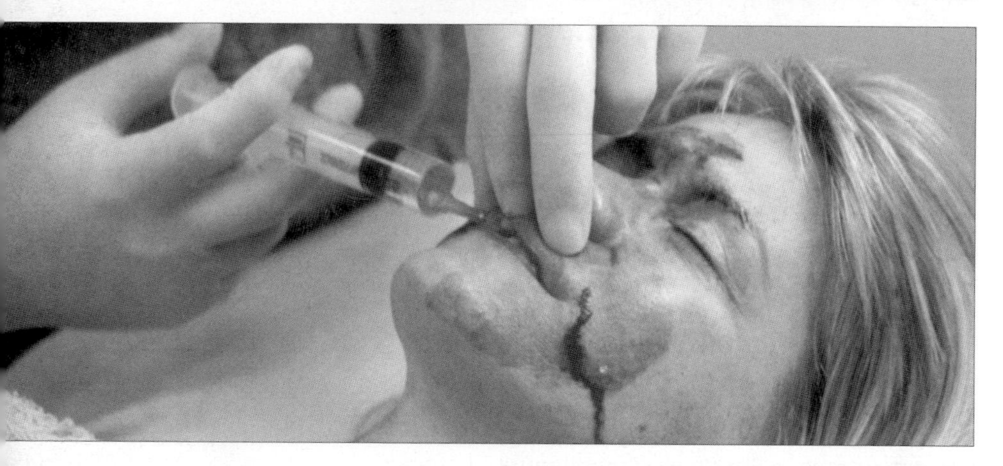

A great deal of work has been done on my lips. (*Top left*) These are the immediate scars after my upper lip enlargement.

Top right: After I had my lips tattooed, I looked like this for three days!

Middle: On the operating table during my lip lift.

Bottom: Undergoing fat injections into my lip.

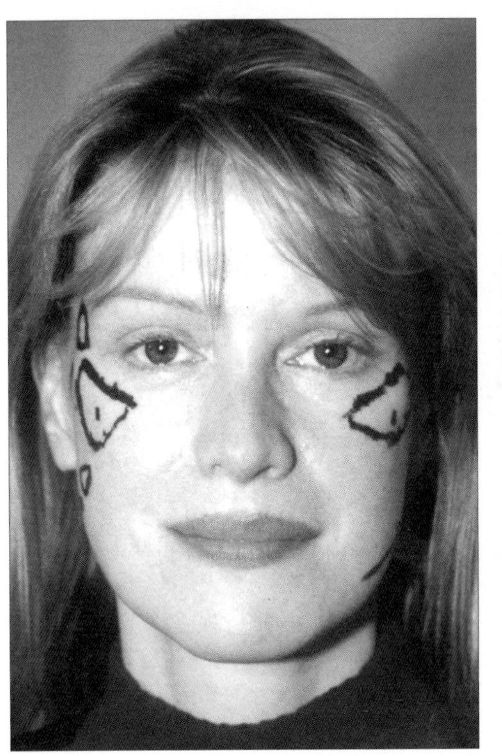
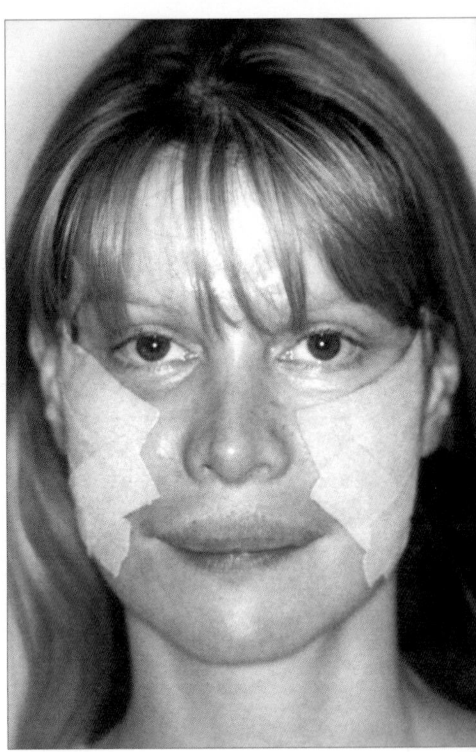

Top: Fixing my cheekbones – before and after the cheek implants.

Bottom: The head-to-toe transformation.

Greek statues all the women's second toes were exactly the same as mine. It's called 'the toe of the goddess' and was desirable in Greek times.

I was fascinated by the street performers in Paris at night. There were mime artists, magicians and all kinds of entertainers who busked for spare change. My favourite one was the Lizard Guy. He would jump out of the shadows waving a rubber lizard and then hold out his cap expecting a tip for scaring you half to death. I thought that showed a lot of originality and was happy to hand over a few francs.

It was a real wrench when Adam had to go back home to Fremont. I was tempted to go back with him. But I had come too far to turn back now. We kept in touch and he still sends me Christmas cards. He eventually married Bubba's sister Miranda, but it didn't work out and they divorced a few years later. He is now happily married to another teacher named Susan.

A few months after Adam went home, I met Marc Burca at a Chelsea wine bar. He was a 25-year-old Romanian baron and drove a shiny purple BMW. I'd never met anyone like him before. He was the most unimaginably glamorous man: rich, devilishly handsome, obviously well-connected and well-bred. When he spoke, it was with an upper-class English accent so posh that I could barely understand him. I went weak at the knees when I shook his hand – he was everything a girl could ask for. I was very shy and completely overwhelmed. I couldn't believe it when he asked me out for dinner.

'Have you got a long dress?' he asked.

'Yes,' I lied. He must have thought that I was dressed so badly as a student statement, but that I secretly had a fabulous wardrobe hidden away somewhere. It was the time when Europeans still thought all Americans were rich. (Maybe he thought I was some eccentric heiress, so I never bothered to tell him I worked in a restaurant.) Truth is, I didn't have enough money to buy new clothes. Marc now calls it my grunge phase. I call it poverty.

'Fine. Put it on and I'll knock you up around 7 o'clock tomorrow night,' he promised. Stunned, I later found out that in England 'knock you up' means knock on your door, whereas to an American it means something else entirely.

I rushed out and bought a green and orange wraparound Indian print skirt at a cheap boutique in the King's Road market for £5. I couldn't afford a new top, so I wore it with a cotton peasant-style blouse from my shabby wardrobe. Desperate to impress him, I gave myself a perm, which, of course, turned my hair frizzy. I parted it down the middle and tried to flatten it down. Marc was too polite to say anything, but must have been horrified by my appearance.

Nevertheless, he whisked me off to dinner at the Mirabelle Restaurant in Mayfair. I had never been to a smart place like that in my life. We sat at a table with around 12 other people, one a mega rich Texan friend of Marc's. I didn't know what to say to any of the others. They all knew each other and were relaxed in their smalltalk, but I was socially way out of my depth. It was a black tie affair and the other women were decked out in designer ballgowns. The famous London socialite Liz Brewer was there. I remember watching her, beautiful and poised in her elegant finery. I thought, 'Wow, she knows everybody'. I knew no one and just wanted to run.

Marc did take me out again a few times after that. We went to the nightclub Tramp – in 1977 it was the place to be – and danced the nights away to the disco music of bands like the Bee Gees and the Commodores. Or, should I say, he danced while I tried my best to pretend I knew the moves. Not only did I have two left feet, but as I'd spent my time at dances as a wallflower watching from the sidelines, I didn't actually know how to dance. I still don't.

Marc and his friends seemed so perfect, which only served to make me more aware of my own shortcomings, including some I didn't even know I had. There are certain social graces to be learned, manners to be polished if you expect to get on in British society. You don't just go seamlessly from pumping gas in hicksville to dining in

Mayfair with the aristocracy. Looking back it seems obvious, but at the time it simply hadn't occurred to me.

Like most of the men I'd dated, Marc never paid me any compliments or told me I was beautiful, and I knew people in his set were making rather disparaging remarks behind my back. Even so, he took me away for a New Year's weekend at a big house in the country that belonged to a friend whose parents were abroad. We young people had the place to ourselves.

'Do you ride?' Mark asked me.

'Of course, I was brought up on a farm,' I said.

'Great. We're all going trekking through the New Forest.'

I had never been on a horse in my life. I had seen a lot of horses back in Ohio but had never actually ridden one. How hard could it be?

We got to the stables and they brought out a massive horse for me to ride. Mark gallantly helped me up into the saddle, and I tried to act as though I knew what I was doing. The others, all accomplished riders, began to take off ahead of me.

'C'mon, horse, let's go,' I said. But it wouldn't budge. It waited until the others had got about 200 yards away and then took off at breakneck speed to catch up. It galloped, jumped over ditches and once it had caught up with the pack it would stop again and then repeat the procedure. To my credit, I managed to hold on until eventually the horse threw me off. I was bruised quite badly but luckily nothing was broken. To this day, Marc doesn't know that I had never ridden before. He thought the horse was a bit daft, not that I didn't know how to ride it.

I felt very smug about life, very proud of myself. There I was with an aristocrat at this great big house surrounded by beautiful English countryside. It was all impossibly glamorous and romantic. But soon after that New Year's weekend he suddenly ditched me in time-honoured fashion: there was no dramatic confrontation, I just didn't get any more calls. I phoned one of his friends and was told that Marc was seeing someone else.

The next thing I knew, he was getting married. It confirmed my worst view of myself. I just wasn't good enough. Marc didn't tell me at the time but, just before he met me, he had also been dumped – almost on the eve of his wedding to a young debutante with whom he was madly in love. I guess he went out with me on the rebound. To him, I was just a fling. I was clearly not in the same league attractive as his other girlfriends.

My self-esteem was at an all-time low. I was left feeling ugly, poverty-stricken and uncouth. I was beginning to think I'd bitten off more than I could chew with this moving to London thing. If I didn't fit in back in Fremont, I *really* didn't fit in here. I wondered what I'd been thinking to come to a place that could reject me on more levels than I ever dreamed possible.

I didn't see Marc again for almost 20 years. In the meantime, I had other relationships with men who were, although not as attractive or as well connected, the kind of men I felt I deserved. It was that matching hypothesis theory at work again.

Chapter Seven

Jackson

I was still fretting over Marc when a waitress at The Stockpot set me up on a blind date, which I had begun to favour because guys would at least have to get to know me over dinner instead of writing me off the minute they saw me.

Martyn was a handsome blue-eyed Englishman who lived in Fulham. He was five years older than me and worked in an antique furniture shop. My friend thought he was the perfect guy for me. He was cheerful and charming and wanted to settle down. Martyn was polite, had perfect manners and was always well dressed. He treated me like a lady and I loved him. In a way I still do, but I am sorry to say that, as with Donny Dressler, I was never passionately in love with him.

He proposed one evening in a pub after we had both drunk more than a few gin and tonics. At the time I couldn't believe my luck. Someone wanted to marry *me*! Next morning, when the sober truth hit me, I was caught in a turmoil of mixed feelings. I was still in love with Marc and the glamorous lifestyle he represented. But a distinguished man like that would obviously never want me. Martyn was a far safer bet. He couldn't hurt me the way Marc did. He would always be good to me. Furthermore, I was on the serious rebound. Here was my chance to prove to Marc and the other men who'd dumped me that I could get a decent man. It was a matter of pride.

I said yes to Martyn, and we got engaged. No harm in that, I thought. I still had time to change my mind. But as the months wore on, I was convinced that no one else would ever want me and it would be hard to find another man like Martyn. Having let Adam Harris walk out of my life, I wasn't about to make the same mistake. No, not me – I was going to make a different one instead.

Marriage to Martyn would be my next big adventure and, at 22, it was time I found a husband, I reasoned. In theory it seemed like a good plan. Getting married to a staid, reliable man instead of falling for heartless brutes who never returned my calls was a grown-up thing to do. Martyn would cherish and care for me. He would never break my heart. Everyone said I was lucky to have him. Maybe marriage was the answer.

Unfortunately I was not nearly mature enough to make the right decision about such an important commitment. I was determined to go ahead with the marriage, but being the dreamer that I was, it was for all the wrong reasons.

I couldn't afford a stylish wedding gown so I was thrilled when some dubious but friendly characters who lunched at the Stockpot presented me with a beautiful cream silk dress as a wedding gift. Luckily it was not too form-fitting. I had been consoling myself with ice cream and fish 'n' chips since Marc dumped me and had gained even more weight.

'Where did you get it?' I asked.

'Don't ask questions. Just wear it and be happy,' they said.

To my horror, I later discovered that they had shoplifted it from

Regine, a boutique in Sloane Street. Perhaps I should have guessed that thieving was how they made a living, but I was rather naïve in those days.

I piled my hair up high, innocently put on my stolen dress and went to take my vows, brushing off a nagging feeling that I was making a big mistake. Just as I was leaving, it began to pour with rain and I arrived at Fulham Registry Office looking like a drowned rat, which I suppose was some sort of omen. I walked in as Cynthia Anne Keepers and emerged 20 minutes later to start a brand new life as Cindy Jackson. Martyn and I became husband and wife on April Fool's Day 1978.

Only a handful of friends came to the ceremony and we all went to a pub afterwards to celebrate. 'Take A Chance On Me' by Abba was playing on the jukebox as we walked in. It seemed such an apt tribute. Pity I didn't understand the irony then.

We moved into a tiny, cramped flat in Chelsea. I found a new job with slightly better pay, as a cashier at Wheeler's, the fish restaurant in Belgravia. Margaret Thatcher was elected as Britain's first woman Prime Minister, unseating James Callaghan.

I also came unseated soon after I bought myself a Honda motorcycle to get around town. I hadn't bargained on how often it rains in London, though, and I was always drenched. And wearing a helmet flattened my hair, making it stick to my head, which did little for my appearance. Eventually I crashed the bike one wet foggy evening by skidding under a double-decker bus on Dawes Road.

I was taken by ambulance to St Stephen's Hospital in Fulham Road, where X-rays revealed a spectacular fracture of my left collarbone. A wing bandage was fashioned around my shoulders and across my back in a figure-of-eight, which I had to wear for six weeks.

I looked like an Egyptian Mummy. With the resulting limited mobility, I moved like one, too. The accident put me off motorcycles for life. The bike was a write-off and I very nearly was as well. Everyone who saw the mangled wreckage commented on how lucky I'd been not to be killed. Acutely aware of just how close I'd come to death, I decided to walk instead.

Martyn was devoted to me and settled happily into domestic life. He hadn't married me for my beauty, and honestly didn't mind how I looked. To him I was exciting anyway. Being American, I was different and kind of exotic. With no one to make me feel that I wasn't good enough and that I must try harder, I was able to relax and think about other things for a change.

But unfortunately there wasn't much to think about. I was bored silly with cooking, cleaning and shopping. Homemaking was neither challenging nor stimulating. Again, I felt that there was something else out there for me. Here I was at 22, a married woman whose life course was supposed to be set, and frankly I found that prospect frightening. Besides, I didn't want to end up stuck in the same rut as my mother.

Sadly for Martyn, I was never going to turn into the little housewife he wanted me to be. Although he was gentle and kind, he was born in the north of England where a woman's place was definitely still in the home. He wanted his dinner on the table and his slippers by the fire when he came home each evening. Martyn wanted children. I couldn't see the point. That was our main stumbling block. (Martyn had no way of knowing that I had an inner child to raise first.)

I just couldn't shake the notion that I was living a life that didn't belong to me. And in a way it didn't. It belonged to Martyn and, like many women, I was expected to adjust my personality to fit in. My decision to leave him was made more difficult by the fact that I have a thing about keeping promises, having been on the receiving end of so many broken ones myself. I had, after all, promised to love, honour and cherish Martyn, forsaking all others 'til death do us part.

But my brush with death had made me determined to make the most of the only life I'd been given. The time came when I had to decide whether surrenderring my entire future for the sake of keeping my word was a fair trade-off. After a lot of soul searching, I walked out on Martyn. We were divorced almost four years to the day after our wedding.

It seemed like I was always being rejected by unsuitable men or breaking up with 'nice guys'. But in every single case – Donny, Adam and Martyn – staying with them and being what they wanted me to be would have meant abandoning my own hopes and dreams in order to help them achieve theirs. My mother did that for my father and he completely took over her life. I wasn't prepared to let that happen to me.

Not a single one of my 'nice' boyfriends knew how to support and encourage my unorthodox visions. Or, as Adam Harris (quoting Hunter S. Thompson) said to me when I eventually started my cosmetic surgery information business 'When the going gets weird, the weird turn pro,' although I prefer Tom Peters' version: 'Crazy times call for crazy organisations.' The truth is, weird or not, I was not willing to be controlled as Mom was by Dad.

My 'nice guys' weren't bad people and I still have fond memories of them. The only thing they were guilty of was perpetuating an old-fashioned, jaundiced view of a woman's role in life, and that wasn't their fault. They're what I call the sandwich generation – men in between. They were raised by women who played traditional roles, stayed home and baked cookies and then found themselves dating the products of women's liberation – independent women with the same aspirations as themselves. Yet they still want a woman who will behave the same way as their mothers. I'm part of a generation of women who were expected to juggle career, marriage and motherhood, while looking beautiful. I fell down on all counts.

Deep in my heart I knew I wouldn't settle with Martyn or spend the rest of my life with him. But we remain good friends and since his mother and father died, I'm the only Jackson left in his address book. We have this little joke as to why I am proud to have taken his name – I hated my own surname with a passion. My maiden name was Keepers. My nickname was 'Creeps'. Kids at school chanted, 'Jeepers Creepers, here comes Keepers,' whenever they saw me. They also called me 'Zoo Keepers' and other strange names. The teenage girl who lived next door to my grandmother in Daleville, Indiana, was called Kathy Jackson. Not only did I envy her having a feller, I also loved her 'normal' name. So at least Martyn made one of my dreams a reality. He gave me the same last name as her.

Even when our marriage was on the rocks we didn't fight or argue. Instead, Martyn has this searching look he used to give me as if he could see right through to my soul and know what I was thinking. I never had to explain anything to him. He always sensed what I was feeling.

There was something else out there for me and I knew it, even if I didn't know exactly what it was or how to access it. Martyn did his best to understand and we simply agreed to differ. I went off and found a little apartment of my own – to start yet another new life.

Chapter Eight

Should I Stay or Should I Go?

One evening, not long after Martyn and I split up, I went for dinner with a girlfriend to an Italian restaurant near her home in Notting Hill. As it was located near the main BBC studios in Wood Lane, we were surrounded by famous faces. It was the same restaurant where Viscount 'Champagne Charlie' Althorp famously tried to remove the DJ Tony Blackburn's slacks. Kensington Palace was also close by and Althorp's older sister, Princess Diana, came in once when I was there.

My friend knew the owner and introduced us. Roberto had swarthy Latin looks and I was instantly attracted to him. When I discovered he owned a silver Mercedes, I took it as a sign. I was flat broke, living hand to mouth and here was a man who owned the car of my dreams. He could also offer unlimited pizza, and he'd already told me that Italians like fat women. I thought I'd found the perfect man.

When Roberto asked me out on a date, I readily accepted. Three months later I moved into the big antique-filled house he owned next door to his restaurant. He didn't exactly invite me to become his live-in partner. It was a natural progression because I was spending so much time with him. I found out he owned other restaurants and some prime London property as well. Maybe finding a wealthy man was the answer. That was before I heard the expression, 'Those who marry for money earn every penny.'

At the age of 26, I thought I was finally ready to settle down. Although I missed my family and friends in the US, in many ways I felt like I was where I belonged. That feeling was reinforced one day when I was shopping in the local delicatessen. I heard on the radio that another one of my childhood idols had been gunned down. John Lennon had been shot and killed in New York City.

At first everything was fine with Roberto, but after a couple of years the rot set in. We clashed big time. A lot of our differences were cultural. Being from the instep of the boot of southern Italy, he was mucho macho.

When I found out Roberto's real age shortly after I'd moved in with him, I was concerned because he was 16 years my senior. I'd never been out with anyone more than five years older than me. He'd lied about how old he was when we first met so I wouldn't lose interest. Still, he saw it as one of the more positive aspects of the relationship. He matter of factly announced that a woman should be half a man's age plus seven. To this day I have no idea how he came up with that equation.

Being old-school Italian, Roberto also believed that men were superior and women should always do what the man decides. 'Women's brains are smaller,' he explained.

Worst of all, Roberto always encouraged me to keep my fringe long because he told me I was cross-eyed. As I had long been acutely aware of every single flaw I possessed and being cross-eyed was not one of them, I immediately recognised his attempt to further undermine my self-confidence.

When I begged Roberto to let me get a rescue kitten, he always said no. Nor was I allowed my own car. He let me drive his Mercedes as long as he didn't need it, which wasn't very often. I thought he would be pleased when I took classes to learn Italian, but I was disappointed to discover he preferred to be able to speak to his friends in front of me without my knowing what they were talking about.

Roberto refused to buy me the Hasselblad camera that I asked for so I could take up photography again. Instead he showered me with expensive (but ageingly conservative) clothes, mink coats and jewellery. I was taken out to expensive restaurants to show off the things that he'd bought me. He thought I was ungrateful, but it was hard to show appreciation when I was being given everything that I never wanted. It was like being a child again and having to pretend to my paternal grandparents that I appreciated their gift-wrapped cast-offs. I thought I'd left all that behind.

As much as Roberto would have liked me to share his interest in keeping up appearances, I found the pursuit totally uninspiring. (Maybe that's what made me go off and join a punk rock band.) He wanted me to put on a show for the benefit of him and his peers. There was nothing in it for me. My mind was numb and my spirit was suffocating.

Roberto never stopped talking about his ex-wife. He said he couldn't marry me because he'd had such a bad experience with marriage the first time around. He was afraid that things would go wrong and he would have to part with half his money again if we divorced. That's why when Prince Charles married Lady Diana Spencer on 29 July 1981 I watched the Royal Wedding on TV alone. Roberto refused to join me, obviously terrified that I would get ideas planted in my head about marriage.

The fact is that I never really wanted to marry him anyway. I just wanted him to want to marry me, if that makes any sense.

In 1982 while we were all wishing we could be as lucky as Princess Diana, Argentina invaded the Falkland Islands and I was embroiled in the emotional battlefield that had become my life with Roberto. During one of our many rows, Roberto boasted that he could get a woman even younger than me. Hitting back, I countered that I could get a man even older than him. I thought I'd made a clever and amusing remark. He thought I was ridiculing his male superiority and showing no respect.

What he was trying to tell me was that even if I wasn't beautiful, at least I had youth on my side, a commodity also valued highly by men. Having always been the baby of the family and younger than my classmates, it had never occurred to me that youth could be an advantage. Now here I was in my twenties being told by a middle-aged man that, not only was I not much to look at, but also there would always be younger, more desirable, women available to him. I already knew that. It was the fact that he coldly spelled it all out while professing to be in love with me that broke my heart. I realised he would never be faithful to me.

Roberto did buy me a fabulous two-and-a-half-carat diamond engagement ring, but it was all for show. To him it was the ideal opportunity to impress his friends with his wealth and to placate my need for a commitment from him at the same time.

It didn't matter how hard I tried to fit into a conventional role, or that I was finally prepared to sacrifice my ambitions to be with him. I even went against the grain and gave up work to take care of his two children and keep the house clean – but still it wasn't good enough for him. Nothing was. He always used to say he was happy the way things were. My unhappiness didn't seem to matter to him and that was what hurt the most.

The crowning insult was that no matter what I did to please him he would still blatantly stare at any beautiful woman he saw when he was out with me. God knows what he did when he went out on his own. He made it abundantly clear that there was an endless supply of women out there he would rather look at than me. And I was incessantly reminded that, unlike his feelings for me, there had once been a woman he loved enough to marry. It was the old familiar feeling of not being good enough or pretty enough. And for the first time in my life I became insanely jealous. Roberto brought out the worst in me.

There's a saying: 'It doesn't matter how many times you end up on the floor as long as you pick up something while you're down there.' Although this relationship brought me to my knees, I have to admit it gave me quite an education.

I learned that there are many subtle techniques a man can employ to try and dominate a woman, including one that appears outwardly chivalrous. This method involves not allowing her to work, paying her way and doing everything for her. After a prolonged period of being cosseted from the real world, her mind is dulled and her instincts become deadened. True to plan, she will eventually be rendered helpless, becoming childlike and dependent – and unable, or unwilling, to survive on her own.

I now know that the benefits of a man parading a younger woman on his arm that he's dressed up to the nines are twofold. First, it's a conspicuous display of his success to other men. Second, keeping a woman distracted with clothes, handbags and shoes means she's too busy offloading her disposable income on the latest fashions to have time to think about accumulating any real assets such as stocks, bonds or property. (And as Coco Chanel said, there's a big difference between fashion and style. Of course, at that point I wasn't very good at either one). It was the early Eighties – not the most elegant decade of the twentieth century. The hugely shoulder-padded *Dallas and Dynasty*-style outfits Roberto bought for me, combined with weekly trips to the hairdresser, made me look like an overly groomed Stepford Wife who could play quarterback for the Chicago Bears. I no longer recognised myself in the mirror.

Roberto taught me how hurtful it can be to a new partner to be constantly reminded of an ex-spouse. As a result, I never spoke much about Martyn.

Finally, I found out that demanding a commitment is a good way of getting rid of some men. (This is a method I have inadvertently employed a few times when it was not actually my plan to end the relationship, although that didn't render it any less effective.) Any man whose intentions aren't genuine will run a mile. Another trick for getting a man out of your way for a few hours is to announce: 'We need to talk.'

Not that I wanted Roberto out of my way or out of my life, but he proved to me once more that every time I tried to be conventional and respectable it was thrown back in my face. I was beginning to understand just how the ugly duckling in the fairytale must have felt as he wandered among all the different animals trying to find out which ones he belonged with, every time either not fitting in, or else being laughed at and rejected.

We argued all the time and I saw echoes of my parents' relationship looming in my own. When I told Roberto I couldn't stand the arguing and wanted to leave, he acted like he didn't know what I was talking about. He said there was no real anger between us, it was only passion we were expressing, and that passion was what everyone else was looking for. I was confused. All my life I'd been told I was overly sensitive and that I took everything too literally and too personally. (Or, as Mom always used to say, it didn't take much to make me come 'unglued'.) So maybe Roberto was right. Maybe it was my fault after all.

In desperation I went to see an eminent astrologer named Tad Mann to get some advice on my relationship with Roberto. He came highly recommended by a friend and had written several well-respected astrology books. Tad was fairly dismissive about this relationship because he told me it was not important and didn't figure much in the grand scheme of things. He said the best part of my life was yet to come – in my forties and beyond. I was horrified – I would be an old woman by then, I thought. He also told me I would become world famous for something I would do that was unusual and as a result of my own personal accomplishments, and then go on to follow a higher spiritual path. Sure, I thought. What I really wanted to know was about

Roberto and me. All he could tell me was that the relationship would end in 18 months. And it did.

I started making plans to leave before my ego was completely crushed and any more years went by. In some ways I was reluctant to be on my own again. I was getting older and I knew the world could be a scary place to be all by myself. That point was brought home to me one morning when I was on the upstairs toilet at Roberto's house. I felt the porcelain tremble beneath me and the floor shake. Although it only lasted an instant, my instincts told me something terrible had happened.

I rushed to the television, and after a few moments a news bulletin came on. Despite being almost a mile away, I had felt the blast from an IRA bomb that had gone off in Hyde Park, killing four calvarymen from the Blues and Royals and several horses. Less than two hours later another terrorist bomb exploded under a bandstand in Regent's Park, claiming the lives of six musicians from the band of the Royal Green Jackets. It's a cruel world for sure, and I was going back out there to face it alone with no job, no money and nowhere to live.

I would also need new friends – I never did fit in with Roberto's. Knowing no one who frequented the trendy bohemian bars I wanted to visit, I employed an old ruse from my days back in Columbus. I would get ready to go out for the evening (later changing into something more downmarket in the back of the cab), telling Roberto I was meeting a girlfriend, then walk into the bar alone and order a drink. I'd constantly glance at my watch and look towards the door. It never failed that within minutes some guy would approach with the usual line, 'Maybe he's not coming,' and offer me a drink. It wasn't long before I had lots of new friends.

That's how I began hanging out with so-called undesirables and misfits just like I'd done ten years earlier back in Ohio. Punk was at its peak, as was its slightly more acceptable close relative 'new wave'. This was music for misfits and they were playing my song.

Everybody and his brother were forming rock bands. One of the guys I met in a bar was a lighting technician who took me to a few rock'n'roll clubs, including the St. Moritz in Wardour Street. There I met Captain Sensible and Rat Scabies of The Damned, former Bay City Roller turned glam rocker Ian Mitchell and the guys from Motorhead, to name but a few. They were great fun and reminded me of my oddball friends back in Fremont. I decided this was the life for me. Roberto was none the wiser. He was far too busy empire building to notice what I was up to.

Roberto was very upset when I left. The day I went to collect the last of my belongings from his house, he tearfully begged me not to go. He asked me to wait one more minute, went upstairs and returned a few moments later with a rescue kitten, a little tabby with white paws. He said it was ours and begged me to stay and look after it. But it was far too late.

Roberto was in many ways a kind and responsible person. I knew he and his sons would take good care of the kitten. My new plans on how to make a living were still sketchy, and I couldn't afford another mouth to feed. So I left the kitten with Roberto and walked out of the door into the unknown – to start yet another new life.

I still didn't know exactly what I wanted. But I sure knew what I didn't want when I saw it.

After I left him, Roberto did exactly what he said he would never do. He got married. True to his bravado, she is even younger than I am and they had a child together. He sold his restaurants and is now retired. But, as with Marc, obviously I wasn't good enough for him. And, as with Chuck, in retrospect I realise he did me a big favour by not marrying me.

One good thing had come from all my misery – I'd lost so much weight that I was skinny again for the first time in over a decade. I could finally get away with just putting on a pair of jeans and a T-shirt before going out. It was just as well, because soon they would be all I could afford.

Chapter Nine

Girls Just Wanna Have Fun

When I'd put the word out at the St. Moritz club that I needed a place to live, someone told me there was a room to rent in a shared apartment in Clapham, south London for £15 a week. I agreed to take it. But I was astonished to find out one of my flatmates was going to be Charlie Harper, the infamous lead singer of the UK Subs. His band was hardcore punk. They were a bunch of ruffians, real hard men who were always coming and going from some tour or another. They probably won't thank me for saying so, but they were all really nice guys once you got to know them.

To pay the rent and have some money to live on, I sold the engagement ring and truckload of clothes that Roberto had bought me. I needed money more than diamonds and dressy outfits. My new friends and I were all broke, and it would have been extremely uncool to be seen posing in big-shouldered frocks at a time when shredded old jeans and distressed leather jackets were the epitome of post-punk chic. So was big hair. We probably spent more on hairspray and black eyeliner than any other wardrobe items, and that included the guys. It felt good to act and look like a young person again after spending four years being a stepmother and playing house with a man who was nearly old enough to be my father.

Finally, here was a look I could pull off convincingly. I had been wearing lots of black since junior high school, and now so was everyone else, except they called it Goth. I could no longer afford trips to the hairdresser for expensive highlights so I bought some shampoo-in dye from the local discount store, which turned my hair white and set off my black clothes nicely. It was even fashionable to be living on state benefits, as most of us were, myself included.

And then there was Wham!. George Michael and Andrew Ridgeley hailed from comfortable middle-class backgrounds. They weren't new wave by any stretch of the imagination. Still, they eloquently expressed the frustration of being young in Thatcher's Britain when they appeared on Top of the Pops singing about unemployment in *Wham Rap*.

I was in my element living such an alternative lifestyle. With my brand new image and arty circle of friends, it wasn't long before I was asked to do backing vocals at a gig at the Greenwich Tunnel Club with a pub band called Winston and the Churchills. So I backcombed my hair until it looked like I'd received a 10,000-volt shock, and put on a mask of heavy make-up and the £5 red and black leopard print ra-ra miniskirt that I found in a second-hand shop. I downed several pints of beer to steady my nerves.

It was a talent contest, which we won, so I was invited to join the band on a permanent basis. Having always been shy, I had never done anything like that before. I even surprised myself. But I've found that you can get away with just about anything as long as you look the part.

Unfortunately, our appearance is what got us pulled over in Lewisham, south London, on the way home. I was driving through the brightly lit high street with three other members of the band when a patrol car spotted us. We must have looked pretty scary because the two policemen inside radioed for backup before approaching our car. After every law enforcement vehicle in south London converged on us, we were searched and I was breathalysed outside the local Marks and Spencer. I was arrested for being over the limit, fined £250 and banned from driving for a year. It was not a pleasant experience and, after seeing what it did to my insurance premium, ever since that night I've left my car at home if I'm going to have a drink.

After a few of gigs with the Churchills, I was poached by Tony Feedback of Long Tall Shorty (a popular London Mod band), and together we formed a new band called Joe Public. First I did backing vocals, then duets with Tony, before eventually being pushed to the front as lead singer. Tony, you see, said he didn't like singing and playing guitar at the same time. So I came in very handy to sing the lyrics.

Once again I was thrown in at the deep end. After I left Roberto I didn't consciously set out to be a rock singer, I just went a little wild as I did back home in Fremont when Dad made me feel bad. Feeling like I had nothing to lose, I decided to stop courting respectability and just go with the flow. For the very first time, I really cut loose and enjoyed life. Having been made to do a man's work from the age of four then going on to hold down jobs outside the home as a teenager, I was expressing an innate *joie de vivre* that had always been suppressed.

I learned what it was like to have fun for the sheer sake of it. What's more, my love of comedy and rock music finally had a combined outlet in the form of my band Joe Public. Our live show was once described as a cross between the joke heavy metal band Spinal Tap and the television puppet band the Muppets. Our sound was likened to "Blondie meets Led Zepplin" in a dark alley.

Although we were pretty outrageous, our band was gentler than Charlie Harper's. We had a floating membership but we always had a drummer, a bass player and sometimes a guy from another band guesting on rhythm guitar, usually Knox from the

Vibrators, one of the original early London punk bands who'd shared the bill with Iggy Pop and the Sex Pistols in the late seventies. Knox is an immensely talented musician – a real guitar hero and gifted songwriter in his own right. Our regular drummer, Eddie, was an accomplished musician and very much in demand. He was the Vibrators' drummer and also played with a rhythm and blues band called the Inmates as well as several other groups such as the Hamsters.

If Eddie had to do a gig with one of the other bands, Chuck, who was a roadie for Geordie punk band the Angelic Upstarts, would stand in on drums. (Chuck died suddenly of the rare form of adult cot death syndrome in 2000.) When the Upstarts were away on tour we borrowed Dolphin, the drummer from Stiff Little Fingers, a band who were coincidently named after a Vibrators song. But regardless of the varying line ups, there was one consistent element: the band always played so loudly that they drowned me out. I always had to shout the lyrics.

We had no manager or agent so I became both, organising our bookings and negotiating how much we got paid. We didn't earn much so we rehearsed wherever we could find that was cheap. We often used a place in Greenwich because it cost £1 an hour less than rehearsal rooms in central London.

During breaks I used to walk over and sit on the banks of the River Thames beside the *Gypsy Moth*, the boat Sir Francis Chichester sailed to complete his single-handed circum-navigation of the globe in 1967. I had previously seen her exhibited at a boat show my father took me to when I was a little girl. We had both come a very long way in more ways than one. It felt good to sit next to her and contemplate our respective journeys. The *Gypsy Moth* stood in the shadow of the famous clipper *Cutty Sark*, which I had also previously seen on numerous bottles of Scotch.

Another of my roles was to badger the music press for write-ups. This was important because fans read papers such as *Melody Maker*, *Sounds* and the *New Musical Express*, as well as people who ran clubs and their customers. The more we were written about, the more we were able to pull a crowd.

National newspapers were also targeted and I often visited the offices of the *Sun* in Bouverie Street when Martin Dunn and Garry Bushell were writing the paper's music column, called Bizarre, and begged them to give us a mention. I also hounded John Blake at the *Daily Mirror*'s White Hot column. (John eventually left music journalism to start a publishing empire - and ended up publishing this book.) Occasionally they did write us up, but it was probably only to get rid of me. At that time I subscribed to the squeaky-hinge-gets-the-oil method of public relations.

The band came over for meetings in my room, where we would discuss what songs we wanted to do and where we wanted to play. Then we'd go out on the town. We often gatecrashed other bands' parties, claiming to be on the guest list. One of us would distract the guy on the door while another looked down the list of names and picked one that had a plus two or three and claim to be that person. (One year I was even named Runner-Up Ligger of the Year in a *Melody Maker* poll, having been pipped to the post by avid partygoers Bananarama.) We ended up at the Embassy Club or Dingwalls every night of the week without fail, never getting home before three or four the next morning.

Sometimes we stayed out all night at Harry's restaurant in Kingly Street or in the VIP Room at the Limelight Club on Shaftesbury Avenue. That's where I met Russell Simmons who owned the Def Jam Record label in the US. Once he brought New York's hip-hop-turned-punk outfit The Beastie Boys over to London and rang me up. The Beastie Boys, the DJ Grand Master Flash, and Run DMC were gigging in Britain. Russell put me on the guest list for their show at the Brixton Academy and afterwards we all went out in a gang. One of my finest moments was when I marched up to the Hippodrome and announced our arrival to the manager Mark Young, who was on the door, 'Cindy Jackson plus 23, please.'

He took one look at my celebrity entourage and hastily waved us all through. They were at the peak of their fame and I had no trouble getting them into every club in town before taking over the entire upstairs floor at Harry's. As a gift, the Beastie Boys presented me with a grey and red T-shirt that had their band logo on the front and 'Get Off My Dick' printed on the back. It was my prized possession. Like my Ben Casey shirt, I wore it for years.

I would do anything for a laugh. One time the owner of Harry's, a guy named Harry, turned up in a *Miami Vice*-style white linen suit, and I have a problem with linen. I think you might as well buy something cheaper and then just sleep in your clothes. The effect is exactly the same. So when Harry showed up swathed in a mass of designer wrinkles, I pressed a pound note into his hand and whispered in his ear, 'Here's a pound. Get your suit pressed.'

Another time at Harry's, I got into a row with the techno-punk band Sigue Sigue Sputnik's drummer Ray Mayhew. He had too much to drink and became verbally abusive to me. I was holding my own until he grabbed a bowl of sugar off a table and tipped the contents over my head. So I picked up a plastic bottle of tomato ketchup and squirted it at him. It landed all over his face, his dyed blonde hair and his silver lurex shirt. A woman came out of the ladies' room and bumped into him. She took one look at him and started screaming hysterically. I guess she must have thought that the bogeyman had stabbed him or that he had been badly injured in a fight. Hearing the commotion, Harry threw him out. Ray was mad at me for ages.

That's what my life had become like. I always came home as the birds were beginning their dawn chorus, had a few hours' sleep, then got up and went out to do it all over again. It was a blast but I have no idea where I got the energy. It's a wonder I'm still alive.

Tony Feedback was the consummate Clash fan. It was from their guitarist, Joe Strummer, that he got the idea for his name. But where Joe strummed, Tony's trade mark was liberal use of earsplitting feedback. Another of Tony's role models was Jimi

Hendrix and, like his hero, he often set his guitar on fire on stage. Occasionally he smashed up his Telecaster at the end of a gig. Tony hated having to come up with a new guitar solo for every number and, just like Hendrix, would play riffs from other songs instead. He used to break into an electric guitar version of 'Strangers in the Night' right in the middle of 'Wild Thing' where the solo was supposed to be.

Tony's lyrics were often politically incorrect. One song, entitled 'I'm Much Better Looking On A Tuesday Morning Than You'll Ever Be On A Saturday Night', he dedicated 'to ugly people everywhere'.

'Is it art, is it music or is it just dreadful? Frankly we're not sure,' declared *Melody Maker*.

We were ecstatic. This was exactly the reaction we were looking for when so many other bands took themselves so seriously.

'When I saw Joe Public recently I described them as rubbish. However, their début single proves I was far too generous ... Joe Public are just what the Great British public deserve. Definitely mega material,' said journalist Garry Bushell, who was then writing for *Sounds* magazine. Another reviewer, who wrote for the *New Musical Express*, summed us up thus, 'Joe Public are so bad, they're good.'

Occasionally two pretty female backing singers called The Raspberry Tarts joined our line-up. They were a duet in their own right so they weren't always available to sing with us. When we had them with us it was a real luxury. And in spite – or perhaps because – of the music press's unkind comments, we built up quite a following. We gigged all over the UK, in towns like Brighton, Birmingham, Aylesbury and High Wycombe. In London we had regular spots at Dingwalls and The 100 Club. We played to a crowd of 2,000 at the now defunct Electric Ballroom in Camden.

But it was at Legends, a club frequented by Adam Ant, Richard Jobson of The Skids and a large selection of rock'n'roll casualties, that we did our most famous gig. I had my moment of glory when I wore a white wedding dress on stage to entertain the Ramones at their end of tour party. Madonna must have liked the idea, because she went on to do the same thing. But whereas hers was probably handmade in Beverly Hills, I got mine at a clearance sale at Peter Jones department store for £15 including a matching veil. (Many years later she even moved to London and married an Englishman, just like I did.) Other times I wore a nurse's uniform. That always got a good reaction. We were wild. Our clothes were wild. Our hair was wild. Mine stood up on end. In fact, my hairdo was very similar to the one worn by one of my childhood heroines and fellow ugly duckling from Ohio, Phyllis Diller.

Joey Ramone came up to me after the Legends gig and shook my hand. However my old friend Lemmy, lead singer with the heavy metal outfit Motorhead, was obviously not impressed. Clutching his trade mark Jack Daniels with Coke and cigarette, he rasped in my ear, 'Your band needs help.'

We had practically become fixtures in the VIP lounge at the Limelight Club by then, along with other regulars such as Boy George, Billy Idol, Mick Hucknall, the guys from Frankie Goes To Hollywood and just about everyone else who made a record during the Eighties. I saw Tom Jones there once but I don't think it was really his scene. When Madonna was in town, we bumped into her band there and they invited us to be their guests at her *True Blue* show at Wembley Arena.

On stage Madonna accidentally kicked the guy who had put us on the guest list, a dancer called Shabba Doo, and took the wind out of him. When we went to the party afterwards at the hotel they were staying in, he had left word that he was ill. We went up to his room and he was lying on the bed in bad pain, so we sat and talked to him instead. Shabba Doo said Madonna felt terrible about hurting him. We never got to meet her personally, but we did get to see her footprint on Shabba Doo's torso.

We also frequented Brown's nightclub in Covent Garden where George Michael would gleefully take over the dimly lit DJ's booth and play his favourite records while people danced to them, unaware of the megastar in their midst. Andrew Ridgley, the other half of Wham!, was more likely to be found upstairs propping up the bar in the VIP room. He used to flirt with me shamelessly, but he did that with every female, so I didn't let it go to my head. Although it was several years before I contemplated cosmetic surgery for myself, I remember being fascinated by his nose job. He had taken a lot of flak from the press but I thought it looked pretty good. I was friends with his younger brother Paul, who played drums on David Bowie's *Blue Jean* video.

We hung out with the guys from The Damned a lot. Dave Vanian, the band's lead singer, drove a big black hearse, which he parked outside the clubs we went to. It matched his deathly white make-up and slicked back black vampire-style hair.

The Damned's bass player, Captain Sensible, kept pet rabbits. One time when I was at his house, Sensible told me to go ahead and put my hand into the hutch to stroke it. When I did, it went for me. He'd trained it as an attack rabbit and never warned anyone beforehand. It bit me, drawing blood. Sensible just laughed. Looking back, I suppose it *was* pretty funny being savaged by a vicious bunny. The Damned's drummer, Rat Scabies, was the most down to earth of the band, and the only one with whom you could have a meaningful conversation.

Joe Public had a regular spot upstairs at the Clarenden in West London, which was an awful gig. The sound was terrible and the audience was often drunk and abusive. I spent many an evening there drinking Shane McGowan and the rest of the Pogues under the table.

My band was also friendly with a Finnish glam/punk band called Hanoi Rocks. They had an outrageous lead singer called Mike Monroe who looked more like Marilyn Monroe. Also in the band was Nasty Suicide on guitar and Andy McCoy on bass. They had an English drummer named Razzle, who always wore a top hat. Everybody liked Razzle. He always had a smile on his face. Tragically, he was killed in a car crash in 1984 in California with ex-Motley Crüe vocalist Vince Neil at the wheel, who survived.

Another good friend of mine was punk rocker Stiv Bators, also from Ohio and resident in London. Stiv led a band prophetically named the Dead Boys, and later formed Lords of the New Church. The last time I saw him he suggested we go out on the town and tie one on. I told him that sounded like fun and to call me. Next thing I knew he was dead, having been hit by a car while crossing the road in Paris.

We did some gigs in the early Eighties at another regular hangout, Foubert's on Carnaby Street. Johnny Thunders and The Heartbreakers often played there. Johnny Thunders was the founder of the New York Dolls, whose new wave style influenced many bands of the era. Johnny was always friendly and easy to talk to and I have fond memories of him. In 1991 I read that he died of a drug overdose in a New Orleans hotel room. He was only 38.

Very occasionally I could afford to go home to visit my family. Gloria and her husband had moved to Illinois, so I made trips to suburbia to see them before moving on to Fremont to see my parents. I enjoyed catching up with my sister, and reading her American magazines and newspapers.

One day when I was sitting at her kitchen table idly thumbing through the *Chicago Tribune,* I came across an article about Phyllis Diller. She'd had lots and lots of cosmetic surgery to change her face completely. A picture of her now beautiful face accompanied the feature. Fascinated, I studied it for ages.

From suburban Illinois, I would travel to Ohio to visit my parents. Dad had since retired. He'd sold the anchor-making business we'd all built up, but of course didn't offer to share any of the profits. True to form, Dad was critical of my bizarre appearance and my exciting new career. He said, 'I suppose you'll be on drugs next, like Boy George,' who'd been in the news confessing to his heroin addiction. Little did Dad know his prediction came about 15 years too late.

Although many of my friends were into drugs at that time, to my knowledge none of my band was. Tony Feedback didn't even drink.

Nor did I actually see much drug taking. Cocaine was popular in the clubs but extremely expensive – far too costly for struggling musicians like us. And I never got offered any. Anyone who managed to score some coke must have been put off by my huge nose and decided against offering me a line. I looked as if I could have inhaled half of Peru.

I enjoyed going back to Fremont, but my misfit status had gone right off the scale and I knew I could never consider living there again. My appearance was beyond 'just a little strange', as it had been while I was growing up. The sight of me in my new wave rock'n'roll persona stopped traffic on Main Street. Bars would suddenly go silent when I walked in, just like in the cowboy movies. People had always given me funny looks and now they finally had good reason.

Back in the UK, Tony got bored with songwriting, so I began to write some of our material. Towards the end of my rock'n'roll career most of the set consisted of songs that I had written. Writing music – good or bad – came easily to me. In the same way that I loved art and photography, it gave me a chance to be creative.

I never saw my complete lack of musical training and limited vocal range as impediments to my rock career. In those days you were 'in' if you couldn't sing or play an instrument properly. As I couldn't read or write music, I simply sang my creations into a tape recorder then took them to a demo guy who had an eight-track studio in Leytonstone, east London. After I'd explained how the song should go, he would work it out and play it back to me on keyboards. Then we'd lay down the tracks in the makeshift recording studio in his spare bedroom, with him playing all the instruments and me singing.

I had no way of knowing that my innocent dabbling in the music business would soon bring some unwelcome notoriety and nearly cost me my life.

Chapter Ten

Wild Thing

My band was thrilled to be offered the support slot on a UK tour with The Exploited, the hardest core punk band ever. Legendary is the only word to describe them. They trashed hotel rooms, beat up bouncers and incited rabid crowds to riot. Mention the name The Exploited to anyone even remotely involved with the band and you'll be provided with a litany of stories about their worldwide trail of destruction. The band once had a pillow and fire-extinguisher fight in a hotel resulting in the entire building needing to be renovated.

As you can imagine, these are not the sort of people to get on the wrong side of. Wattie, the band's lead singer, was really crazy. He wore his hair in a foot-tall lime green Mohican. As he hailed from a rough part of Edinburgh, I couldn't understand a word he said. In fact, every member of The Exploited came from a colourful Scottish background and had an indecipherable accent to match.

We travelled all over Britain, sleeping on acquaintances' floors, never once in a hotel. Everyone had a friend of a friend who had a place, with varying degrees of hygiene, where we could stay. Why spend money, they reasoned, when you can crash somewhere for free? And who was I to argue?

But things turned really ugly when we played The Dome in Brighton. The audience was in riot mode and, as Joe Public was on first, we were just about keeping everything under control. As I sang on stage I could see Wattie in the wings with the rest of the band out of the corner of my eye. They were teasing me and pelting my band with sandwiches from their dressing room refreshment tray. It was near the end of the tour and we were all pretty close friends by now.

We went off, The Exploited went on and, before they could finish their opening number, the audience went berserk. What little security there was couldn't hold them back. They rushed the stage and smashed all the band's equipment to pieces. Bits of broken drum kit and amplifiers were tossed everywhere. The Raspberry Tarts were not on tour with us so I was the only woman on the bill. In a blind panic, I ran into the ladies' bathroom and locked myself into a cubicle. I was sure I was going to get hurt. A couple of Wattie's band members needed hospital treatment. They didn't sense that the stage was about to be stormed by so many demented people and couldn't move fast enough to get out of their way. Eventually the police calmed things down, but as we drove away I was shaking. The place was surrounded by emergency vehicles. It was a miracle nobody was killed. I guess my Guardian Angel is a music fan.

There was another life-threatening incident when we played Blackpool in Lancashire. Someone had poured lighter fuel over one of the punks in the audience and set him on fire. He burst into flames and was quite badly burned. To this day I don't know whether or not he survived his injuries. We had to stay at the venue all night. The police wouldn't let anyone leave until they had taken statements from and questioned every single one of the several hundred people there.

But the time I was really convinced that I was going to die was after we left the final gig of the tour in Scotland. Tony Feedback and I were in my car, and the rest of the guys were in the tour van. As we drove down the A1, the blizzard from hell started blowing. The van had taken a different way, so when my engine stalled somewhere in the Cheviot Hills, we were on our own. We were in the middle of nowhere and the snowstorm got worse and worse. There was no way out of it. It was white wherever we looked. We couldn't even tell where the road was.

Eventually another car came along and stopped. A couple got out, came over to us and said, 'We're lost. We're really scared. Do you know where we are?' We didn't have a clue so we decided to stick together. My car finally started, and we crept along behind them at around five miles an hour. The conditions were treacherous, especially as we had to negotiate steep hills and valleys. It was truly terrifying.

We eventually got back to civilisation. We'd never met the couple in the car before and we never saw them again. But whoever they were, I'll never forget the way we all stuck together. By this time my Guardian Angel must have been wondering what she had done to deserve being assigned to me.

Next, we recorded a cover version of 'Wild Thing' as a duet with Reg Presley, the original lead singer of the Troggs. It was one of the songs I used to hear being played at the park dances that I wasn't allowed to go to as a teenager. Our new version wasn't a hit like the 1966 one, although it did receive a good review by the *New Record Mirror* in its Singles of the Week column: 'Nifty EP featuring the best Troggs cover I've heard in a while,' it read. It was also reviewed in the heavy metal magazine *Kerrang* by Adrian Smith from Iron Maiden, who said, 'It's quite good, but I don't know if that's due to her.' (That's just typical – the whole idea was mine and I even produced the track.)

We were lucky that the record was even released. When we recorded it, GWR Records were going to put it out but when I called them to negotiate the contract they said, 'Sorry, we're not going to do it now because Jeff Beck has brought out a version of "Wild Thing" and we can't compete.' After all the initial excitement, naturally I was upset.

Then, when Paul Ridgeley, Andrew's younger brother, invited me to Wham!'s final concert at Wembley and the party afterwards at the Hippodrome, who should be there but Jeff Beck?

'Excuse me, you've just screwed up my record deal,' I said to him.

'What are you talking about?' he asked, looking confused.

'You've brought out "Wild Thing" and I've just recorded it with Reg Presley. You've had hits. I've never had a hit. Thanks a lot,' I explained, more frustrated than angry.

'I'm really sorry, I didn't know,' he apologised.

A week later I bumped into Jeff again at Dingwalls. He bought me drinks and we talked all evening. It was obvious that he was doing his best to be charming and amusing. Like me he is an animal lover and strict vegetarian. I thought we were kindred spirits. When he invited me back to his West London apartment for a drink, I went willingly.

He obviously has a thing about feet because, as soon as we got inside, the former Yardbird took my shoes off and began playing with my toes. My first thought was: 'Oh no! I hope I don't have any toe jam'. The famous fingers that had strummed the chords of 'Hi Ho Silver Lining' were now toying with my humble (but, hopefully, not smelly) feet. Soon his hands were all over me. I succumbed to his advances and spent the night with him.

But when I went into his bathroom, I was in for a nasty shock. There was women's underwear on top of the linen basket and feminine cosmetics on the shelves. Either Jeff Beck was a cross-dresser, or he was living with a woman. Later I discovered that it was the latter. His girlfriend was Julia Smith, who went on to marry the rugby star, Will Carling, who in turn became friendly with Diana, Princess of Wales. He obviously didn't tell Julia about me because when I ran into the pair of them one evening at the Kensington Roof Gardens and tried to say hello he ushered her along and wouldn't even acknowledge me. It goes without saying that he never called me again. Jeff Beck, along with both our versions of 'Wild Thing', disappeared without a trace.

Reg Presley, meanwhile, went on to become a leading expert on the origin of crop circles. He resurfaced on the music scene again in the Nineties to collect massive royalties for a song he wrote in the Sixties, 'Love Is All Around', which featured in the hit movie *Four Weddings And A Funeral.* (Contrary to popular belief, Reg didn't write 'Wild Thing' – Chip Taylor did.)

But it wasn't because of my duet with Reg or my liaison with Jeff Beck that I became infamous overnight. I hit the headlines when I was accused of breaking up Noddy Holder's marriage in 1985. I was pictured kissing the Slade frontman on one of my wild nights out.

I met Noddy just once before at Bryan Adams' post-gig party on 27 April 1985. Bryan Adams is one of my all-time favourite performers, so I was thrilled to be asked along to Brookes restaurant in Shepherd's Bush after the show. There were lots of Radio One DJs there, and among the celebrities was The Who's Roger Daltrey.

'I thought you'd be taller,' I said to him. He looked much bigger on television.

'I was tall once but I've worn down over the years,' he replied dryly. Guess he didn't die before he got old after all, I thought.

I had a long chat with Noddy and told him I sang in a band. We talked about the possibility of Joe Public covering a Slade song. He was quite flirtatious with me but nothing more than that.

Then one evening I ran into him again at a gig at the Ad Lib in Kensington. He was with a crowd of people and he said, 'Come along with us, we're going out on the piss.' We went to all sorts of places, drank the night away and got totally rat-assed. We kissed. Someone took our picture. That's all there was to it.

But the guy who took our picture sold it to the *Sun*.

Next day the headline screamed: NAUGHTY NODDY! WHAT WILL HIS MISSUS THINK?

'Sexy songbird Cindy Jackson, caught in a raunchy nightclub embrace with veteran rocker Noddy Holder, talked yesterday of their red-hot romance,' the article said. What red-hot romance? We only kissed.

The article had been written by Nick Ferrari, one of the paper's music journalists whom I'd often hassled for write-ups.

It went on, 'The 23-year-old [I was really 30] blonde said of the Slade singer, "He makes me tingle with his sizzling passion. He's a really good kisser, I'm looking forward to one hell of an affair with him. He's so cuddly and sweet. He's the perfect man."' I promise I didn't say that, although I must admit he was a good kisser.

'Noddy, 34, is currently working in London – and has left his wife Leeandra at home in Wolverhampton to look after eight-year-old daughter Charisse.

'Cindy, singer with a group called Joe Public, admitted, "Noddy told me he wasn't married. But of course I know about his wife. I'll wait for him to tell me about it – I won't confront him."

'Leeandra, 30, said recently, "Noddy often talks to women, but that doesn't mean anything."' Well, it certainly meant nothing as far as I was concerned.

Noddy and his wife had already filed for divorce. But everyone thought I had moved in on him and stolen him from Leeandra. To set the record straight, I gave an interview to the *Sunday Mirror*, in which I announced that I had never slept with him. In fact, I had never actually been alone with him. It was the truth, but I couldn't convince anyone to believe me. I liked Noddy, he was a laugh. But I certainly didn't break up his marriage.

Noddy agreed with me. 'This was a one-off kiss at a party. I haven't seen this girl Cindy since and I have no plans to see her again. Our divorce had been planned long before,' he told the *Sunday Mirror*. Leeandra added, 'We filed for divorce two months ago. There is no other woman involved – and certainly not THAT one.' I was a little hurt by that – I can think of worse people he could have kissed.

But the damage was done. From that day on, breaking up Noddy Holder's marriage is what I was known for in the rock world. A lot of doors were slammed shut in my face – just at a time when every girl singer and band were getting signed up. It was a shame because Joe Public was beginning to do really well. I'd worked hard to get the band to this point, but none of that mattered now. Noddy and his gang were so popular and well connected that suddenly my name was mud in the music business, even though I'd done nothing wrong.

The truth is I had had so much to drink that I can barely remember that kiss, and I never saw Noddy again except on TV. Over the years I've always hoped he harboured no hard feelings and didn't believe what the tabloids claimed I'd said. And anyway, I came out of the situation a lot worse than he did.

For example, I was invited to appear in the audience of a mock Wham! concert for the George Michael and Andrew Ridgeley video of their single, 'The Edge Of Heaven'. It was reported in *Sounds* magazine: 'When we arrived at the recording studios in Twickenham, I was stunned to spot ... a French tourist who thought he'd been catching a London Tourist Board sight-seeing bus, a *Sounds* cleaner, and even legendary kiss'n'tell girl Cindy Jackson, all mingling with the audience (themselves a director's nightmare of punks, oddballs and degenerates).' Well, little did they know that their attitude was nothing new.

And when another member of the music press accused me of being a man in drag, it wasn't the first time my gender had been mistaken. (I didn't actually mind, since it was John Peel, who also played the opening mandolin on Rod Stewart's 'Maggie May'.

That song is a *classic*, and anyone who played on it can call me anything they want.)

Then *Melody Maker* ran a picture of me with Bryan Adams, Noddy Holder and Neil Murray from Whitesnake. 'These famous superstars reached the highest number one spot – except one. Can you spot the loser?' Of course they were referring to me.

Having been the subject of vitriol all my life, I didn't expect much else. I may not have reached number one in the charts but many of my friends had. I felt happy and privileged that they let me hang around with them, even though at one time I was so broke that I was forced to live in a run-down apartment in Holloway – a violent and notoriously crime-ridden area.

That's where I was living when the CID used my apartment to stake out my upstairs neighbour. Apparently he'd stabbed a minicab driver to death within yards of my apartment. This time when I came home and the authorities were waiting for me, I knew the drill. But when I volunteered the keys, they told me they didn't need them. They'd already been inside my place. And just like the time back when I lived in the green breeze-block apartment building in Columbus, the suspect was not at home. But he did eventually turn himself in and is now serving a life sentence for murder.

I was also burgled while I lived there. My treasured Minolta SRT 101 camera that Dad had bought for me was one of the things that was stolen. The burglars must have been annoyed that they went to the trouble of breaking down my door only to find there wasn't much worth taking, since I really owned next to nothing. I wasn't happy about living like that, but I didn't have a whole lot of choice. Every time I saw a bag lady living in squalor on the streets of London, I was haunted by the possibility that I, too, could easily end up like that one day.

By the time I moved, yet again, into a shared apartment off Green Lanes in Haringey, north London, I'd redeemed my reputation somewhat and become a minor celebrity on the cult music scene.

Sounds magazine described my latest living arrangement this way: 'Cindy Jackson's recent move into the godforsaken hovel that passes for the home of ex-*Sounds* photographer Steve Payne is the very last stop before Skid Row.' I'd began sharing a flat with Steve Payne and his girlfriend Chrissie. Although I'd never been more destitute, I remember it as one of the best times of my life.

We had a crazy time while I lived at that apartment. Steve, being a rock'n'roll photographer, took pictures at gigs; that's how we met. I called him The Executioner because he always cut off the top of people's heads in pictures. (To this day we still argue the artistic merit of including the entire head in photographs.)

Chrissie had a more unusual occupation. She was a mudwrestler. I'd come home from nights out with the band and go into the bathroom to find a trail of mud. No matter how many times I asked Steve to tell Chrissie to rinse the mud out of the bathtub when she got home from work, the task always fell to me.

When heavy metal band Wasp came to town, Chrissie was asked to be Waspwoman on their UK tour. This involved wearing a skimpy leather outfit and being lashed to a rack while lead singer Blackie Lawless pretended to torture her on stage. Chrissie didn't get much recognition for the role, though, since she had to wear a leather mask throughout the show.

Next she decided to become a snake charmer. She bought a snakeskin leotard and got a six-foot-long python named Oscar, which she kept in a huge glass case. One day I got home to find both my flatmates beside themselves. Chrissie was crying and Steve was trying to comfort her. 'Oscar's gone missing,' she sobbed. We searched but couldn't find him anywhere.

A couple of weeks later Oscar came home. 'We have to take him to the vet immediately,' I announced upon seeing his thin body. He was very dehydrated and it was obvious he'd come home to die. We gave him water and offered him some live crickets, which he refused. Chrissie was convinced that Oscar would be OK. But the next day Oscar was dead.

Steve's family lived in Devon in the south of England and his sister was training to be a taxidermist. His mother was coming up from Devon to visit him, after which she would be taking the train back home. We tried to work out how to get the dead Oscar down to Devon so Steve's sister could stuff him for extra credit. 'My mother won't take a dead snake. She'll freak,' said Steve. On his sister's instructions, Oscar had been kept in the refrigerator all this time so he wouldn't decompose. I put forward the idea that we should gift-wrap Oscar and send him home with Mrs Payne as a present for his sister. So we put him in a box, wrapped it in some festive foil paper and topped him off with a nice bow.

'Don't open it. It's a surprise,' we said. She took poor dead Oscar home on the train with her, none the wiser.

A few days later, as a joke, I draped a toy rubber snake in the refrigerator among the cheese and bacon and waited for Steve and Chrissie to come home. They went for a midnight snack and I heard a bloodcurdling scream before they hammered on my door yelling obscenities. I had almost given them both a heart attack. They thought Oscar had somehow come back.

We were ardent fans of the Eighties' band the Undertones. When one of our friends got a job working as an operator for a cab firm near the Undertones' singer Fergal Sharkey's Finchley home, she copied down his telephone number from the company's records. After a few beers, we'd all huddle around the telephone, each of us straining to get our ears nearer to the receiver, and call him up. We were far too star-struck to say anything. We just wanted to hear the great man's voice. To his credit, Fergal was always incredibly patient and polite. In his distinctive Irish accent he said things like, 'Come on, you've gone to all the trouble of dialling my number, now what do you want to say?' But every single time he was greeted with stunned silence. (Mr Sharkey, if you are reading this, please accept my sincerest apologies. And I still consider 'Teenage Kicks' to be one of the greatest classic pop songs of all time.)

Steve and Chrissie eventually split up and Steve now lives in Hollywood, California, where he's a movie cameraman and runs a video business. Every time he sees me on US television, he sends me an e-mail. Last time I heard from Chrissie, she was living in Hawaii, where she was originally from.

While my own music career was going nowhere fast, someone I knew intimately was riding high in the charts. He was Ultravox drummer Warren Caan, a Canadian, who was my boyfriend for two-and-a-half years during the time I was with my band. Unfortunately, I wasn't the only woman he was dating, although he wasn't to know that I knew about the others, or that I kept tabs on him. A girlfriend and I regularly bought sandwiches and a six-pack from the local 7–11 then parked at the end of his street to watch his house through a pair of binoculars. I wrote down details of all the comings and goings in a special notebook.

I tolerated his indiscretions – after all he was a rock star, I reasoned – until one day I'd had enough. As I drove past his house, he pulled up on his Harley Davidson with a beautiful girl in a miniskirt and cowboy boots on the back.

I went home and called him up, and he pretended he was there on his own. I said, 'I'm on my way over. I'm in the neighbourhood and I need to pop in and give you something.' He started to protest that it wasn't a good time as I put the receiver down. I immediately phoned six mini-cab companies, giving them Warren's address and saying it was a fare to Heathrow. Then I ordered several pizzas with toppings I knew he hated, such as anchovies, onions and garlic, and had them delivered to him. Next I ordered Chinese and Indian meals on his behalf. In fact, every outlet in Finchley that did home deliveries was sent to his house with a takeaway.

He lived in a quiet cul-de-sac and, as one after another of my deliveries arrived, a traffic jam formed in the street. I figured that every time he heard the doorbell ring he would think it was me and make the girl hide in a closet. It was my way of getting even with them both. I didn't have the nerve to turn up myself and tell him I knew what was going on. But he guessed it was me, because he called to thank me for the pizzas. I think he was being ironic.

The worm was starting to turn. I'd had enough of men treating me like dirt. I split up with Warren. It was time to move on again.

Chapter Eleven

The Living Years

My father contracted a rare illness called mesothelioma, a form of lung cancer caused by asbestos exposure. From the time of the initial diagnosis he was aware that it was terminal, but managed to gain some comfort from the fact that the same disease had also claimed the life of another man from rural Indiana, whose hobbies included piloting his own airplane. The actor Steve McQueen had died of mesothelioma in 1980 at the age of 50. Dad pointed this out at every opportunity. Maybe he thought it added a much-needed touch of glamour to his otherwise grim predicament.

Because I was living abroad, we all agreed that I would visit Dad while he was still alive. We thought it made more sense than waiting until the end and then making the trip home to attend his funeral.

Dad wanted to make his peace, but it wasn't the cleansing experience I'd hoped for. Towards the end he was weak and frail, a shadow of his former self. He had lost his hair and all of his force. The chemotherapy had also made his throat so dry he couldn't yell any more. It was shocking to see a man who was always so powerful and scary suddenly seem so small and vulnerable.

Despite his physical weakness, he nearly made medical history. Most people live no more than six months after being diagnosed with mesothelioma. Dad survived for over two years. He didn't want to die and fought as hard as he could until he finally lost his grip and slipped away in 1988 at the age of 74.

True to his nature, Dad insisted on being in control of all events leading up to the time he was finally laid to rest. He had carefully (and, I thought, morbidly) outlined every step of the exact procedures to be followed from the moment of death. Every detail was there, from when the county coroner was to be notified, to his funeral and eventual burial next to his parents in Indiana. Typical of Dad, it was not an extravagant affair. No one expected it to be.

I had a dichotomy of feelings that scarred so deeply I couldn't even address the pain of losing him. In spite of all our conflicts and the turmoil he caused, he was still my father and responsible for my very existence, as well as having had a profound influence in shaping my destiny. I'll never know if the woman I have since become could have found a way to reach out and communicate with him.

Dad left me $100,000 in his will. He'd gambled the house on the stock market during the Eighties, as we discovered after his death. Being so reckless, he could have lost everything, but at that time the markets were as strong as his obsession with hoarding money. As a result, he'd secretly squirrelled away a small fortune. If he could have taken it with him, he would have. Since he couldn't, Mom, Gloria and I each received a lump sum.

After Dad's death, I returned to Fremont to help dispose of his effects and sell the family farmhouse, which would have been too much for Mom to look after on her own. She went to live in suburban Chicago with Gloria and Carl, who now had a little girl. Six weeks later I returned to London with what was left of my legacy, having paid $11,000 inheritance tax to Uncle Sam. Receiving the money was like being handed back-wages for all the hard work I had to do as a child. (Had I been given a choice, however, I would have preferred a childhood instead.)

Although I had never before considered cosmetic surgery and knew absolutely nothing about it, it didn't take me long to decide that's how I was going to spend my inheritance. If Phyllis Diller could do it, I thought, so could I. After pondering the options, it seemed the wisest investment. I could, for instance, buy a small flat, get a new car, take a trip around the world or get a decent wardrobe. On the other hand, I thought, in theory, if I had the right face and body, I could get all those things as well.

Unlike Dad, I didn't need to take things apart to see how they worked. When you live life on the sidelines, you become one of life's observers. My time had been spent watching, listening and learning. I had the advantage of seeing life from every angle. It's those who occupy centre stage that often have a blinkered view because they can't see beyond the glare of the spotlight. I'd seen a lot of life – at times I felt I'd seen *too* much.

I moved into a nice apartment in north London's Highgate, which is where Rod Stewart is from. My new flatmate, Juliette McCrimmon, was a student at stage school and training to be an actress. She was also only twelve years old. We had previously been neigbours and Juliette and I had become such good friends that her mother let us share their London flat when she decided to spend more time at their country base. I did the school run every day with the other 'mothers' but our home life was far from normal. A typical evening would consist of Juliette practising her tap dancing homework in the kitchen while I phoned in to report suicides to Archway Police Station. We had a perfect view of Suicide Bridge, the Archway Road overpass from which people regularly leap to their deaths. Fate may have dealt me a tough life and an unattractive face, but I had never considered that particular option. I've always been aware that there are a lot of people who are much worse off than I am. Having to cross Suicide Bridge and seeing the flowers and notes placed by loved ones of 'jumpers' on the anniversaries of their deaths was a daily reminder of that.

Instead, I had learned to live with my misfortunes, but it was beginning to show. My rock'n'roll lifestyle combined with a lifetime of hardship had taken their toll. At 33, I looked and felt like a haggard old woman. And people treated me accordingly – not only like a drudge, but like an *old* drudge.

Having already determined that no man would control my life and finances, I now decided that nature was no longer going to dictate my destiny just because I missed out on the genetic lottery. All my life I had watched pretty girls get what they wanted – the men, the jobs, all the attention – and it was clear that nothing I was capable of achieving would ever rate as highly as simply having been born with a pretty face. Experience had taught me over and over again about the direct association between looking attractive and being popular and successful. I felt I had as much right to that as anyone else, even if it meant risking life and limb to get it.

Experience had not been my only teacher. I'd read about the 'halo effect' in several of my self-help books. The halo effect is the distorted perception that people form based on their general impressions of others. An example is the way we may perceive a beautiful, smiling well-dressed woman. On no further evidence we are likely to believe that she has a happy personal life and lives in a nice house. Or on the other side of the coin is the example of Mr Goodier. That was the negative halo.

People also use stereotyping to categorise others. When they see a person bearing the hallmarks of a certain group they mentally assign that individual to the group on no other evidence. Mr Goodier's appearance also caused me to stereotype him. The stereotype was reversed when I found out who he was. I then automatically formed a completely different set of assumptions about him.

Psychologists have estimated that human beings form opinions about each other on the following formula: 55% visual, 38% auditory and 7% content. If that were true, it would explain why it didn't matter what I said or did, and it never would as long as I didn't have the right look.

My plan was to take control of those perceptions and finally make them work *for* me instead of *against* me.

Unlike those whose appealing looks entreat the world to cosset them, not once in my life had I ever felt safe. Prettier girls reaped all the rewards in life, whereas I had to live like a pauper. Others were offered a helping hand when they needed it, but not me. Because of my appearance, everyone assumed that I could look after myself. Eventually that became a self-fulfilling prophecy, albeit one borne out of necessity.

Instead of the rude awakening that some pretty girls get when they turn 45, I learned very early on that you can't count on anyone for anything, nor can you rely on nature. And that it's better to obtain power for yourself than to spend your best years helping someone else build up theirs, because they may just leave you high and dry one day when somebody who better matches their hypothesis comes along. You're much better off securing your own resources in order to look after yourself and your loved ones. A woman in control of her destiny, her finances and her career wields the power of the goddess, the matriarch and the crone. Downtrodden and helpless she is not.

While other kids had to study for hours to get good grades, I achieved them effortlessly. (After learning to cheat on mathematics tests, that is.) I had more ambition than most, but no matter how hard I worked at my various occupations, I could never seem to get ahead. What more evidence did I need that the only thing missing was the right looks? And there are plenty of academics who will back me up.

'Society's obsession with beauty is the beast you can't ignore,' wrote Teresa Wiltz in the *Chicago Tribune*. 'Whether you have it in abundance or it forever eludes you, you can't deny its power. Wars have been fought over it. Fortunes have been lost over it. Men have been brought to their knees by it. Women seek it everywhere from cosmetic counters to plastic surgeons' offices.'

I had witnessed the multi-faceted power of beauty myself countless times over the years. Beauty is like a brilliant beacon pulling in a myriad of emotions: love, jealousy, admiration, fear, lust and avarice. It's important to remember that just because someone is attracted to you, it doesn't necessarily mean they have good intentions. Attraction begets an indiscriminate audience.

Most of us are still not aware of the extent to which men are influenced by the way a woman looks. And, politically correct or not, it's still a man's world – for the time being. That's why to be beautiful is to live in a dangerous paradise. It was, after all, my mother's stunning beauty that caught my father's attention, which in turn caught her in a lifelong trap. Her thoughts and opinions were always irrelevant; he certainly didn't marry her for her culinary or domestic skills.

Dad saw Mom's primary source of power, her beauty, as something to be possessed, controlled and kept safe from the eyes of other men. Yet her beauty was condemned to fade under a life sentence of guarded isolation. If the power of beauty were ever mine, I would never surrender it to a man who simply wanted to add it to his already overflowing male arsenal, rendering me powerless yet again.

And there were practical benefits. It's well known that if you are plain you don't get as good a job. Attractive people receive lighter jail sentences if they commit an offence. They have an easier time of it in general. These are the research facts, but I also knew them from a lifetime of observing those around me.

Living in London, I was aware of a glittering world out there, literally just around the corner, to which I wasn't allowed admission. I wondered what would happen if I turned myself into a top-of-the-range 'Barbie', who represented the contemporary feminine ideal to which I aspired. And what is considered 'ideal' is dictated by society, not me. These things are very easily quantified, so my masterplan would leave nothing to chance. The Barbie image was a safe bet. It had been tried and tested and, unlike me, widely accepted.

Symbols send potent nonverbal signals in our society. I was told that I had a similar profile to the Wicked Witch of the West. And as much as I wanted to be as beautiful as my childhood role model, Barbie, I also wanted to be like Glinda, the Good Witch in *The Wizard of Oz*: kind, virtuous and on the side of justice. She happened to be very beautiful, whereas the Wicked Witch was really ugly. That was no coincidence and the symbolism certainly wasn't lost on me. By projecting an image that sent out a different set of signals, I reasoned, the reactions I invoked would shift accordingly.

Having first been powerless around my father, then with other men and finally the world in general, I decided to gain some power for myself by embodying the image that we all preferred. I wasn't trying to be superficial or vacuous.

On television, I've been asked, 'Why don't you forget your looks and work on the inside?' Considering the fact that no one would let me forget how I looked before the surgery, and having now changed from that appearance to one that is more acceptable, I would like to rephrase that question and direct it back to the world: 'Why don't *you* forget about the way I look and see who I am inside?'

Another question I'm repeatedly asked is why I had so *much* surgery. The answer should be obvious: it's because there was so much aesthetically wrong with my face. It was never a question of merely getting rid of a big nose or a double chin. Since I had more than one problem, I was going to need more than one solution. The final look I was after couldn't be achieved with just a couple of procedures. Besides, I didn't just want to look better. I wanted to look fabulous. And I had a very long way to go.

Having become a member of Mensa, the high-IQ society, back in the Seventies, I had finally been recognised for my intelligence. But little good it did me when I'd always been denied the opportunity to make the most of it. I know looks aren't the answer to everything, but all my life I'd seen doors fly open for those who were more attractive than me. Those same doors were slammed in my face. All I needed was one lousy break. It was clear that I'd have to level the playing field a little to get it.

Some psychologists maintain that true intelligence can't be measured by standard tests. The most widely accepted definition of intelligence is the ability to solve problems. This aptitude can be revealed by how well you score on problems posed in day to day life, as well as on IQ tests. And, while everyone may not join me in regarding my transformation as a stroke of pure genius, they certainly can't deny that it solved the problem.

Still, no matter how much sense it made to me, a good deal of my plan was still theoretical at that point. Even if it *were* possible to change myself by scalpel into a different form, in the future would I be noticed by 'quality' men: attractive, professional, educated, intelligent – the sort of men who had so far eluded (or should I say avoided) me? Would it make a difference to my career? Could it possibly win me new friends and improve my standard of living? And most importantly, *would people be kinder to me?* Could all those things be mine simply by altering the way I looked? Again, regardless of what the answers to those questions would eventually be, I had nothing to lose by trying. After all, I'd exhausted every other possibility available to me and been rejected at every turn. Cosmetic surgery was my last chance to get out of the rut I'd been born into. It was also the only way of making the matching hypothesis work in my favour.

At that time, cosmetic surgery was still very much the domain of the rich and famous. That's one reason I'd never considered it before. Another was sheer economics. Cosmetic surgery is expensive. Never in my wildest dreams did I expect to be left a lump sum to do with whatever I wished.

Having been given the opportunity to change my life for the better, cosmetic surgery seemed the logical route. I would annihilate my current image and turn it into something else. A transformation borne out of destruction. It would be like ripping apart one of my old hand-me-downs and using the finest sewing skills to make it into a dress fit for the Queen of the Prom. (Considering my clumsiness with sharp instruments, it was just as well that I wouldn't be the one doing the cutting and sewing.)

I was accustomed to leaving behind things that weren't working for me. First my home country, then stagnant relationships, and now my own face and body. But leaving is a two-way dynamic: in walking away from one thing, you're also walking towards something else.

Cosmetic surgery was the answer I'd been seeking all my life. I couldn't wait to get started.

Chapter Twelve

Changes

It may seem ironic that I used the money Dad left me to get rid of the family resemblance, but I had been so frustrated and downtrodden during my childhood that I created a Walter Mitty-style world for myself. Like lots of little girls, I acted out my dreams through the fantasy life that I created for my doll. No one ever questions the rationality of girls who play house with baby dolls then grow up to get married and become mothers. But I played with Barbie instead – and it was finally *my* turn.

I took a long hard look at myself in the mirror. What I saw staring back at me was an aging hag with a harsh face, with whom I simply could not identify. I remembered reading about Michelangelo back in art school, and I began to understand how he must have felt when he gazed at a block of marble and pictured what was to be his future masterpiece trapped inside. Like Mike, I would also need to do a lot of careful chiselling to set free the image I saw in my mind's eye.

I'll change my face and body, buy a wardrobe of new clothes, and create a whole new image for myself, I decided. It was obvious that my cosmetic surgery list would take a while to achieve: fuller lips, smaller nose, larger eyes, smoother skin, higher cheekbones, smaller thighs, slimmer waist, slender knees, a less jutting chin ... I also wanted just the one chin. I was beginning to develop the double variety.

For years I'd employed all the time-consuming tricks of the trade to make the best of myself using camouflage make-up and concealing clothes, but they never were very convincing. If they had been, I wouldn't have needed cosmetic surgery. Besides, I wanted to wake up ready to greet the world with a minimum of effort.

Another thing I remembered from my art school days was Leonardo da Vinci's theory of the classically proportioned face. For further guidance, I turned to anthropology and discovered two more templates for human beauty: the baby in its first year of life and the female temptress in her late teens. Babies don't have big eyes, full pouting lips and upturned noses (to facilitate breast-feeding) by accident – there's something innately programmed into the human psyche to bring out the protective, nurturing instinct. (Even the endearing 'cute' qualities of domestic animals such as puppies and kittens are biological ruses to increase their chances of survival to adulthood so they can reproduce.)

Add to this a cocktail of unlined skin, a defined waist and shapely bottom (large breasts aren't as important as a lot of women think – it's the lips and hip to waist ratio that attracts a man). Blonde hair, though not essential, implies youth because hair tends to darken with age. And anything you do to elongate the legs is good, like wearing high heels, because the best breeding age is late teens, when women's torsos haven't quite caught up with their legs. Mix it all together with da Vinci's dictates and you get a very powerful image intentionally designed to elicit a specific and predictable human response.

When I started looking at the world of cosmetic surgery I saw a plethora of opportunities. I had a detailed mental image of what I wanted to look like, but I had no idea how close I could come to matching it. So began a long journey that continues to this day, because changing my looks to conform to a set of biologically predetermined criteria is the only thing that has ever brought me any kind of lasting success.

I was told early on in my quest that there were three intractable rules in cosmetic surgery:

> *1) You cannot change bone structure.*
> *2) You cannot make a plain person look pretty.*
> *3) You cannot take more than ten years off a face.*

I went on to break every one of those rules and set a world record.

During my transformation, I became accustomed to achieving changes that I was told were impossible, or that I shouldn't attempt. As I was used to being dictated to by my father and had inherited his determination, negativity presented a challenge rather than acting as a deterrent. It didn't happen overnight but, almost a decade and 27 procedures later, I was to achieve results not only above my highest expectations, but beyond my wildest dreams.

I was aware of the risks involved and didn't underestimate them. Being human, I don't like pain. And the thought of having my face cut open and something going wrong during an operation filled me with sheer mortal terror. But having admitted those fears to myself, I was even more apprehensive of the life stretched out before me if I didn't go ahead with my plan. I felt I stood to gain more than I had to lose. The chances of anything going wrong during my operations were so small, I reasoned, that it was worth the risk. Even so, I always made sure my apartment was neat and tidy before being wheeled in to the operating theatre. After all, it would be Gloria who would have to come to sort out my belongings in the event that something went fatally wrong and I didn't want her to find everything in a mess.

Having cosmetic surgery was a similar experience to deciding to come to England, despite my crippling fear of flying. After the church steeple incident over Cleveland, my dread of airplanes hit an all-time high. Yet still I took the risk and boarded several planes to cross the Atlantic. I'd rationalised the trip by thinking that I could either die (of boredom) in Ohio or else on a plane bound for somewhere else. And statistically my chances of survival were excellent.

By much the same token, as I embarked on my marathon of cosmetic surgery procedures, I thought, I can either suffer a path of life that I'm unhappy with or I can take a risk and try something new. And, let's face it, I wasn't exactly tampering with perfection.

I could almost hear my Guardian Angel sigh as I got on the phone and asked my GP about cosmetic surgery. 'I really don't know much about it,' he said apologetically. In fact, he was clueless. This, I learned, is quite normal. GPs aren't supposed to be cosmetic surgery experts. They know a little about everything and aren't intended to be in-depth specialists in any one field, particularly this one. Many of them don't even approve of cosmetic surgery in the first place.

Everywhere else I tried I got the same response. None of the medical organisations are allowed to say who the top surgeons are in any particular area of specialisation. No one could, or would, give me the information I needed. I ran up against one brick wall after another.

After making further enquiries, a photographer friend said he knew a surgeon in London that a model he knew had been to. On this recommendation, the only one I could get, I went to see the doctor at his clinic. He agreed to perform my first couple of operations.

And so to the surgery itself. My eyes were the first to be cut and reshaped. He removed the bags and then took up the slack by slicing strips of flesh from both my upper and lower lids. This had the added effect of making me appear wider-eyed. While he was at it, I asked him to vacuum out the excess fat from the inside of my knees by liposuction. I hated my chunky farmgirl knees that had been the butt of so many cruel comments. 'They'll just have to find other ways to pick on me,' I said to myself. Little did I know how prophetic those words would prove to be in years to come.

When I woke up from the anaesthetic, I felt dizzy and nauseous. After throwing up into the bedpan, I pulled a compact out of my handbag and looked into the mirror. Although my face was badly swollen, I could see through the stitches and bruising that my eyebags had disappeared and my eyes were open wider. Even though I felt dreadful and knew it would take some time to heal, I was thrilled. My first thought was: What can I have done next? When it came to deciding, I was, of course, spoiled for choice.

I stayed in the clinic overnight and went home by taxi the following morning. Five days later the stitches were removed. On day six I carefully applied make-up and went out with my friends to the Hippodrome. Funnily enough, I was never self-conscious about being seen during my healing phases. Having been through scenarios like the pie pans on the cherry trees, I was beyond embarrassment.

The friends in whom I'd confided about my operations were aghast and told me not to have them. They said I looked fine as I was. It was a common reaction, but I ignored it because I knew I was beginning to make real progress. I wasn't going to turn back now. Eventually I stopped telling anyone about my upcoming operations until after they had been performed. This meant that Gloria and Mom didn't worry. It also meant that I was very much alone in my quest. However, it was a lot easier to face the operations by myself than to try and convince everyone else of the validity of my plans. I needed to preserve my energy for getting through the operations, not exhaust it defending my actions to others.

Next, I had a chemical peel in the doctor's office, under a local anaesthetic. An acid solution was brushed on to my face that basically fried off the top layers of skin. My face turned into one large scab and when it dropped off my skin was very red underneath. It didn't worry me. The result was similar to the one achieved when Mom smeared Vaseline on my face, thinking it would protect me from sunburn. After two weeks the redness disappeared and I was left with a fresh, smooth complexion. My farmer's freckles had gone along with some superficial wrinkles and old acne and chicken pox scars. I was elated.

After starting an unofficial network by talking to patients in waiting rooms, I was becoming more and more knowledgeable about the efficacy of various procedures and who excelled at them. All the surgeons I met expected patient loyalty. But my loyalty was to my plan and nothing was going to stand in my way. Every time a surgeon argued, 'I'm not really sure you need this procedure ...' I thought: 'Well, I take your opinion on board but if you won't do it, I'll go somewhere else.'

At that time I told no one about my overall plan, especially not the surgeons. I changed one or two features at a time, randomly working my way from top to bottom and back again.

No matter how hard I searched, however, there was one procedure that no one wanted to perform, and that was the operation to reshape my jaw. I knew the proportion of it was mathematically wrong. It was something I had lived with since the realisation occurred to me during my art school days. Yet I couldn't find a surgeon in the UK who was prepared to put it right.

I read in a beauty magazine that brushing dark powder around the jawline would make it appear smaller. I admit to having done this for years, but it probably only made me look as if I had a five o'clock shadow. Just as unconvincing was my habit of drawing my lip liner way outside my mouth, to give the impression that my thin lips were fuller. I wasn't fooling anyone.

After my chemical peel healed, I couldn't wait to get back under the surgeon's knife. Within months I had my nose made smaller and underwent abdominal liposuction to get rid of excess fat and give me a waistline. Since the liposuction operation to my knees was relatively easy and pain-free, I was led into a false sense of security.

That's why I was taken by surprise after having abdominal liposuction. The surgeon had done nothing wrong, yet every time I moved I was in agony. All the surrounding muscles were badly bruised during the procedure, and I soon learned how many simple movements involved using those muscles. If I sat still I was fine, but it was painful to stand up. I hobbled around bent over double for ages.

As for my nose job, that was also uncomfortable to say the least. The surgeon broke my nose in two places and rasped down the bone to make it slightly smaller. When I came round after the anaesthetic, it felt like I had about a mile of gauze crammed into my nostrils and I coughed up a lot of dried blood. I was violently ill after the anaesthetic and had to wear a cast on my face for a week that made me look like Hannibal Lecter. When the dressings came off I was disappointed. Whereas my liposuction was a great success, my nose was neither small enough nor the shape I had wanted. In other words, it was not the nose I picked.

It didn't put me off. The next procedure I went for was a lower face-lift and jawline liposuction to get rid of my saggy jowls and double chin. While my double chin had disappeared, my bone structure remained the same; my remaining chin seemed to jut out even more without the fat underneath to soften the angle. I also had collagen injections to make my lips fuller. At that time I was still unaware that the problem with my lips was not merely one of being thin, but they had no shape. They were just straight lines. Plumping them up only resulted in a duck-like effect. Besides, I found collagen injections expensive and the effects short-lived. It seemed I was taking two steps forward and one step back. The changes I had undergone weren't nearly radical enough.

My old pop columnist friend Martin Dunn thought they were. When I ran into him at a party at Stringfellows. A year had passed since I'd started having cosmetic surgery and he commented on my new looks. I didn't want my picture all over the papers, but when he offered me £1,000 for my story I thought, What the heck, nobody I know reads the *Sun*. Martin turned my story into a double page spread with the headline: I SPENT £10,000 ON A BODY SWAP.

There was a scantily clad picture of me, shot by top Page Three glamour photographer Steve Lewis with the caption: 'This is rock singer Cindy Jackson's £10,000 new look – the result of 14 months under the plastic surgeon's knife.'

The article continued, 'Cindy, 27 [I was really 33], decided she didn't like what nature had given her. Now Cindy says, "It was worth every penny. My rock'n'roll lifestyle had taken its toll. My eyes had huge bags from too much drinking and late nights and I had a beer gut."'

It set the publicity machine rolling. Unbeknownst to me, the *Sun* had syndicated the story all over the world. It was the summer of 1989, and I was immediately invited to go on Sky's *Derek Jameson Show* to discuss my surgery. Also on the show was Gerry Marsden from Gerry and the Pacemakers, who I'd been a big fan of while growing up in the sixties. Next I appeared on *Wogan*, Britain's most popular talk show at the time. Although both Derek Jameson and Terry Wogan are seasoned professionals who did their best to put me at ease, I was a nervous wreck in front of the television cameras – despite encouragement and coaching from little Juliette, who went along with me to the BBC studios. Nonetheless, I felt that I'd done OK and got away with it, never expecting to be asked to appear on television again. At any rate, I wasn't keen to repeat the experience.

Meanwhile, Mom, Aunt Katherine, Aunt Sibby and her husband Uncle Bob came over to visit me for the first time. Mom and I went to Paris where we finally got to speak French to French people instead of each other.

Shortly after my relatives left, the BBC contacted me again.

They asked if I wanted to have breast implants while being filmed for the *Ruby Wax Show*. I never really considered having a boob job. It wasn't part of my plan. But, as I was in the process of having everything else fixed, I thought, Why not? Ruby Wax, a fellow American, took me for lunch at the BBC canteen. I remembered her from the *Girls on Top* TV series and I was delighted to meet her. She was very friendly, asked me about my background and we discussed the surgery I was to have for the show. I was quite nervous about it all and said, 'This is a very personal subject.'

'Don't worry. We'll edit the film together,' she said. 'Anything you don't like we'll take out.' She put my mind at rest so I agreed to go ahead.

On the day of the filming of my operation, which was mocked up for the cameras, Ruby turned up with the crew and helped wheel me in to the operating theatre. The BBC wanted to film on that particular day, which wasn't convenient for the surgeon, so I didn't actually have the operation until much later.

When I went to the studios to film the interview about my allegedly enhanced figure, which was entirely thanks to padding from the costume department, I was quite shocked by Ruby's tone. She read a tirade of nasty comments off the autocue. 'Where are you from?' was one of her questions.

'I was brought up on a farm in Fremont, Ohio.'

'Oh, so you're poor white trash,' she replied.

'I'm not that white,' I quipped.

When she had finished verbally chewing me up and spitting me out, Ruby presented me with a little medal that said: 'I Got Fixed.' All well and good but, when I tried to contact her to ask when we were going to edit the film, I discovered she didn't mean it. The subjects of her shows were never allowed anywhere near the editing room, I was informed. Despite the fact that I'd kept my end of the bargain, including pretending that I'd really had the operation (even until now), Ruby didn't keep hers. I realised that I'd misplaced my trust once again.

Fearing the worst, I mounted a pre-emptive strike. I called up my pal Martin Dunn at the *Sun*. Meanwhile, I'd had my boob job with the BBC's money.

'The BBC has bought me a boob job,' I told him.

'You're not kidding me, are you?' he gasped.

The operation cost £1,500 and the BBC had sent me a cheque for that amount before I went under the surgeon's knife. Luckily I photocopied the cheque before I banked it. Photocopying cheques was a habit I retained from my poor past – I couldn't afford to have a single one go missing without a trace. Martin sent a motorcycle courier to collect the copy as proof that I had received the money.

Although I had sold the story to the *Sun*, I could hardly believe my eyes when it appeared as a front-page splash. NEW BOOBS ON THE BEEB, it yelled, a play on words referring to the then popular hit band New Kids On The Block. The article was accompanied by huge 'before' and 'after' pictures of me in a pink bikini. They'd also published the photocopy of the BBC cheque.

'Cindy Jackson, 27 [I was still really 33], had her breasts enlarged by two inches for a TV show,' it said. 'BBC chiefs faced a storm of protest last night as MPs accused them of wasting licence payers' money.

'A cheque drawn on the BBC Accounting Services Television account arrived at Cindy's north London home. Two days later, she booked into a clinic.

'Cindy said, "My boobs were 34A. Now they are 34D. They look terrific."

'Tory MP Alistair Burt said, "The payment is totally wrong. If the BBC wishes to do programmes about cosmetic surgery there must be many people they can talk to without fixing up the breast enlargement themselves."

'Fellow Tory Ian Taylor said, "I am not sure that we pay our license fees to enable young women to have their breasts made bigger."'

I phoned Martin Dunn.

'Are MPs really outraged?' I asked him.

'No, but they will be when they read this,' he replied dryly.

And so will everyone else when they now read that the real operation was not even filmed, but faked for the cameras.

I heard afterwards the BBC were actually quite pleased with the publicity, but said they wished I had waited six weeks to tell the story nearer to the airing of the show. In response, I sold another story to the *Sun* saying how Ruby Wax had lied to me. I fought fire with fire.

If Ruby had been honest and told me she was going to make a mockery of me, I would have been fine about it. I have a sense of humour and I don't have a lot of ego attached to my surgical transformation. I was upfront and said to her, 'Look, if we're going to have a laugh out of this, please just let me know.' But she insisted it was a straight show. The dishonesty left a very bad taste in my mouth. It was unfair and unnecessary. Like some men who treated me badly, she must have thought I was a nobody who didn't matter anyway.

When the show finally aired, my suspicions were confirmed. Ruby's caustic remarks to me, now accompanied by hysterical canned laughter, were left in and my witty responses ended up on the cutting-room floor. She was the only one allowed to have a sense of humour and she used it to ridicule me. I could hold my own, but I wasn't allowed to. The result was that I came across looking pretty stupid.

Researchers from her shows have contacted me during the intervening years, but I haven't appeared with her since. You can't expect to cross bridges that you've already burned.

Meanwhile, I had no shortage of upcoming television appearances – or cosmetic surgery operations.

Chapter Thirteen

Fade Away and Radiate

I heard about a surgeon who was very good at upper face-lifts. As I'd had the lower part of my face lifted, I wanted the top of my face to match. My eyes were also still saggy underneath, despite the first operation, and needed to be tightened again. He performed both procedures under what is called a twilight anaesthetic, which means you're conscious, but unable to feel anything. By that time I'd become a cult celebrity again – this time on the cosmetic surgery scene. As the surgeon drew his scalpel down the side of my face, I heard him say to the operating theatre staff, 'If I make a mistake on this girl, my career is *over*.' We all chuckled nervously.

He didn't make a mistake, and I was pleased with what he did. But when I told him I was disappointed with my nose job and asked him if he could make it smaller, he said no, adding that he thought there was nothing wrong with it. I smiled at him and said, 'Never mind, maybe it's not so bad after all.' Time to change surgeons again, I thought to myself.

Meanwhile, I'd taken my young flat mate Juliette, now 13, to have cosmetic surgery. She'd always hated her prominent ears so we had them pinned back. Juliette was a pretty young girl and it was the only thing she needed done.

Due to the publicity I was receiving, prospective cosmetic surgery patients from all over the world began contacting me via the BBC, the *Sun* newspaper, Sky Television and everywhere else I'd been interviewed in order to ask for my advice. I met up with them in cafés, pubs, restaurants and doctors' waiting rooms to talk about what worked and what didn't, and to discuss which surgeons were doing the best work and those whom it was wiser to avoid. Despite the fact that we all saw the power potentially available to us, a confusing maze of misinformation and medical establishment politics stood between our goals and us. Unless we pooled our knowledge, we were all in danger of falling victim to them.

In addition, many of us had experienced a particular breed of bossy, hard-looking women who seek to control beauty in much the same way men do. Ironically, they often come in the form of cosmetic surgery advisers or beauty therapists. They hang around the peripheries of cosmetic surgery, hoping to make a quick buck. The ones who've had surgery often look scary, and the ones that haven't make you wonder why they don't practise what they preach. Either way, the consensus was that even if they had the wisdom we were seeking, they were not about to share it with us. Had that been the case, we'd have looked no further.

It was through this untapped demand for factual and empowering advice that the job eventually fell to me. The beauty of the situation is that I also benefited from this exchange of information. That's how I ended up getting the best surgery. One girl I met who wanted to speak to me about breast implants had exactly the pert, gently curved nose I coveted. She showed me her 'before' picture and, prior to surgery, she had the biggest hooked nose I had ever seen. It had really ruined her face, but now she had an absolutely perfect nose that suited it. What's more, it didn't look at all like a nose job. I took the name of her London surgeon and wasted no time scheduling an appointment. Little did I know I was making a date with destiny. I was about to meet the man who would eventually transform my face and body – and my entire life.

When I met the surgeon, Edward Latimer-Sayer, I was struck by how kind and gentle he seemed in contrast to some of the more aggressive doctors I'd met. Not that personality is any indication of ability, but I found it reassuring nonetheless. After an intense hour-long consultation, he agreed to give me the nose I'd always wanted. It was so exciting. But when the plaster came off to reveal the nose of my dreams, it made my chin look even bigger. The big nose and big chin had actually balanced each other out. Now that I had a cute nose, my chin took over. I asked the same surgeon to fix it.

'Oh, no,' he said. 'I'm a cosmetic surgeon. I don't perform sliding genioplasties. You need a maxillofacial surgeon.'

'Please have a go, you're really good,' I begged.

But, quite rightly, he wouldn't perform a procedure that was outside his field. He did, however, agree that having the procedure would improve my facial aesthetics. I was resigned to being stuck with my chin until I found a top maxillofacial surgeon.

Meanwhile, Edward Latimer-Sayer did agree to help me with my lips. He lifted my upper lip by cutting a margin of skin away from it and closing the wound, creating a new lip line. This had the effect of making my lip wider from the front and fuller from the side view. The leftover margin of skin was sliced in half and implanted vertically between my nose and upper lip to create the little trough that most people have naturally.

My upper lip had been very thin and the space between it and my nose was vast, giving a simian effect. The procedure that he did solved both problems and left me with a perfect Cupid's bow. When I asked him to do the same to the lower lip, he explained that it wasn't appropriate and that it would pull my lip down to expose my lower teeth. Although he had succeeded in convincing me it would look worse than having a small lower lip, I still wanted it made bigger somehow, and I realised I would have to wait for the right technique to come along.

Next I asked him to remove my BBC breast implants. They had always felt uncomfortable and the right one had gone hard as a rock. My silicone sacs were removed under local anaesthetic, and I took them home with me. (Today I use them as paperweights in my office.) I was relieved, not only because my false bosoms had given me such discomfort, but also because I had realised they didn't really suit me. I'm not a busty, blousy sort of person and, frankly, I was a little embarrassed by them. What's more, I discovered that most men don't really like the idea of breast implants anyway.

I had a theory that if I kept my breasts bandaged tightly up high for six weeks the scar tissue would form a bond with my chest at that level, resulting in my bosom being higher and more youthful. It worked. When I took the bandages off I had exactly the shape I predicted. But now that I had a less voluminous chest it made my hips seem pear shaped, so I decided it would be better to aim for a more athletic figure rather than a voluptuous shape at this point.

While the Allied forces were planning Operation Desert Storm, I was planning another operation – to fight the battle of the bulge. My surgeon had secured one of the new ultrasonic liposuction machines that had only just been introduced in Britain. I asked him to use it to reshape the sides and backs of my thighs and shrink my 'love handles'.

Ultrasonic liposuction is unique in that it causes an injury to the underside of the skin and the resulting scar tissue shrinks as it heals. This gave a lift to my thighs and hips by tightening them, as well as removing excess fat. It still left the backs of my thighs swollen and bruised for a while though, as I realised when using the bathroom for the very first time after the operation. Not realising I needed to lower myself gently, I sat down as normal. The impact of the porcelain suddenly making contact with my newly operated-on thighs resulted in severe pain like an electric shock shooting through my entire body. I was nearly the first woman on the moon.

Over the years, when patients I had got to know went in for their operations, they would often ask the surgeon if I could accompany them and watch the procedure being performed, which involves getting to wear the entire Ben Casey-type outfit complete with surgical mask. Instead of being grossed out while observing operations, I was fascinated. It also made me even more acutely aware of how critical it is to select the right surgeon and anaesthetist, because patients are so vulnerable on that operating table. I resolved never to entrust my life to just anyone.

It also meant that I had yet more privileged information about the entire cosmetic surgery experience from start to finish. It seemed I was spending every waking hour researching cosmetic surgery from both sides of the knife. I was becoming quite an expert and began to be recognised as such.

The constant trickle of enquires I was receiving from people seeking advice became a deluge. I would be up until all hours of the night writing out personal replies to each and every one of them by hand. (I didn't even have a typewriter at that point.) But the time came when I had to choose between ignoring the mountain of mail that was beginning to take over my life and charging a fee for my hard-won knowledge. That's when I decided to turn my new-found wisdom into a business, the Cosmetic Surgery Network, which I still run today.

It was 1991 and Margaret Thatcher, having bid farewell to Downing Street, had been replaced by John Major the previous year. Britain was in the throes of a deep recession. I could not have picked a worse time to start a business, yet that is exactly what I did.

With no credit references, I was unable to secure a loan to help me get started. The only form of credit I had was a Visa card with a £5,000 ($7,500) limit, so I took the entire amount out in a cash advance that I made regular repayments against each month. That allowed me to buy essentials such as postage stamps, stationery, a typewriter and a fax machine.

Not knowing the first thing about running a business, I bought a few paperback books by corporate strategist Tom Peters, who is my kind of businessman – completely off the wall. Some of the titles that caught my eye included *Thriving on Chaos, The Pursuit of Wow!* and *In Search of Excellence*. Having always been a voracious reader, it seemed quite natural to just get a few books by an expert on the subject then simply apply what I had learned. That is, after all, the theory behind higher education.

I enjoyed running my own business. It gave me yet more scope to be creative and made me feel very grown up, especially since I got to have an accountant. That was quite a big step, considering that only a few years earlier I was living on unemployment benefit and could keep track of my finances on one hand.

In the early days I charged £15 ($25) for people to consult me on the telephone at home during certain times of the day. In return I gave them sensible advice and doled out cautions about all the different procedures. I compiled fact sheets on each operation with information I got from doctors, medical books, feedback from other patients and my own personal experiences, which I photocopied and sent to those who were considering changing their looks.

Basically, I told prospective patients what I wish someone had told me. I explained the details of each procedure in plain English. If they asked which surgeon had performed a specific procedure on me I told them, but I never recommended a particular surgeon. Instead I taught them how to choose one for themselves, like I had. Nor did I encourage anyone to go ahead with surgery. I emphasised the risks, the possible pitfalls and the usual causes of disappointment.

If someone was determined to follow in my footsteps when having cosmetic surgery, then they needed to know the whole process I went through to attain successful results. This involves, among many other things, taking responsibility for the outcome of the surgery by finding out as much as possible about the procedure and then interviewing several surgeons.

When I first embarked on my transformation, I had never met anyone who'd had cosmetic surgery. Even though it's become much more mainstream now, it's still very much an elitist privilege to know who the very best surgeons are. In the beginning I had no inroads into that world so I had to learn the hard way – by trial and error.

After a while, the crucial knowledge I'd amassed was in huge demand from others. I was overwhelmed that there were so many people in the world who, like me, got negative feedback from the world about the looks they were born with. Thousands of men and women from all over the globe wrote (and still do, in droves) saying how miserable they were with the face and body they were given and, because of a lack of information, begged for insider knowledge. Here's a typical letter:

Dear Cindy,

I am considering cosmetic surgery but, due to lack of information, I don't know how to take the first step. The two forms of surgery I am considering are to my face and eyes. I have a fuller face (chubby cheeks) and was hoping that the excess fat from my cheeks could be removed through liposuction but I am unsure if this certain surgery exists. Also my eyelids tend to sag over my eyes. Can you possibly put me in touch with any surgeons who specialise in these two fields?

I have suffered from low confidence for years but I am now determined to change the way I feel. However, I do understand that cosmetic surgery will not transform me into a supermodel, but it will make me more confident. I would appreciate your help.

Others contacted me saying how disappointed they were with the surgery they had already had:

Dear Cindy,

Two years ago I had surgery with a London surgeon. I wanted my undereye bags removed and he suggested 'tidying up my upper lids' at the same time.

The result has been disastrous. He removed a lot of the soft tissue from my upper lids resulting in my eyes looking sunken and small. The skin is discoloured and generally my eyes feel uncomfortable. My eyebrows seem to have dropped down into the sockets.

Needless to say I am extremely unhappy with my present appearance and discomfort. I have not seen the surgeon since surgery (his nurse removed the stitches). I feel as though I have been disfigured and even paid for the process (£2,000).

I am thinking about approaching another surgeon with a view to repair work but obviously feel extremely apprehensive about this. Perhaps you could offer some advice?

I knew the answers to their questions, but there was no one for me to turn to when I wanted to take my transformation to the next level. Thinking I'd struck lucky when I came across two British women who'd had operations to reduce the size of their chins, I was aghast when they both turned out to be horror stories. One of them was desperately disappointed because the surgeon she employed had simply sawn off the front of her chin, leaving it completely flat and shapeless with a flap of redundant skin underneath.

The other patient had been left with little feeling in her lower face and limited control over her mouth muscles, which meant she drooled constantly. She bitterly regretted having ever contemplated having the operation in the first place. It made me even more wary of the procedure. (I subscribe to the old adage, 'A smart man learns from his mistakes. A wise man learns from other people's mistakes.')

I felt bad for patients like that who had been damaged beyond repair, and it made me all the more determined to obtain and distribute the very best information to those whose surgery was still in the planning stages and to take extreme care over my own future choices. As someone who listens to her own advice, I was forced to live with my jutting chin for some time to come.

I attracted more and more attention from the media, who

dubbed me the 'Living Doll', a title that stuck and has been used at every available opportunity since. However, the vacuous-looking modern Barbie dolls with ankle-length platinum hair they compared me to had little in common with my old classic 1960s Barbie – or me. Whenever there was a TV programme featuring cosmetic surgery it was always me they wheeled out. Suddenly I was getting calls from America to appear on talk shows there.

The *Maury Povich Show* was the first in a long line of American talk shows on which I was featured. Playing on the 'Living Doll' angle, the researchers asked me to bring along a Barbie doll dressed the same as I was. I didn't want to splurge out on anything new – I was spending my entire legacy on rent and surgery. Funds were getting desperately low. My favourite dress was purple, so I found a purple sock in my drawer from which I made Barbie a matching garment. The sewing skills I learned as a little girl saved the day.

My appearance with Barbie on that show did yield some rewards. Although I didn't receive a fee, they flew me via Chicago on my way back to London so I could visit Mom and Gloria. This circuitous airline routing became my standard 'payment' for appearing on American television shows. After all the years I had been hard up while living in London, it was good to get to spend time with my loved ones again. Even if it meant appearing on shows like *Sally Jessey Raphael* and *Jenny Jones*.

Incredibly, the hosts with the worst reputations for being tough – Jerry Springer, Howard Stern and Anne Robinson – were the nicest to me. All three of them flattered me and made me feel good about appearing with them. Figure *that* one out.

American tabloid talk shows are not a pleasant experience. Audiences called me every name under the sun and treated me like an absolute freak. I was crowded by fat men and women spilling over their chairs, spitting venom, jumping, shouting, beside themselves with rage, simply because I'd undergone lots of surgery. 'I'm fat and I'm happy!' they yelled. 'You should give your money to charity instead of spending it on your looks!' It was always the same reaction whatever shows I went on. 'You're a bimbo! An air head!'

Meanwhile they'd bring on some rabid pop psychologist to parrot the usual clichés about looks not being important and pronounce me insane. If I modelled myself on Barbie, I guess this bunch modelled themselves on Trolls.

Having lived in England – the home of understatement – for so long, whenever I went to the US it seemed, in many ways, more like a foreign country than it did home.

After appearing on those dumbed-down programmes, I'm often asked how I can sit there and take all that crap; people write to me to say how much they admire my composure. The answer is that it's very easy – I tune them out, just like I did when my father yelled at me. However I did keep in mind one thing that Dad had always shouted at me – 'It's only a TV show, damn it! It's not real!'

Besides, rising above that type of behaviour never fails to make them look even more lowdown by contrast. I refuse to give them the satisfaction of stooping to their level. There's a saying where I come from, 'If you get down in the mud and wrestle with a pig, not only do you get yourself dirty, but the pig likes it.' I rest my case.

Having cosmetic surgery became a way of life during that period. Despite the regular visits to my family, every time I turned up I looked different from the last time they'd seen me. Carl joked that I should wear a name tag so he would recognise me when he came to pick me up from the airport. Mom didn't say too much about her changing daughter. 'I liked you before,' was her stock observation. She was getting used to seeing me on TV, so my transformation wasn't too much of a shock. In fact, she got so accustomed to my being on TV that, if she was channel surfing and she saw me on a programme she'd seen before, she would surf right on by.

Gloria rarely admits being related to me. Not out of shame particularly, but she has her own life in the small, conservative Midwestern suburban town where she lives. Her Barbie-loving daughter Adrienne, however, is a different story. One day when

Adrienne was playing at a friend's house, a re-run of a talk show I had done came on. Adrienne looked up and announced, 'That's my aunt.' Her playmate's mother said, 'Now, Adrienne, that lady might look like your aunt, but that's not your aunt, honey.' To which Adrienne replied, 'Yes it is,' and continued playing.

The incongruity of the outrageous personality on a tabloid talk show claiming to have had serial cosmetic surgery to look like a Barbie doll being related to modest mild-mannered model citizen Gloria was beyond imagination, and she flatly refused to even entertain the possibility. But when Gloria came to pick her daughter up she volunteered, to the astonishment of the entire neighbourhood, that her younger sister had just been on TV and asked if anyone had caught the show. I maintain that Gloria also has an outrageous side, which you can catch rare glimpses of if you watch very carefully. But then, how could she not, considering the gene pool from which she originates?

Meanwhile back in London I had a mask face-lift. It is so named because my face was detached and lifted off like a mask, re-draped to make it completely wrinkle-free and stitched back into place. In fact, it was lifted so much around my eyes that my eyebrows went straight up and back, so I looked like one of Mr Spock's Vulcan relatives on *Star Trek*, but that didn't last beyond the healing phase.

Nonetheless, my eyes remained almond shaped, and I no longer looked anything like I used to. Now we were getting somewhere. Edward Latimer-Sayer also tightened up my chin and transferred fat from my abdomen to my upper lip and used what was left to fill out my nose to mouth lines whilst I was on the table. Before bandaging me up and bringing me round from anaesthetic, he used a rotating wire dermabrasion wheel to sand off any remaining surface wrinkles, and then sliced off two facial moles with his scalpel. (I know exactly how it was all done because I have it on video.)

While my beautification plan was going from strength to strength, things on the home front were turning ugly with my latest boyfriend, Phil. He was five years younger than me and a musician who, unlike Warren, never got his big break. Phil was a balanced individual; he had a chip on *both* shoulders.

I met him just after my first few operations in 1989, at which time he was the good-looking one whereas I was still working on becoming attractive. When I say 'good-looking', I mean Phil was gorgeous. I must admit that his looks are what first attracted me to him. But I should have looked deeper. He had a cruel saying that should have set alarm bells ringing: 'Ugly girls have to try harder.'

When I began to look prettier than him and started to make a name for myself, I think he felt upstaged. His response was to become resentful and try to tear down my new-found self-esteem. He kept urging me to get rid of my long blonde hair – one of the few assets I'd always had. 'It would look better darker and really short,' he insisted.

When I first had the idea to set up my business, the Cosmetic Surgery Network, he gave me a sour look and pronounced, 'It'll never work,' ignoring the mountain of post on my desk and the telephone that rang non-stop.

The one area where Phil actually gave me encouragement was when it came to giving up my band. The meagre success we'd enjoyed was more than he could stand, having failed to get anywhere with music himself. But I didn't quit the band for him. Instead, I was determined to make cosmetic surgery research and information my career and it was more than a full-time job. The band would have to go. After being in one band or another for almost nine years, I played my last gig at Bootleggers in 1991.

Phil's bitterness grew. He kept telling me how lucky I was to have him. 'No one else will want you because you've had so much surgery,' he said. 'You're beginning to look like a man in drag.'

The fact was that I looked a lot more masculine before my surgery. He began to try and undermine me at every opportunity and I reacted very badly. After witnessing my mother's self-confidence being worn away, I wasn't prepared to let any man do the same to me.

Phil was broke. I never cared about that. He certainly did,

though. Any success I had was met with sarcasm and put-downs. He never failed to find a way to ruin things for me. I learned to play down my accomplishments and keep my triumphs to myself.

I had more than a little trouble getting rid of Phil. Every time I tried to break up with him he wouldn't agree that we should part. He threatened to tell lies to the press about me, and even demanded money to go away, menacingly calling it 'insurance'. It felt like I was living in a nightmare from which there was no waking up. I was horrified to realise what sort of person I had let into my life.

In the beginning I always said he was too good to be true, and I should have thought through the implications of that statement. I'd been completely taken in by his good looks and false charm. But, as Robert Palmer warned in his hit song 'Doctor, Doctor', 'A pretty face don't make no pretty heart.' It was a valuable lesson. Phil was the best-looking man I've ever dated, but unfortunately he didn't have the personality to match.

In the end I employed lateral thinking and started treating him exactly as he treated me in the hope that he would go away. Finally he got the message. Funny how he wouldn't tolerate the very things he expected me to put up with.

Out of necessity, my whole childhood was spent developing strategies to outmanoeuvre my father. It was now second nature for me to try to work out people's motives for acting a certain way and, because of my early traumas, I still spent a lot of time analysing what makes the male of the species tick. I surmised what their reaction was likely to be if I would act or speak a certain way. It was something I practised from a very young age.

My father had all the power: the guns, the house, everything was under his control. I felt so powerless the whole of my childhood. Powerless to help the animals he shot. Powerless to help my mother when he was so unkind to her. Powerless to help myself. The only real escape for me was to grow up and take control of my life. The surgery was a means to an end. I wanted to look beautiful and to have the power of beauty. Now I was beginning to get the looks I wanted. I had my own apartment and was running my own business.

Unlike my father, Phil had no real hold on me and his intimidation tactics didn't scare me. It was a lot easier to walk away from him than it would have been to stay.

In 1994, soon after my escape from the jaws of hell, my own jaws came under the spotlight. The world's most eminent dentist, Ronald Goldstein of Atlanta, Georgia, contacted me out of the blue. He'd seen me on TV and said he was coming to London and asked if he could see my teeth. I went to his fascinating lecture at the Royal Academy of Medicine in Harley Street and he invited me for a drink afterwards.

Meeting Dr Goldstein reminded me of the first time I met Edward Latimer-Sayer. Here was another kind and gentle man with whom I immediately felt at ease. (Their accents, however, could not have been more different.)

When he looked at my teeth, he said they weren't bad, but he could improve them quite a bit with bleaching and a little reshaping. My lower teeth resembled tombstones and he said he would remove the overlapping top edges with a diamond drill to make them appear uniform. There also was a small gap on each side of my upper teeth he wanted to eliminate using a simple bonding technique. I got out my diary then and there and made an appointment to see him in Atlanta after the New Year.

When I got to his office I noticed a signed photograph of Phyllis Diller. By coincidence, the woman who inspired me to have cosmetic surgery in the first place was also a patient of Ronald Goldstein's.

It was just as well that the treatments were surprisingly pain-free, because they were done in the full glare of the spotlight. The Atlanta-based television channel CNN followed the progress of my dental treatment for one of their medical reports. Next trip, Ronald and I appeared on NBC Extra together.

I loved the South. While it seemed that all of America was glued to the television to follow the OJ Simpson trial, I was making regular visits to Atlanta to shop, hang out with my new friends there and continue with my dental appointments. I always stayed at the Buckhead Ritz Carlton, which had become my unofficial US office. It was there that I turned on the television one day to see horrific reports on the aftermath of the bombing of the Murrah Federal building in Oklahoma City, which killed 168 men, women and children and shook the whole country.

Although I had made a life in England, my roots will always be American and I shared the sadness and outrage felt by the nation, as well as being deeply moved by Bill Clinton's televised emotional speech from the scene. Events such as that tend to humble us all and remind us to count our blessings.

When my dental work was complete I was thrilled beyond words. I especially liked the way Dr Goldstein had used 'cosmetic contouring' on my lower front teeth. With just a little reshaping, he'd created the illusion that they were perfectly straight. Although I'd never given it much thought before, I began to appreciate the importance of straight white teeth and how well people respond to a broad, confident smile.

Eventually I confided to Ronald Goldstein that I wanted my chin reshaped. Like most of the medical élite I was now dealing with, he understood aesthetics and was sympathetic to my predicament. He agreed that it would be a big improvement and encouraged me to go ahead with the operation. And he knew just the man for the job.

Dr Goldstein recommended a friend of his, Dr Louis Belinfante, also in Atlanta, who was one of America's top maxillofacial surgeons. I immediately arranged an appointment for a consultation with him.

'We'll take it back a bit,' said the surgeon. 'But if I take it back to the exact proportion you're talking about it might make your nose look too big.'

'I don't care, I'll get my nose fixed again,' I said.

'I do not want to do an operation that is going to precipitate another operation,' he insisted.

'If my nose looks too big, I'll get it fixed,' I repeated. 'I want my chin to be perfect. I want it right in line with my upper lip and not a centimetre over. If you err, please err on the side of a receding chin.'

Here was a man who could fulfil my dearest wish. I knew all the risks and through my top-level medical connections I had finally found the surgeon I trusted to do it perfectly. Having seen pictures of his work, I was aware of the wonders he had done for those with severe deformities. And, like my now regular surgeon in London, not only did he make them look normal afterwards; he actually made them good-looking. There was no way I was going to let him turn me down.

I carried on pleading my case and he finally relented. A few days later I was admitted to a hospital in Smyrna, Georgia, hometown of superstar Julia Roberts. I arrived at the prescribed time of 5.30am. It was still dark and I was groggy from lack of sleep so I didn't notice the sliding glass doors. I thought they were wide open but they weren't – they were just very clean. I walked straight into the glass and bounced off, nearly knocking myself out. I cursed my accident-prone genes. That surgeon came very close to getting to fix a broken nose as well as doing my chin.

At least the pain took my mind off the serious operation I was about to undergo, as did the seemingly endless procession of people who appeared at my bedside with clipboards bearing form after form in quadruplicate requiring my signature. In England I was used to being asked to sign a single consent form, but America takes its red tape very seriously. They also take credit cards for cosmetic surgery, so I charged the operation on my Visa card. (Nowadays I joke that if I had a pick-up line it would be, 'Do you take plastic?')

Dr Belinfante made an incision inside my mouth at the base of my lower teeth and stretched the skin and muscle down and back to expose my chin bone. (Taking this particular route ensured there would be no external scarring.) He used a circular saw to cut through my chin and disconnect it from my jawbone. He then slid my chin bone backwards until it was in line with my upper lip just as I'd requested. Then he drilled holes in the bones on either side of the crevice and threaded surgical steel wire through them to secure my chin back on to my jawbone.

After putting everything back where it belonged, he sewed up the hole inside my mouth. It was a major procedure to say the least: get this one wrong and, instead of people drooling over me, I'd be the one drooling uncontrollably for the rest of my life, like the patient I'd met back in London. I had to take a lot of drugs afterwards: steroids, painkillers, antibiotics, you name it. I hadn't seen so many pills since the Sixties.

After being discharged from the hospital, I was holed up at the Ritz Carlton while I recovered. I was sick as a dog and my chin was so swollen I looked like a bullfrog – I was puffed up right down to my chest. When I rang the UK to check my messages, there was a call from a Melbourne TV show. They wanted to fly me to Australia.

'I'm recovering from surgery, I don't know if I can,' I told them.

I asked Dr Belinfante what I should do. 'I want you to stay and rest in Georgia for five days before you go anywhere,' he advised.

I packed my chin with ice. Five days later I packed my suitcase. I couldn't resist the opportunity to visit my third continent.

Chapter Fourteen

Doctor My Eyes

A researcher from Network 7 met me off my Qantas flight when I landed in Melbourne. 'Who else is on the show?' was one of the first questions I asked her. She told me there would be a woman who, at that time, was one of the world's foremost laser cosmetic surgeons. Laser surgery was a new innovation, something I had yet to try, and I was thrilled that I was going to get the chance to meet her. So keen was I to make her acquaintance that I asked the researcher to call her from our car as we were driving away from the airport. The surgeon had a cancellation that afternoon, so I dropped off my suitcase at the hotel – they had booked me into a fabulous suite at the Rockman Regency, where the Doobie Brothers were also staying – and went straight over for a consultation.

She explained how her method of surgery worked. My skin could be rejuvenated, she said, with the use of a high-energy laser beam which pulses on and off in microseconds. It was claimed that lasers are more accurate than traditional methods when used to treat lines and wrinkles, because practitioners have more control when using a tiny beam set to penetrate to a specific depth than is possible with skin peels or dermabrasion. I wanted to have my forehead resurfaced, where I had, not surprisingly, begun to develop some worry lines. I couldn't wait to try it, and we arranged for the surgery to be done the morning after the TV show.

I spent just five days in Melbourne. It's a beautiful city and I would have loved to stay longer. On the second day I was invited to go on a girls' night out with the television researchers. Although I was desperate to go with them, instead of relishing their warm Australian hospitality and savouring the city's café society, I was reluctantly forced to stay in bed with the worst case of jetlag I had ever known. Crossing the Atlantic between England and America was bad enough but the effects of going all the way to Australia hit me like a ton of bricks. Not to mention the major operation I had only just had in Atlanta, which made me feel very weak. In fact, I felt like I was going to die.

The next day, although I was still feeling shaky and listless, I rose early and went jogging to get some fresh air and a rough idea of the city's layout. After a quick shower and fresh fruit breakfast via room service, I went on a whirlwind tour of Melbourne, taking in the tree-lined boulevards, its trundling network of trams and the Yarra River meandering lazily through the town centre.

The following day was also my own and the guys from the television channel asked me what I would like to do. I didn't have to think long: I really wanted to go into the bush and see some of the indigenous animals. They generously arranged a VIP tour of the famous Healesville Animal Sanctuary, 41 miles to the east of Melbourne. Opened in 1934, the Sanctuary provided a brief opportunity to immerse myself in the sights, scents and sounds of the Australian bush. It is home to more than 200 species of native birds, mammals and reptiles. A path weaves through the Sanctuary taking you through large habitat areas where wildlife can be seen in its natural environment.

I was shown around by a bushranger who introduced me to hundreds of colourful birds, kangaroos, emus and dingoes. He took me behind the scenes to see sick and orphaned animals being lovingly tended by dedicated staff. I got to cuddle a baby wombat named Isabella whose mother had been killed by a car. When I put her back in her pen and started to walk away, she pushed against the bars and cried for me to come back. Her desperate plea for affection brought tears to my eyes. I went back and picked her up again, but it only made our inevitable parting worse for both of us.

If it hadn't been for the compulsory six-month quarantine all animals had to face upon entering the UK at that time, I would have enquired about taking her home with me. But Isabella had been through enough already. Still, like so many animals that have touched my heart, I'll never forget her.

I didn't get to hold a koala, though. Apparently there are laws against that because koalas, which by the way are not bears or even related to the bear family, are so sensitive that they can suffer severe trauma from encounters with people. (Perhaps I was a koala in a previous life.) Australian law allows touching koalas only when they require veterinary assistance. I took pictures instead.

Next on the agenda was the television show. I was an old hand at speaking on camera by this time and everything went without a hitch. Near the end of the programme, they showed me a picture of some guy and had me narrate the procedures I would use to make him more attractive, while a computer operator manipulated his image to my specifications on the TV screen. I quite enjoyed that part. It wasn't until I had finished rearranging his face to a much-improved version that they told me that the guy was the Australian Prime Minister. So much for Anglo-Australian relations.

My laser surgery was scheduled for the following morning. Even though the procedure is relatively painless and a general anaesthetic isn't necessary, the surgeon had instructed me not to have anything to eat or drink after midnight the night before – so what did I go and do?

After the show I went out on the town with the guys from Network 7 and ate and drank like there was no tomorrow. Not being long out of my band era, I still had a somewhat rock'n'roll attitude when it came to out-of-town gigs. Television researchers all over the world who have been in charge of entertaining me have invariably commented on this. They always tell me they expected some kind of snooty lady-who-lunches health fanatic, but instead got someone whose excesses would have made the Sixties line-up of The Who on tour look like a grammar school outing. I had, after all, learned how to fight for my right to party directly from the Beastie Boys. (I've calmed down a lot since then.)

I eventually crawled into bed at around four in the morning and turned up at the laser surgeon's clinic at 6am horribly hungover and reeking of alcohol. I was terrified that I would spontaneously combust as soon as the laser beam hit me, but it was too late to back out now.

The surgeon prepared me for the procedure by covering the lower two thirds of my face with aluminium foil and placing gauze over my eyes. (At which point my Guardian Angel probably covered her eyes, too.) Feeling nauseous, I swung one of my legs over the edge of the trolley and put my foot firmly on the floor to try and stop the room from spinning. She administered a local anaesthetic and I braced myself as the laser beam began incinerating the skin on my forehead, producing a crackling sound like bacon frying and filling the room with acrid smoke accompanied by the unmistakable stench of burning flesh. I swallowed hard over and over again to prevent myself bringing up the Chinese meal and gallons of sake that had gone down so easily just a few short hours before.

When it was over, the surgeon wrapped a large gauze bandage

around my forehead and I went back to my suite at the Rockman Regency looking like Rambo in drag. The next day the wound was raw, swollen and oozing lots of runny yellow pus. Because the surrounding skin was completely numb, in the days to come I couldn't feel it when the pus had built up under the bandage and begun to trickle down my face until it seeped into my eyes and impaired my vision. The procedure had caused my eyelids to turn red and puffy so it was impossible to apply make-up. The swelling on my chin had gone down dramatically, but it still had a long way to go before it would look normal again. I suddenly realised that during the course of a few short weeks I had circled the entire globe and had cosmetic surgery on three continents. To say I was looking the worse for wear would be an understatement worthy of the English upper class, to whom subtlety is a revered art form.

I have never been a particularly vain person. Vain people look in the mirror and think they look pretty good. Whenever I look in the mirror I always see room for improvement. In recent years, the amount of room I've seen has fluctuated according to the stage I was at during my cosmetic surgery transformation. Since I was neither accustomed to being pleased with the reflection I saw in the mirror, nor to receiving positive reinforcement for the image I presented to the world, my various post-operative healing stages merely represented a temporary return to a less attractive state which still felt like home. (Kind of like visiting Ohio.) It's entirely due to this lack of vanity that I never thought twice about going out in public during my healing phases. Or as Ogden Nash put it, '... it's those in front who get the jolt.'

Therefore, regardless of how ghastly I looked as a result of the combined effects of jet lag and the aftermath of two major facial surgical procedures, I was determined to make the most of what little time I had left in Australia. So I carried on sightseeing during the day and doing some serious partying in the evenings with my new friends at Network 7. The morning before my flight back to London I even woke up in bed with the show's host, Derryn Hinch. Nothing happened – he'd come up to see me to my suite and we carried on raiding the mini bar until we both passed out.

As a popular radio and television personality, Derryn is well known in Australia for his controversial views. He also devised a weight-loss programme that helped him lose more than 42lbs over an eight-month period. He gave me a copy of his diet book inscribed with the words 'Nothing personal.' To shed the pounds, he said in the book, 'I did not stop eating. I did not stop drinking alcohol. I did not stop having fun. I did not stop going out to restaurants for lunch. I did not stop going out to restaurants for dinner. I continued to eat such "banned" food as fried dim sums. I continued to eat pizza, pies at the footie, bread (heaps of bread), French fries, fried chicken (including the crispy skin), Indian pompadoms and oily nan bread. Even fortune cookies at my Friday Chinese luncheon. And not a day went by on this diet when I did not drink beer and wine. Not one.' Hmmm ...

When I first moved to London I dreamed of seeing the world and thought I would start by visiting most of Europe – to an American it all looks so close on a map – but economics decided otherwise. During my early years in London I could barely afford to cross the English Channel to France, much less venture further afield. Going home to see my family on a regular basis was completely out of the question. One Christmas Gloria even had to buy me a round-trip airline ticket so I could finally spend a holiday with her and Mom.

Cosmetic surgery changed all that. Not only have I seen much of the world, but I got to travel First Class with all expenses paid and was given spending money, known as 'per diem' in television expense account language, on top. The great thing about flying First Class is that they provide unlimited champagne before take-off and throughout the flight, which helps me forget my fear of flying, as does the inevitable grilling about cosmetic surgery techniques by the flight attendants.

Over the years I've made regular trips to Germany to take part in television discussions about cosmetic surgery, which I always enjoy immensely. Not only are the Germans wonderful hosts, but they have the best beer in the world and every other car is a Mercedes – even the taxis.

My wardrobe has also been greatly enhanced. One time I realised I was wearing shoes I bought in New York, underwear from a trip to the South of France, a dress I got in Geneva (with a sushi stain down the front that I gave myself in Tokyo), the bracelet I picked up in Frankfurt, a jacket I acquired in Toronto and I was carrying a handbag I purchased in a Melbourne market, all set off nicely by a Los Angeles suntan. I was in Scotland at the time. Whenever I visit a new country, I always buy something to take home to remember my visit. There has been only one exception.

On my way back to London from Australia there was a stopover in Thailand. Bangkok airport was almost as shocking a sight as I was. Apart from a serious shortage of clean restroom facilities, I was saddened to see shop after shop laden with items made of, or decorated with, ivory. It sickened me to see the shameful array of tacky tourist trinkets produced from the senseless murder of beautiful, peaceful elephants. On principle, I left Thailand without buying a single thing, just as I boycott animal-tested products and real fur.

When I got back to London, I couldn't wait to show Edward Latimer-Sayer the results of my latest operations. While he was suitably impressed with my new chin, it was obvious that he was horrified by the condition of my forehead.

'Before I decide about investing in laser equipment, I'm going to have to see how you recover from this,' he said grimly.

It took four months for the swelling and blistering to disappear and I was left with unsightly scarring. Edward Latimer-Sayer had to perform dermabrasion to rid my forehead of the ugly marks. Laser surgery didn't work for me. All it did was destroy my skin. I did try it again a few years later with a different type of laser, and the results were still disappointing. Nowadays I stick to dermabrasion and cosmetic peels, which have always given me excellent results.

Next I began to notice that, because of all the face-lifts, my hairline had dramatically receded above my ears, so I went along to see a hair transplant surgeon. After injecting local anaesthetic into various parts of my head, he cut out a strip of hair-bearing scalp from the back and closed the wound. Next he made tiny incisions into which he planted hairs one hair follicle at a time, known as micro-grafts, into the scar tissue left by my face-lifts. Then he filled in the area above my ears, bringing my hairline back down where it belonged. I was given some potions to apply and warned to be careful not to damage the newly implanted follicles when washing or brushing my hair. A few weeks later the transplanted hair fell out as expected, but the re-growth was permanent, so the procedure was a success.

Not long after my hair transplant, I was able to complete the bone structure changes I wanted. Under a general anaesthetic, Edward Latimer-Sayer made incisions inside my mouth above the upper teeth and inserted two solid silicone cheek implants. Afterwards, the effect of the swelling was reminiscent of an overzealous squirrel gathering nuts for the winter. Again, it didn't stop me from going out. It was nearing Christmas and there were lots of parties to attend. I just looked a little cheeky.

When the swelling finally went down, I was delighted with the results, which came as no surprise. Ronald Goldstein had already fed my picture into his computer back in Atlanta and manipulated my face to give me a sneak preview of what I would look like with cheek implants. It had been his idea for me to get them in the first place.

All was not plain sailing, however. After a few months the implants were slipping a little and one of them had begun to curl under. This is not terribly unusual and some patients opt to have the operation reversed. But not me. I loved the way they looked and wasn't willing to part with them.

The problem was mainly on the left side, where my underlying cheekbone was more flat than the right one, a result of my skull forming asymmetrically in the womb. Therefore the implant did not fit over and cup the bone like it was designed to. It just slid around under the skin. They would need to be sewn to the bone. My surgeon said, 'Well, if I'm going to go in there to straighten things out, I might as well lift your face a little more because both procedures involve the same incision.' Guess I should have waited a while before having that hair transplant.

That was the face-lift that finally made me look so much younger than my years. Some people who have had multiple old-fashioned face-lifts just get their skin pulled back repeatedly, making them look false and overly stretched, famously known as the 'wind tunnel' effect. But having a series of dramatic mask face-lifts where my face was lifted off, re-draped and replaced progressively higher resulted in my looking younger each time. With regular maintenance, I intend to continue to look at least twenty years younger than my age for the rest of my life.

All the while I was catching planes like taxis. At least once a month, TV stations were flying me to places like Los Angeles, New York or Toronto to appear on their shows. While I wasn't exactly being paid a fortune for the privilege, at least I got to see my family far more regularly. Having lived abroad and gone home rarely in the previous two decades, it was great to get to know them again.

Mom was spending a lot of time down in Arkansas with Aunt Sibby, who was also a widow by now – Aunt Sibby's husband Bob died after a long illness called myasthenia gravis, the same disease that claimed the life of Aristotle Onassis. As difficult as losing a partner may be, it was as if Mom had suddenly been let loose from a long spell in a dark, dank prison. Having been heavily guarded by Dad all her married life, she was making the most of her new-found freedom.

Among their many outings, Aunt Sibby had driven them to Oklahoma to go to gambling casinos and to Graceland in Tennessee to visit Elvis's memorial. Mom's older sister, my aunt Katherine, died of stomach cancer. Another of Mom's sisters who lives in Indiana and we see far too little of is Aunt Priscilla, who is a real treasure. She is a sweet and caring woman, and extremely religious. She can work any conversation back to the word of the Lord. She was the first of the sisters to be widowed. Her husband, Hershell, died when I was a little girl.

Aunt Priscilla's son-in-law trains pilots on the Top Gun team at the Pentagon. Aunt Sibby and a couple of my other aunts once drove to Washington DC to visit him at his office. They were given a VIP tour but when they came out, they went into the huge parking lot and couldn't remember where they had parked the car. After they had wandered around for ages, becoming even more lost and flustered, Aunt Priscilla finally said, 'Look, there's an attendant.' She walked across to a tall black man in uniform.

'Excuse me, son, can you help us find our car?' she asked him.

'Ma'am, don't worry, just jump in my car and we'll drive around until we find it,' he replied helpfully.

A long, black chauffeur-driven limousine with tinted windows pulled up and the driver got out to open the doors for them. Once comfortably seated, the ladies had another look at the 'parking lot attendant' and noticed he was sporting an awful lot of medals on his uniform. Family legend does not specify which one of them realised first that he worked inside the Pentagon building and not in the parking lot, but they all had seen rather a lot of this man on television over the years. It was none other than General Colin Powell, the man who helped conduct foreign policy decision meetings for three presidents and led the Gulf War effort on the

US political front. He is obviously also a compassionate man who not only likes to help aging widows but also has a great interest in cars. As a hobby, I have since learned, he spends hours rebuilding junker Volvos, his professed love affair with automobiles having developed when he was growing up in a poor immigrant household in New York.

'Cars, unlike people, lack temperament,' he wrote in his autobiography *My American Journey*. 'When working on them, I was dealing not with the gods of the unknown but the gods of the certain; not the gods of abstraction but the gods of the concrete. If something malfunctioned in the engine and I proceeded logically, I could identify the problem and fix it, the only area in my life where I had that kind of control. I found these mechanical puzzles absorbing and relaxing.' Well, he certainly solved Aunt Priscilla's puzzle and very quickly located her car.

Mom had suffered a cerebral aneurysm back in 1981 and had undergone major brain surgery. Aunt Sibby had one nearly ten years later, which took the wind out of her sails for a while. Strokes and vascular weakness is a genetic problem in our family and, for this reason, I take a 75mg aspirin every day to help thin my blood. It's wise to try to pre-empt these things if you can.

Meanwhile, my business was growing so rapidly that I realised that I needed to conduct it in a different way. I couldn't possibly talk to everyone who called my hotline – I was receiving an average of 200 telephone calls a week from women and men wanting support and advice and there weren't enough hours in a day. Since most of them had the same questions, I decided to write and publish a comprehensive cosmetic surgery guide. I became a credit card merchant so I could send these books out by mail order. For those seeking more personal advice, I thought I had the perfect solution.

Chapter Fifteen

Substitute

Many of the people I'd spoken to on the telephone had expressed a desire to see me personally. Likewise, I was keen to meet other patients, see their results and share information face to face.

The north London hospital where most of my surgery was performed agreed to let me use an office where I could give private consultations to patients who sought my advice. The floodgates opened and I was immediately booked several months in advance.

Prospective patients of every conceivable description found their way to my office – men, women, young, old, gay, straight, rich, poor, celebrities, models, politicians, medical professionals, secretaries, drag queens and even those undergoing gender reassignment. You name them, I got them. It was great.

For all our diversity, we shared a common bond. We saw cosmetic surgery as a tool that could help us get rid of the sticks other people were hitting us with.

Many of them told me they identified with me and felt able to speak openly for the first time, confiding their innermost fears and personal hang-ups about the way they looked. Together we talked and we listened; we laughed and we cried. I may never have been prom queen, but those patients certainly made me feel like the queen of cosmetic surgery.

Although I'd finished most of my transformation, I continued to undergo regular maintenance procedures, such as filler injections in my lips and having my eyeliner and eyebrow make-up tattooed on. In addition, when the new synthetic lip implant came out, I was the first in England to have one put into my lower lip. It seemed like I was always having *something* done, and the patients who came to see me during that time shared the details of those experiences as they were happening, just as they shared theirs with me. It wasn't unusual for clients to find me clasping an ice pack to my face or looking bruised and battered from my latest treatment.

On these occasions I always apologised for my appearance but they didn't care how I looked during the process or what gruesome sight they were confronted with – we were all after the same thing. What they were concerned with was whether I was happy with what I'd had just done and, if so, should they consider having the same. I was the only one they trusted to be honest with them. Well, you can't say I didn't put my money where my surgically enhanced mouth was. Besides, just about any procedure you could name, I'd already tried and could give you the full run-down on.

I also got to know the work of the world's cosmetic surgeons. For years I sat in my office and watched a non-stop parade of their results. *Everybody's* patients came to see me. It got to the point where I could identify certain signature procedures and name the surgeon who'd performed them. (Of course, the very best cosmetic surgery is undetectable.)

My reputation for having a non-judgemental attitude and

sky's-the-limit approach spread far and wide. The cosmetic surgery industry was still notoriously taciturn at that time. Because I saw no reason why it shouldn't be more accessible, my presence ruffled more than a few feathers. Nonetheless, it wasn't long before I'd single-handedly pushed back the boundaries of traditional cosmetic surgery and precipitated several previously unknown trends. And for once they weren't borne of media hype or some clinic's public relations machine. They came from genuine patients.

First there were the clones. After a lifetime of wanting to look like other women, I was amazed to discover that other women began to want to look like me. It's not unusual for a prospective patient to write to me expressing a desire to have a particular feature like mine. After all, I have had most of the available cosmetic surgery procedures, and many women use my face and body as a kind of shopping catalogue. They say, 'I want my lips done like yours', or 'Tell me what kind of face-lift you had,' or 'How can I get rid of my flabby thighs?' It was probably only a matter of time before I ended up having my very own army of 'clones'.

When Isobel Hayes first walked into my office at the Cosmetic Surgery Network in the summer of 1994, she looked me in the eye and said, 'I want your nose.' She was a striking woman but there was no denying that her large nose was a distraction. I sympathised. She was obviously trapped, as I had been, behind a face that sent out the wrong signals; although only 28, she dressed conservatively and seemed shy and inhibited.

After we chatted for a while, Isobel admitted that she also wanted to get rid of a few moles on her face and some old acne scars. I recommended dermabrasion, where the skin is sanded off with a rotating wire brush. This could be done at the same time as her rhinoplasty.

When she had her £3,000 operation that autumn, I went along. Her rhinoplasty and dermabrasion – by the same surgeon who did mine – went as planned. For the first week she looked terrible and refused to leave her house: her nose and forehead were encased in plaster and the skin around her mouth was red and raw. But when the plaster came off, she was thrilled with her small, upturned feminine nose – just like mine, though tailored by the surgeon to fit in with her facial proportions. The dermabrasion took two weeks to heal, but left her with a flawless complexion.

Over the succeeding months, we became friends. It wasn't long before Isobel was commenting on how often men complimented me on my lips. To achieve the right fullness, I'd had two operations – one to lift my upper lip and another to fill it with fat taken from my backside during a liposuction session. Fortunately for Isobel, her lips were not as thin as mine had once been, so she did not need to have her upper lip turned partially inside out; she settled for a fat transfer like I'd had.

She was also dissatisfied with her thighs and wanted to have ultrasonic liposuction on them, as I'd had done on mine. So a year-and-a-half after her first operation, she was back in the operating theatre for new lips and hips, costing £3,500.

Even before those two procedures, she had begun to look uncannily like me. When she let her hair grow and began wearing it in the same style as mine, people started asking if we were sisters. My standard joke was, 'No, we're not even Catholic.'

Obviously, I didn't take these comments very seriously. That is, until Isobel and I went on vacation to the USA together.

One day we decided to go shopping in downtown Chicago with Gloria. We were in the Escada store on Michigan Avenue when the saleswoman approached Isobel and me as we were holding up matching dresses in front of a mirror.

'Are you twins?' she asked.

I laughed. 'Twins? We're not even sisters! This is my sister,' I said, pointing to Gloria, who had just joined us at the mirror. The saleswoman, however, gave me a distinctly frosty look and walked away, clearly convinced I was having a joke at her expense.

Gloria, who doesn't look anything like me, was not amused. She has never understood my desire to change the way I look (she won't even have her ears pierced) and here, suddenly, was someone who looked more like me than my own flesh and blood.

After that I couldn't help noticing that, whenever Isobel and I went out, she would buy the same make-up and clothes as me. Before her surgery, she had worn a lot of lace and Laura Ashley-type dresses; now she had entirely changed her look to copy mine. Once, when I returned from Paris with a fabulous rubber raincoat, she made me ring the Left Bank boutique and order one for her.

I had no problem with her behaviour, as long as she didn't start wanting to *be* me. If she had changed her voice or manner to imitate mine, that would have been a little alarming. But our personalities are completely dissimilar; she is quiet and home loving, whereas I am more outgoing and daring, and we have utterly different tastes in men. As I saw it, the clothes and make-up I wore enhanced my new looks to their best effect so it made sense for her – now that she had many of my features – to copy everything else.

I don't feel proprietorial about my looks. They are merely a means to an end; a way of making me feel more confident using a tried and tested formula. Before having my own surgery, I would have worried about losing my individuality if someone had wanted to look like me. (I would also have questioned their sanity!) Now I just feel flattered.

The features I have are a kind of uniform, specifically tailored according to scientific principles to make me look as appealing as possible. Why should I mind if other women want to achieve the same results?

At last count there were at least a dozen other Cindy clones – most of whom prefer to remain anonymous – dotted around the world. But it is not my intention to encourage women to have surgery that makes them look like me. They decide what they want. Through my advisory service, I help others to find their best look; if that happens to be a doe-eyed blonde with turned-up nose and full lips, so be it. What does it matter? Perhaps if more of us looked the same, men might begin to care more about the aspects of a person that really matter – the character, intelligence and spirit inside.

Isobel explains why she became my double like this: 'Until I saw pictures of us taken together wearing the same clothes, I never realised how much I looked like Cindy. It was quite a shock. Although we have similar features, I only used to notice the differences: look carefully and you'll see my face is longer and wider than hers is and I'm quite a bit taller,' she says.

'After the pictures were shot, Cindy and I couldn't be bothered to change our clothes so we went out to dinner in Hampstead, north London, dressed identically. It was the only time I have ever consciously tried to look exactly like Cindy and we caused a sensation. Everyone gawped and the proprietor bought us champagne.

'Being a clone was fun for an evening but it's not something I'd want to do on a regular basis. I'm not interested in the limelight; Isobel Hayes is not even my real name – I've changed it here because I value my privacy. I don't want to become a "freak," wheeled out for spots on breakfast television. I have always been judged on my appearance and I've had enough of it now.

'At first, when I was a child, my problem was not being pretty enough. At primary school I remember a friend telling me I was ugly but that it didn't matter because there were plenty of ugly men out there who would like me.

'Despite such comments, I didn't really worry about my appearance until I reached puberty. Suddenly, my nose seemed to grow bumpy and out of proportion to the rest of my face. The boys even nicknamed me Schnozzle Durante. When I saw photographs of myself, I couldn't believe that tough-looking, beaky woman was me. Inside, I felt softer and more feminine; I imagine it's almost how transsexuals must feel – completely at odds with their own exterior.

'My lack of self-confidence caught up with me in my early

twenties. I hid behind my hair, wore discreet make-up and dressed conservatively, usually in trousers (never skirts) and a blouse. Being looked at was the last thing I wanted. This is not to say I was a gibbering wreck. I never had any difficulty attracting men; the problem was mostly in my head.

'I used to feel cosmetic surgery was for image-obsessed stars, not ordinary women like me. Then, one night early in 1994, I was watching television when Cindy came on to talk about what she'd had done. Her new nose was exactly the sort I wanted. Eventually, I plucked up the courage to go and see her.

'I wanted her to convince me to have a nose job but she said it had to be my decision. While we talked, I kept glancing at her nose. I was terrified of ending up with one of those Hollywood piggy buttons stuck on the end of my face but Cindy looked completely natural. My family didn't know about my plans. I knew they would only try to dissuade me; whenever I complained about my looks, I was told that I was making a fuss about nothing. The only person who understood how I felt was Cindy. Our chats on the telephone became more and more friendly and we began meeting quite regularly for lunch.

'Cindy is a very confident woman. Gradually, her "if you've got it, flaunt it" attitude began to rub off on me. [I also say, "If you haven't got it, get it."] Instead of buying dowdy clothes, I began to adopt a more fashionable look. I wasn't consciously copying her; we just had the same taste. Sometimes, we would go out shopping separately and buy identical outfits.

'On the day of the operation, I was terrified. But two weeks later, when the plaster was removed, I knew the risk had been worth it. Eighteen months after my nose job, I had my lips plumped up a little and had some stubborn fat removed from my thighs. These were the finishing touches; I don't intend to have any more surgery, except perhaps a face-lift one day.

'The last thing to change was my hairstyle. I had been dyeing my hair blonde from the age of 18 and always wore a fringe to make my face look smaller. Now, I was confident enough to brush it off my face. I also grew my hair longer because I felt more womanly.

'Coincidentally, Cindy has the same hairstyle. We also share wide lips, high cheekbones and small noses but that isn't surprising when you consider that we went to the same surgeon. He has a favourite profile he likes to create and there are quite a few women around wearing Cindy's nose.

'I certainly didn't set out to resemble her. If we had had the same lifestyle, maybe I would have tried harder to accentuate our differences. But we don't, so it doesn't really matter.'

I met another Cindy clone when the deputy editor of *Woman's Journal* contacted me and asked if I would be photographed with her for the magazine. Her name was Linda Briggs and she had seen me in the media over the years. As a result, she decided to take the bull by the horns and change her look as well. But, unlike Isobel, I'd never met her before and she went to a different surgeon.

Not all surgeons have the same ideas about beauty. Linda doesn't have a single feature that is remotely similar to mine, so she actually looks nothing like me at all. From what I could tell, the biggest change she made was having her short red hair dyed blonde and false hair extensions put in, which softened her image. I encouraged her to grow her own hair longer.

It's not only the new Cindy Jackson that some people wish to look like. Many simply want to turn back the clock and look like they did when they were younger. In that case I always suggested they take an old picture along to show the surgeon so he can get an idea of the task at hand.

As for those who wanted to change individual features, I encouraged them to do the same thing they did when they wanted a new hairstyle – go through some magazines and find a picture of someone with a feature they like and take it along to show the surgeon. That would enable them to express to the surgeon in concrete terms exactly what they wanted. In turn it gives the surgeon an exact idea of that prospective patient's personal aesthetics, so he can tell the patient if he thinks that particular feature would suit them and whether or not he felt capable of successfully performing the operation. Little did I know I was starting yet another new trend in cosmetic surgery that would soon sweep the globe.

One man came to see me clutching a picture of his idol, Elvis Presley. Under my guidance, several operations later he began to resemble the King.

A few years later I was contacted through my website by a man who'd bought my cosmetic surgery book and used it as a shopping catalogue instead of a reference guide. Miles Kendall, a young man working as a web-designer, was keen to be completely transformed. He wanted to get rid of his prematurely aged face, large nose and crooked teeth. I couldn't resist the challenge. Together we chose a collage of features chosen from the very best Hollywood had to offer. We selected Tom Cruise's eyes, Brad Pitt's nose, Johnny Depp's cheekbones, George Clooney's lips, Russell Crowe's chin and Jude Law's teeth.

But funds were limited. He confided that he had nowhere near the money I'd spent on my own transformation. I reassured him that, knowing what I know now, I could have done it at a fraction of the price, since I wouldn't repeat my expensive mistakes. We would use that knowledge to make his transformation a reality using careful planning and a minimum of operations. And we did. He was over the moon with his new image.

Another patient, Maureen Howard, brought several photographs of Ellen Barkin. She ended up sacrificing her house to fulfil her biggest dream: to look just like her favourite movie star. Maureen, an unhappy divorcée from Doncaster, told me she had spent years mulling over the possibility of going under the knife to change her looks. But she never thought she'd go through with it.

'The first time I saw Ellen Barkin was a turning point in my life,' says Maureen. 'She starred in a movie called *Sea of Love* several years ago and I sat in the cinema completely spellbound by her beauty. She had exactly the look I wished I'd had. But I couldn't afford surgery, so I made do with styling my hair like Ellen's and copying the way she applied her make-up.'

Then one day Maureen read a magazine article about me. 'The feature told how Cindy overcame all odds to achieve her goal, and there were dramatic before and after pictures,' says Maureen. 'I thought, If she can do it, why can't I? So I wrote to Cindy.'

Maureen came to London and had a nose job, breast implants, an eye job and fat transferred from her thighs to her lips. The total cost of the surgery was just over $15,000. 'The result was worth every penny,' says Maureen. 'The surgeon helped me achieve my most cherished dream. My friends and family are astounded and strangers do double takes as I walk down the street. And when I look in the mirror I no longer see a world-weary haggard face. Instead I see a superstar.'

I know exactly what she means, although I certainly don't see myself as a superstar.

Strangers have always done double takes when I walk down the street for one reason or another. Who knows why they still do – maybe they recognise me from the media or perhaps they're just looking for the 'joins.' Or, with any luck, some of them might just find me attractive.

But, as I've previously explained, attraction is indiscriminate. I was about to get a major reality check on the uglier side of human nature that would change everything – and bring me face to face with the bogeyman.

Chapter Sixteen

Every Breath You Take

My celebrity status became official when I acquired stalker. He started a vendetta against me, making malicious calls, screaming down the phone that I was going to die. Or he would send abusive letters containing sexually obscene material and death threats through the mail. It was a nightmare. Because stalkers have been known to attack and even kill their victims, I was uncomfortable going out alone knowing there was a sick person out there who was obsessed with me. Since I had no idea what he looked like, any man in the street could have been him.

Oddly, he was also obsessed with my advertisements in women's magazines. He went on and on about them in his letters, and how he intended to stop me from placing them.

He even wrote to *Vogue* magazine, where I had been a regular advertiser for years without so much as a single criticism about my service from patients. When *Vogue* wrote to me saying they had received a complaint, they inadvertently enclosed a copy of this man's letter. It had his name and address on it.

Two can play this game, I thought to myself.

I decided to hire a private detective to watch every move he made until I had all the information I needed. It was only a matter of days before I knew a lot more about him than he'll ever know about me.

My stalker turned out to be a man in his twenties living in Hounslow, Middlesex. He'd had a nose job carried out by an NHS consultant plastic surgeon and he was bitterly unhappy with the result. He'd tracked down the surgeon who did my second nose job, Edward Latimer-Sayer, and asked him to perform a corrective operation. During the course of the consultation, the surgeon became wary of the man's temperament and would not consider treating him. After being told there was nothing to be done to change his face again, he turned nasty and switched his attention to me. This was purely because the surgeon had put my unsatisfactory nose job right and would not do the same for him.

I made an appointment with a detective sergeant at Hounslow CID. In the interview room I handed over the private detective's report along with the stalker's letters. They examined everything and made copies for their files. Since it's a criminal offence to send obscene and threatening material through the post, they took my complaint very seriously and wasted no time in paying him a visit at home. There the CID officers found the pad on which he had hand-written his letters. The detective sergeant in charge of the investigation told me that the man had confessed and then broken down and cried hysterically, pitifully begging them not to tell his parents, as he still lived at home. He promised the police he would never do it again. But it was all just an act – he didn't stop.

As soon as I received the police report, I pounced on the fact that he didn't want his parents to know what he'd been up to. I sent copies of the lawyer's letters and the police report by special delivery to his father at his place of work (in case the stalker intercepted the mail), having got the address from my private detective. Enclosed was a covering letter explaining that his son's illegal actions were affecting every waking minute of my life and he had to be stopped. I threw in some photocopies of the obscene mail he'd been sending for good measure.

My local police were aware of his activities so I was on the priority response list in the event that he physically attacked me. I never went anywhere without a personal alarm and could not walk down the street without looking over my shoulder. After all I had been through to take control of my own life, suddenly some creep who I'd never even met had power over my every move.

I decided to take matters into my own hands. Since I had all his personal details, including his telephone number, I called him up. 'I think you had better come and talk to me, show your face, stop sending me anonymous letters,' I said.

He came to see me at the hospital and, as he was also writing spiteful letters to my surgeon, I arranged for him to join the meeting. Besides, not knowing what this man was capable of, there was no way I was going be alone in a room with him. Edward Latimer-Sayer recognised him immediately.

'Yes, you turned me down,' the man said to him bitterly. It was obvious why my surgeon wanted nothing to do with him. Operating on someone who was clearly so menacing would have been dangerous. There have been several cases around the world of cosmetic surgeons being stalked and even murdered by patients.

I could barely stand to look into his hateful face. There was something very disturbing in his eyes that haunts me to this day. 'You have caused me a lot of anxiety and you've cost me a lot of money,' I explained to the stalker, trying to hide the fact that I was shaking with fear. Apart from hiring the private detective I had sought legal advice about having him prosecuted, and the lawyer had written him a letter on my behalf, reserving the right to press charges if he continued plaguing me. Because he knew I was a woman living alone, I had to spend a small fortune on increased security on my home in the form of a more sophisticated burglar alarm, an armoured door and metal bars on every window.

The stalker again pretended to be full of remorse and promised to stop.

Like many stalkers, this man has repeatedly changed his *modus operandi*. He began typing his letters and mailing them from different parts of town, but I still knew it was him. He was like a cockroach that had become immune to pesticide.

At the moment he's still around and still obsessed with my advertisements – and everyone else's as well. The fact that I've had a stalker was in the newspapers and soon others involved with cosmetic surgery who'd been receiving hate mail contacted me. In every case, when I was shown the letters they'd received, I immediately recognised his handwriting. It gave me great pleasure to hand over a copy of the thick file I had on him so they too could take matters further.

Incredibly, my stalker has now joined forces with the British Advertising Standards Authority, despite the fact that I'd made them fully aware of his criminal activities and after he wrote to them and admitted that he had supplied them with 'incorrect information' about me. It's things like these that reinforce my lack of faith in the establishment. But that's not the worst of it.

The British government obviously don't know his track record, because he's praised in a House of Commons Select Committee Report entitled, 'The Regulation Of Private And Other Healthcare – Cosmetic Surgery and Other Activity In Small Clinics' produced at the end of 1999. Maybe you can't blame them – he's such a good actor that the police told me they believed him when he broke down and swore he'd leave me alone. Considering that those men are trained to spot guilty criminals pleading innocence, you'd think they would have seen through him. But they didn't.

Because of the obsessional and frightening behaviour of this man, I began to think twice about seeing patients face to face. With my increasing fame, I was placing myself in serious danger.

Anyone could walk into my office posing as someone who was interested in cosmetic surgery.

And anyone did. A British newspaper set me up. A reporter from the *Sunday Mirror* came along to see me pretending to be a patient wanting a nose job. I gave her the same advice as anyone else but the paper ran a fictitious piece that made me look unprofessional and irresponsible. Edward Latimer-Sayer was also mentioned in the article. He immediately began libel proceedings. Mirror Group Newspapers settled out of court. They ended up paying his legal costs, substantial damages, printing an apology and a Statement in Open Court was read out. The success of his case also vindicated me.

I felt exposed and vulnerable. Although I was determined to carry on my work, after my stalker and the newspaper incident, I couldn't tell who was a genuine patient anymore and who wasn't. I honoured my commitment to all the people who had booked with me in advance and reluctantly stopped seeing patients personally. It was a great shame because we'd shared so much. Jealous and spiteful individuals had ensured that we no longer carried on. I felt a terrible loss at having the one thing that I'd finally found that I could do well, and that was appreciated by others, taken away from me. However, little did they know that I'd learned to thrive on adversity. How could I not? I had known nothing else. (There was also the problem-solving thing.)

Determined to provide the best and most up-to-date information about cosmetic surgery, I decided to expand on my existing cosmetic surgery guidebook. It would be fully illustrated and contain a wealth of inside information – from *both* sides of the knife. The book would be the absolute and ultimate bottom-line guide to cosmetic surgery. Every word had to be correct, medically as well as in terms of practical advice. All the information was checked and double-checked by top surgeons as well as by patients, so I waited for their feedback before making it available by mail order. It took me over a year to complete the project, but everything I'd been telling patients in person was there. What's more, that information was now available on a global basis. I also made an accompanying 50-minute educational video.

Finally, no one could stalk me or set me up. Genuine patients are not out to do that. They simply need information. The book, called *Cindy Jackson's Image and Cosmetic Surgery Secrets,* is sold over my website, www.cindyjackson.com. New editions come out several times a year. (Any cosmetic surgery book in the shops was written at least 12 months previously, meaning that the information is out of date in this rapidly changing industry.) It is now so comprehensive that it has taken the place of the video. Praised by patients and the medical profession alike, it represents more than a decade of research into hundreds of thousands of case histories.

In the book, I don't urge anyone to follow my – admittedly extreme – example or, indeed, to rush into surgery of any kind. In fact, I go to great lengths to advise anyone who wants to change their appearance to wait, research their options, think about it and talk to several surgeons. I explain how to conduct a consultation with a surgeon anywhere in the world, arming them with a set of questions to ask. I explain what each cosmetic procedure involves and give advice on how to pick a surgeon. The most basic rule is that if a surgeon is unable to produce before and after pictures a patient should run a mile. There is no way anyone can know what a surgeon is capable of without seeing the evidence.

Such straightforward advice really seemed to upset some people. The truth is that many surgeons don't have before and after pictures to show patients because they haven't conducted enough procedures. Or if they do have pictures they obviously don't want anyone to see their results. It's little wonder that these surgeons don't appreciate me imploring patients to insist on seeing them.

In addition to seeing before and after pictures, I would also need to know that the surgeon had been primarily practising cosmetic surgery for the last five years, had performed no less than one thousand cosmetic operations and be currently performing no less than two hundred documented cosmetic surgery cases per year.

Trying to find a suitable surgeon can be confusing. For example, in Britain, patients are sometimes advised to only let a National Health Service consultant operate on them. However, considering that cosmetic surgery is not normally available on the NHS, exactly where would their experience come from? NHS plastic surgeons are primarily trained to treat burns, congenital deformities and the disfigurements of accident victims, which does not automatically make them experts in face-lifts or tummy tucks. In fact, it could mean they have never performed a single cosmetic surgery procedure in their lives.

Then there is the Specialist Register. The only way to be a Specialist and on the Register in Britain is to have been trained in this speciality in the NHS. (See previous paragraph.) But that means, in theory, that a British surgeon who left the NHS over twenty years ago to set up in private practice, may have trained all over the world and been performing cosmetic surgery ever since, would not be eligible for the Specialist Register. This is because it was only introduced after he would have left the NHS, which obviously does not specialise in cosmetic surgery. By the same token, newly accredited surgeons who are on the Specialist Register may have performed very little cosmetic surgery. (Having surgery by a doctor on the Specialist Register offers no guarantee whatsoever that you will be happy with your results. I have never met a patient who understands how the Specialist Register works or how it is supposed to benefit them.)

Personally, I've never been operated on by a surgeon who was an NHS consultant or by one who is on the Specialist Register, but that is by no means meant as a comment on the abilities of those particular doctors.

Another thing you often hear is that you should go to your

General Practitioner for advice on cosmetic surgery. Most GPs, mine included, are not exactly authorities on the subject. They will usually refer you to your local NHS plastic surgeon. This referral is based on proximity – where you happen to live. Your GP may have no idea how many face-lifts or nose jobs the guy has carried out or the level of his competence. Yet by sending you to a surgeon whose work he may never have even seen, your GP is doing his job.

There are two sensationalist assertions about cosmetic surgery that are regularly trotted out, which manage to both insult the intelligence of cosmetic surgery patients and divert attention away from the genuine issues at the same time. One is the claim that any member of the public can call himself a cosmetic surgeon and needs no medical qualifications to operate on people. I have never heard of this actually happening. Nor would hospitals be able to grant such a person admitting rights. Another old chestnut is that, although you have to be a veterinarian to cut open an animal, anyone can operate on humans as long as they give their consent. (They have obviously never heard of Huntingdon Life Sciences, who perform all manner of invasive procedures on thousands of animals annually in Britain, and certainly not by veterinarians). Again, I don't know of any examples or hospitals that would allow it. And of course those who recite these theories never present any actual case histories. Yet they make it sound like people all over Britain are unwittingly having facelifts by the local greengrocer on the kitchen table, while realities such as vivisection, abattoirs and factory farming do not exist.

Some surgeons don't like me. Before I came along there was no one with whom their patients could compare the results of their surgery. Because I wanted the best possible surgical outcome for myself and got it, I've inadvertently raised the standard of acceptable cosmetic surgery results way beyond the reach of many surgeons. A surgeon once said to me, 'If one more patient comes to me and says, "I want a nose like Cindy Jackson" or "You gave

ɒ *left*: Two aficionados of the cosmetic surgeon's art – me with Michael Jackson.

ɒ *right*: Out on the razz with Terry Major-Ball and Burt Kwock – perhaps you
:ognise him from the Pink Panther movies (*above*); and in the recording studio with
: original wild thing, Reg Presley from The Troggs, and Tony Feedback (*below*).

ttom left: Sharing an intimate moment with Shane McGowan. Neither Shane nor I
nember this picture being taken – but of course he must have been drunk to kiss
:! (*Inset*) The beautiful couple a few years later…

ttom right: With Noddy Holder – both of us a little the worse for wear (*above*); and
h Howard Stern in New York, just after appearing on his show (*below*).

Top left: With Shirley Bassey at a London cocktail party.

Top right: With the Duchess of York after my modelling stint for Children in Crisis.

Bottom left: With Simon Le Bon in Cannes during the film festival.

Bottom right: Me with the cream of the mid-eighties punk scene – (*above, left to rig*
the late Joey Ramone, the late Dee Dee Ramone, the late Phil Lynott, Charlie Harp
of the UK Subs, Lemmy from Mötorhead, the late Jeffrey Lee Pearce and me. I am
also pictured modelling with Jilly Johnson (*below left*) and at the BBC with Robert
Kilroy-Silk and my beautiful cat Cato (*below right*).

p left: Chatting with Prince Michael of Kent at the Knightsbridge Barracks, Hyde rk. The subject of conversation? Cats, of course.

p right: With 'Mrs Merton' – Caroline Aherne at a post filming party Manchester.

iddle left: With Glen Campbell on the set of *This Morning*.

iddle right: With Darryn Hinch in Australia.

ttom: Jer-ry! Jer-ry! Jer-ry! With the King of Chat at Stringfellows, London.

Top left: James Hewitt and Cato.

Top right: With celebrity hairdresser Charles Worthington (*left*) and Jacques Azagury Princess Diana's designer (*right*) at my video launch.

Middle left: All smiles with Ivana Trump in the South of France.

Middle right: With Joan Rivers at CBS studios in New York.

Bottom: Christmas 1997. I'm on the left and my sister Gloria – aged 44 – is on the right

eing Barbie. (*Top left*) This picture was taken in Switzerland at an international arbie doll festival. (*Top right*) In Berlin, right after the wall came down. On this casion I was being Barbie for a German TV show. (*Bottom left*) With M. G. Lord ho wrote the Barbie biography which devotes an entire chapter to me. Here we are her New York City book signing. (*Bottom right*) Me and my shadow – two Barbie lls together!

The band, then and now. (*Top left*) Me performing at the Embassy club in 1985 at the Ramones' end-of-tour gig. (*Top right*) At Dingwalls in 1985 – Eddie on drums, Knox on guitar, me on vocals. (*Bottom*) I've recently put the band together again – The Dollz, 2002: (*left to right*) Robbie Tart (*bass*), Juliette McCrimmon (*backing vocals*), Knox (*guitar*), me – looking a little different to my mid-eighties persona (*lead vocals*), Isabel Scott (*backing vocals*) and Eddie (*drums*).

p: Spot the difference! With the woman who has undergone surgery to look like
:. That's me on the right, in case you can't tell…

ttom left: Barbie and Ken – cosmetic surgery's not just for us girls…

ttom right: With Maureen Howard – my surgically created Ellen Barkin lookalike.

Top left: This is a computer-enhanced image of how I would look today had I not undergone surgery.

Top right: Personally, I'm rather happier with the way I actually look…

Bottom: Was it all worth it? You decide – this is me in my birthday suit, on my fortieth birthday!

me a face-lift so why don't I look as good as Cindy Jackson?" I'm going to scream.' Luckily he is a good surgeon and he was laughing about it. But if certain less talented surgeons have a bad week they blame me rather than looking at their level of patient satisfaction. I side with my fellow patients and my first responsibility is to those people who ask for information.

Witnessing my success, a crop of wannabe 'surgical advisers' set up shop, hoping to cash in. Since it isn't that easy, they have quite a high turnover rate. One woman, who has since gone out of business, claimed to have had a lot of surgery, yet she looked no different. She went on to copy my *Vogue* advert nearly word for word, using exactly the same layout. But what was spooky about the whole thing was that she claimed to have a similar life story to mine, but it was all fabricated to attract business. I found that pretty weird.

Another appeared in a spread in the same women's magazine that I had done the previous year using before, during and after photographs of her face-lift, just as I had done with my own surgery. She heaped praise on the surgeon and his work, but she soon fell out with him. At last count she was on her third surgeon, having publicly declared each one 'the best'. I wonder what happened to the women who, after reading about her in the press, went to the first or second ones and are now as unhappy with them as she is.

Yet another wannabe has borrowed heavily from my business forms and mail-out material, but had to use her own picture, for obvious reasons. While I don't wish to be unkind, her photograph does beg the following questions: 'How would someone who looks like that and carries so much excess weight have the nerve to advise others on beauty and liposuction?' and 'If she's such an expert, why doesn't she take her own advice?' (Intriguingly, the wannabes are often odd-looking women.)

Some of them charge more for consultations than fully trained surgeons. For their money, they ask you what kind of surgery you're interested in, then recite their stock script, parroting the most fundamental of medical details. Some also hand over a standard list of local surgeons under the pretence that it's been specially tailored to your needs. In both cases they're charging an arm and a leg for readily available information and laughing all the way to the bank.

The media tend to promote these women because they're both playing the same game. That's why the wannabe adviser's alleged credibility often comes from amassing and displaying a stack of meaningless press cuttings and quotes, which is quickly and easily done in this age of misinformation.

An ironic twist in this tale is that these ladies who blatantly imitate my business model sometimes make disparaging remarks about me to clients. I suppose they see me as the competition, whereas I see them as unwittingly helping to keep me in business due to the confusion they spread. (But, like the surgeons who don't like me, they can't fault my surgical results, so the gripe is obviously personal, despite the fact that they've never even met me.)

The media, which has an indiscriminate hunger for new angles on cosmetic surgery. I understand that they can't quote me every time, even if I do have more facts than anyone else. I also understand that the media regard cosmetic surgery as entertainment and, to them, publicising typical case histories and factual medical information is boring. That's why you'll only see polarised articles – the 'life-changing' successes and the horror stories – rarely anything in between.

It's a frustrating state of affairs. Just about every cosmetic surgery feature I see in the press or on TV is incorrect, incomplete or fabricated. Sometimes all three. Patients would do well to remember that if they had a serious disease and needed medical advice, the last person they would trust their lives to would be a reporter. ('I've just been diagnosed with a life-threatening illness. Better buy some women's magazines and turn on the TV to get some advice.') Cosmetic surgery should be no different.

Here's one of the more amusing examples of how the media get their cosmetic surgery information. One day back in 1994, during a telephone conversation with a journalist from a tabloid newspaper, I was asked how many people undergo cosmetic surgery annually in the UK. I replied that there is no way of knowing because the figures aren't reported to a central organisation. But she persisted. 'Would you say 100,000?' I told her that sounded a little high. 'How about 20,000?' she asked. I said that was a little low. 'In that case I'll split the difference and say 60,000,' she declared.

That figure, which had literally been plucked out of thin air, was duly published and, to my utter amazement, has been solemnly quoted in practically every report about cosmetic surgery in the UK ever since. Unbelievable? Look up some press cuttings.

There are countless examples of misleading cosmetic surgery stories. Again, it's we patients who suffer. When a reporter from one of the more respected newspapers contacted me for information on Trilucent (soybean oil) breast implants, which had just come on to the market, I gave her detailed and correct medical information. I explained that the doctors I had spoken to about them were not very impressed and that the results weren't as good as other implants. Most importantly, their two main selling points – that they were safer because they were made of a natural material and that they made it easy to interpret a mammogram – were reneged in the manufacturer's literature. Instead, there were warnings of possible fat embolism, which can be fatal, if the implant ruptured and of impaired ability to interpret mammograms of breasts that had been implanted with them. (All this information had immediately been made available to patients in my book under the Breast Implant section.)

The reporter thanked me and I looked out for the article. When it appeared a few days later I couldn't believe my eyes. It consisted of a case history of a woman who'd had the implants and did nothing but rave about them and how much safer they were than other implants, and that with them she had no worries about future mammograms. It was no better than an advertising promotion. Not a single word about the safety issues or mounting dissatisfaction with them by surgeons and patients alike. It was that polarisation thing again.

That article prompted large numbers of women to opt for Trulicent implants. I know, because it was me they wrote to when they were banned and patients were urged by the British government to have them removed without delay. What could I say in response, except that they should have written to me before going ahead? I had the information several years earlier. But do you think anyone (besides me) would publish it *then?* (Needless to say, the same newspaper that had so blatantly promoted the soybean oil implants reported their being banned in screaming headlines followed by yet another case history – this time of a woman whose Trilucent implants had been a disaster.)

Nonetheless, I still co-operate with the press, although these days I prefer to appear on live TV shows (because they can't be edited), and write cosmetic surgery articles myself. Most journalists who write slanted articles are only doing the job they've been told to do by their editors. I know this because they tell me – some of them have become good friends. In many cases I've bonded with journalists while helping them get through their cosmetic surgery operations. Regardless of what they write or say, it's me they contact when their *own* health and safety is at stake.

Despite being set up by newspaper journalists a couple of times and having appeared on a few TV shows with less than honest agendas, I think I've done pretty well considering how many hundreds of media interviews I've done over the years. I'm lucky to have had so few bad experiences. I've enjoyed most of the material that's been written about me. The press have been an integral part of my life since 1989 and I am grateful to them for their help.

The media and wannabes aren't the only ones who've been known to spread misinformation. I shared the stage with a prominent TV personality on one talk show who went on and on about how marvellous her breast implants were and how she'd never be without them. However, in the hospitality room afterwards she confided to me that she'd had endless problems with them and told me how painful and troublesome they'd been. To this day I still can't figure out why she lied like she did.

It's a personal triumph for me to be able to talk on television. I've come a long way since I was a painfully shy child with such a bad speech impediment that I couldn't even speak in front of the class. Perhaps it was necessary for me to achieve so many of my own ambitions before I could help others achieve theirs. Yet sometimes I am still the subject of poison.

The *Observer* newspaper launched an unprovoked professional attack on me, using a good deal of their news page and two prominent pictures of me to do so. I was devastated. It was public humiliation on a scale I never knew existed. Everyone wants to be liked – why should I be any different? I've spent my whole life seeking approval; it's one of the reasons I subjected myself to the surgeon's knife in the first place.

The bottom immediately fell out of my business. My phone stopped ringing. Nobody asked me to appear on TV and patients stopped sending off for my information. I asked myself why. I asked others why. I got the answer from a friend who was a seasoned journalist on another paper. She explained, 'It's simple. You've had a lot of positive press. Newspapers know that some people will like you – or *any* person in the public eye – and some won't. They want to sell newspapers to both.'

'But it was all lies,' I protested.

'Then you can sue them for libel,' she announced.

Although I had nowhere near the required funds for a lawsuit, a lawyer friend, Graham Atkins, thought it was an open and shut case from a legal standpoint. He volunteered to represent me on a contingency basis (no win/no fee). The *Observer* caved in pretty quickly, as they had no defence.

My out-of-court settlement allowed me to buy the home of my dreams. The downturn of my business, which turned out to be temporary, gave me time to write this book. The fact is, I came out of the situation better than I went in. As Gloria always says 'When somebody hands you a lemon, just make lemonade.' Once again, it was my fellow patients who were the real victims. The following year I heard from several who'd seen the libellous article and were put off getting the facts from me and so went on have disastrous surgery.

A couple of old-fashioned establishment feminists have also snarled at me. They usually take the form of middle-class university-educated women who've never even got their hands dirty, much less done men's work in factories. These busybodies insist that I've bought wholesale into the beauty myth and believe me to be misguided and dangerous. What they don't know, among other things, is that what I've done is the ultimate feminist statement.

No one except me is going to control my life. It's my body and it's my right to do what I want with it. Isn't feminism about restoring the balance of power? It may on the surface seem politically incorrect but beauty does give women power, so who are they to dictate what form it takes? After all, we have to play the game being played, and I was merely playing out the only hand I'd been dealt. (I wonder what *they* would have done had they been born into my circumstances?) The fact that we have the power to create a better life simply by changing our looks is too simple a concept for a lot of people to grasp.

But none of these people matter. In every single case I wasn't the first object of their venom, nor will I be the last. I've learned that some just like to gripe and criticise others. It doesn't mean they have any better alternatives on offer. Likewise there are negative and toxic people out there who are best avoided – I've also learned that misery truly does love company. That's why they hate anyone who breaks ranks, because it makes them look bad for staying where they are. Some people think I belong back on the farm: a downtrodden, middle-aged housewife who looks 50, not 25. But some people also voted for Richard Nixon.

Want to know the great thing about all of them – my stalker, the newspapers that set me up, the wannabes, the feminists and all the others who made it their business to be my detractors? None of those people were attacking *me*. They didn't even know *me*. They were attacking a *mask,* for crying out loud. How smart does that make them?

For over a decade I watched these angry people shadowbox with their own personal demons while deluding themselves that it was me (or what I stood for to each of them) that they were fighting. They blamed me for anything and everything: their bad surgery, their physical shortcomings, their career failures and even mankind's inclination to reward beauty and the very biological imperatives that dictate human behaviour. But all I was really guilty of was showing them the mirror.

And, just like trainee guard dogs that savage effigies in place of bad guys, their viciousness was wasted on a likeness. I had already left the building.

Chapter Seventeen

I'm In with the In Crowd

Leaving the bogeypeople behind to wallow in their own bitterness, I went off to get a life. After all, that's why I had cosmetic surgery.

Before my stalker and the *Sunday Mirror* put me off seeing people personally, the patients I had been meeting and helping through their surgery included of a lot of major celebrities, politicians and public figures. At their request, I often accompanied them into the operating theatre and observed the procedure being done. Mine would be the first face they saw when they came round from the anaesthetic.

I continued with this, and eventually went on to specialise in it, for the sole reason that at least you know exactly who you're dealing with when it's someone famous. An added benefit was that it enabled me to keep my finger on the pulse with as many patients as before. It wasn't long before the *Daily Express* called me 'the woman who helps keeps the beautiful people beautiful.'

Little by little, many of these celebrities became friends and began introducing me to their friends and inviting me to their homes and their parties. Sharing such a personal experience with someone does tend to break down certain barriers. Doors that had always been closed to me suddenly burst open. Having been the girl who was never asked out by anyone decent and had no choice but to hang out with undesirables, overnight my presence was being requested at all sorts of glittering celebrity parties and society events. On these occasions I was often photographed by the paparazzi and pictured in the gossip columns.

This is how I came to be labelled a 'socialite' by the press – something I could never have planned in a million years. Next thing I know, I was listed in *Who's Really Who*, the unofficial guide to London society. Although I was now living yet another element of my childhood fantasy life, the route that eventually took me there would have stretched even my fertile imagination.

The gay community also embraced me. By that time, however, I was no stranger to the name 'Fag Hag'. Even as far back as high school I'd had close friends that were gay men. We share a common fondness for aesthetics and a similar sense of humour, as well as idolising glamorous female icons. I've been called 'camp' more times than I can count. (I do not, however, care much for show tunes.) Sadly, I've lost many of those friends in recent years.

My new face and figure even attracted modelling jobs, which I found irresistible. (Barbie had been a teenage fashion model and I just had to try it.) Much to my amazement, I even found myself sharing the catwalk with supermodel Jerry Hall. We were both modelling Isabella Kristensen couture at a charity fashion show.

Jerry and I were alone backstage when, noticing I was having trouble with my fluffy pink stole, she came over to me. In a motherly gesture, she adjusted the stole and fluffed out my hair. She must have sensed how unsure of myself I was feeling. But then again it was probably written all over me. The 'hair people' had woven miles of false braids into my own hair and piled it up in an outlandish pagoda shape on top of my head, then rendered it immobile with plenty of lacquer.

My dress, which was too big for me, had been taken in a few moments earlier and was held together (just about) with dozens of dressmaker's pins, all poised to stab me every time I moved.

Jerry reassured me in her lazy Texan drawl, 'Just give it plenty of attitude, honey, and you'll be fine,' opening the backstage curtain for me to go out on to the runway. I wished Mick Jagger had treated her better. She seemed so kind-hearted.

Looking out at the waiting audience, I wondered once again why I thought I could do this. Here I was, someone who was so uncoordinated that I could have done with walking lessons, about to attempt catwalk modelling. As the music boomed and the crowd's eyes fixed on me, I begged my Guardian Angel not to let me trip. When I got to the end of the platform, I curtseyed to Sarah, Duchess of York, who was in the audience. She beamed at me and started off the applause for my outfit. I got away with it and have done many times since.

Next time I modelled for Isabella Kristensen was in Scotland at Duns Castle. Ivana Trump supplied the jewellery from her own line, personally decking out each model with baubles from her collection. When she'd finished fastening my bracelet she patted me on the arm and said, 'You look faboolus, dahlink.' That cracked me up. Moments like that are priceless to me.

At the formal dinner that evening, I found myself sitting at a ridiculously long dining table next to gazillionare coathanger magnate Peter Shalson. When I looked down at my place setting, I was amazed to see silverware stretching out for what seemed like several feet in each direction on either side of my plate. Then the first course arrived.

I nudged Peter. 'Psst! Which fork do I use?' I asked.

'It's soup. Use the spoon,' he replied dryly, not realising I was joking.

When I looked across the table at Liz Brewer, who was hosting the dinner, she was too engrossed in conversation with Ivana to hear. So I'm repeating it here because it fell on deaf ears the first time. (Liz, by the way is now a good friend of mine. She doesn't remember meeting me the first time, though.)

I also got to meet Joan Rivers, who is one of my favourite comedians. She congratulated me on being so open about my surgery, saying she didn't think much of celebrities who have procedures done and then deny it, because they are misleading other women and presenting themselves as unrealistic role models. Then she asked how I got the money for all those operations. 'Were you hooking?' she implored. Joan Rivers just kills me.

When I appeared on her afternoon talk show at the CBS studios in New York, I was astounded to discover that Tony Little was on just after me to discuss his latest fitness video. What are the chances of two people from Fremont, Ohio being booked on the same episode of the *Joan Rivers Show* without anyone knowing about it until afterwards? Tony and I grabbed a quick chat in the green room, then he had a plane to catch.

Another unlikely coincidence was revealed deep in the Georgia woods, where I was attending a cocktail party at a southern mansion with my friend Neil Shulman. He wrote the book on which the hit movie *Doc Hollywood* was based. Michael J Fox played the leading role. The plot concerned a country doctor on his way to California to become a cosmetic surgeon, who got waylaid by a car crash in a hick town.

Neil spotted someone he knew across the room and motioned for him to join us. Just before the man sat down, Neil introduced us, 'Cindy, I'd like you to meet Jim Hotz. He's the real-life Doc Hollywood – the guy I wrote the book about.'

There was a stunned silence. 'What?' asked Neil.

'He's from my home town. We're both from Fremont, Ohio,' I explained. Jim was Gloria's age and had attended the local Catholic high school. We caught up on some Fremont gossip while Neil tried to figure out the odds of that happening.

When Ronald Goldstein introduced me to the eminent University of Southern California academic Gordon Patzer, author of the classic textbook, *The Physical Attractiveness Phenomenon*, we had a lot to talk about, and not only because we shared the same professional interest.

It transpired that, unbeknownst to me, Gordon had actually lived in Fremont after I left town. He had been engaged to a good friend of mine. When he told me who it was, I treaded very carefully, since I knew that she had committed suicide the year before. He did the same, not knowing if I knew. When it eventually became obvious that we both knew, we talked long into the night, sharing the happier memories we both had of her.

And there have been incredible chance encounters with the rich and famous. Once when I was getting out of a taxi to go into London's Caprice restaurant, a man ran up and asked me if he could have the cab. It was George Hamilton. I said sure, I didn't need it anymore. He smiled (and I was nearly blinded), before asking if I was from America. He must have picked up on my accent.

I said, 'Yes.'

'What part?' he enquired, still not getting into the cab, despite the pouring rain.

'All of me,' I answered.

Laughing, he finally got into the taxi saying, 'That's the funniest thing I've ever heard,' and disappeared into the night.

I got to meet Michael Jackson at a private lunch given by Peter and Polly Shalson when he was in England to address the Oxford Union. I told him that my parents were Hoosiers, too, and he laughed. I knew it was a term he wouldn't have heard lately.

Several newspapers reported that meeting and I have been asked countless times what I think about his surgery. Every patient's motivation is different; if he's happy with his results, then the procedures have been a success. Reams of unkind things have been written about Michael Jackson's appearance. However, little or no thought has gone into what it must feel like to be him. Why does he want to look like he does?

My theory is that it reflects what he feels like on the inside. Maybe he doesn't identify with being a black man from Indiana and doesn't want to look like one – perhaps on the inside he feels neither black nor white. As a former child star, it may be that he sees himself as neither young nor old. Having grown up with a tough taskmaster of a father, it's possible that he doesn't wish to appear hard and masculine in the traditional sense. So what image has he created? One that is neither black nor white, old nor young, male nor female. Michael Jackson's staggering talent and incredible life mean that he is clearly not like the rest of us. His surgically created look reflects that.

San Lorenzo is one of my favourite London restaurants. It's also a well-known celebrity haunt. Nonetheless, I was still taken by surprise one evening as I was putting my coat on to go out of the door. A bearded man rushed over out of nowhere to open the door for me. When I turned to thank him, I was looking Steven Spielberg in the eye. (The next day I read that he was in London to attend Stanley Kubrick's funeral.)

I would have completely missed that if I hadn't turned to thank him. Good manners cost nothing, I always say.

Steven Spielberg is also a former Ohio resident. They turn up everywhere. One New Year's Eve at the exclusive Brown's nightclub in London, while waiting in line to go to the ladies' room, I noticed Chrissie Hynde in front of me. Feeling obliged to make conversation under the awkward circumstances, I said hello and told her that, like her, I was from Ohio (she's from Akron).

Her face lit up and she asked me all about my hometown and questioned me about what I did in London. Because she's someone I admire so much and I thought she might disapprove of my surgery, I played it down.

She told me very forcefully that if that was what I wanted to do and it worked for me, then I should go for it and not apologise to anyone. I hung on every word she said as I cowered in her great presence. She joked that she could probably do with some herself. Being accustomed to people covering insecurity with self-deprecation, I reassured her that she didn't need any surgery and told her that she was very pretty. I swear she blushed.

I was only being honest. Chrissie Hynde is a very attractive woman in person, but that isn't why I've admired her for so many years. Besides having considerable musical talent, she's very outspoken on political issues that are also important to me, including animal rights.

I regularly travel to Dublin to appear on Irish television shows, where I always stay at the Shelbourne Hotel and at night walk along Grafton Street to Ireland's premier nightclub, Lillie's Bordello. It's *the* place to go in Dublin. All the major bands that play the local stadium stop in for a nightcap after their concerts.

One time when I was there Bruce Springsteen smiled and said hello as he brushed past me in the crowded bar. Unlike most of the megastars who frequent Lillie's, he didn't make use of the VIP room, known as the Library, instead preferring to mix with the club's regular members.

Me, I *like* the VIP room. The next time I was in Dublin I was in the Library, working on a pint of Guinness, when my absolute favourite rock'n'roller, the Groover From Vancouver, Bryan Adams, came up to me and introduced himself. Like Bryan Adams needs an introduction. (I didn't let on that we'd been pictured together in *Melody Maker* in 1985.) He said I looked like Barbara Eden in TV's *I Dream Of Jeannie*. I told him I'd been in a band, and we talked about music for a while. He asked me if I'd been to his show that night, and I told him that I was in Dublin to appear on a TV show, which I'd only just finished. When I recounted details of the last gig I'd seen of his at the Hammersmith Odeon in London, he looked at me in disbelief and said, 'But that was in 1985,' implying that I would have been too young to have been there.

A moment later, a member of his band rushed up to us and said to me, 'I've seen you on TV. Aren't you that woman who's about 50 but looks 20 because you've had so many face-lifts?'

Gratefully, I replied, 'Yes, that's me!' Although I was several years off being 50, I wanted Bryan to know I was telling the truth about having been at the Hammersmith Odeon in 1985. Next time they played Wembley Arena, I was on the guest list. There's nothing like a live rock'n'roll concert to blow the cobwebs out of your brain.

A few months later I got a phone call from one of his roadies saying, 'You've got to help us. Bryan's band has a bass guitar that needs to come from London. We've left an All Access pass for you at the gig in Brighton tonight. Please do us a favour and bring the guitar?' The bass guitar was duly dropped off at my house in London and I delivered it backstage in Brighton. Bryan is as nice a guy as he is a brilliant performer. He is also a fellow vegetarian and actively supports environmental groups including Greenpeace and Save the Whale. We both shop at Waitrose on King's Road, where, unlike me, he claims he never gets recognised.

It was after Bryan's Brighton gig that I had an in-depth conversation with his manager, Bruce Allen. He urged me to write my autobiography. (Here it is, Bruce.)

I also appeared on the *Jerry Springer Show* in the US, when his show was new and his guests were not nearly as outrageous as they are today. Jerry also has strong links with Ohio, having once been mayor of Cincinnati. I met him again at his party at Stringfellow's to launch the show in the UK. He had one of his flunkies approach me and hand me a note asking me to call him at the Meridian, the hotel he was staying at in London. I never did.

Another time on the *Leeza* (Gibbons) *Show* in Hollywood, I sat next to Bob Mackie, who as we know designed a lot of Cher's outrageous costumes, as well as a number of Barbie's outfits. Ruth Handler, Barbie's originator, was also on the show, and she autographed my old Barbie from the Bargain Barn, which I still have and treasure. The show's producer had asked me to bring her along. They placed Barbie on a shelf behind me. She was wearing one of her original Sixties dresses, which was by now old and tattered. By contrast, I was wearing a glittering replica of one of her new costumes. We had truly switched places. But I'm still not sure which of us took the other to Hollywood.

Chapter Eighteen

Any Man of Mine

Meeting celebrities became an everyday occurrence and after a while I wasn't nervous about talking to them. But it was a different story when I ran into Marc Burca again.

Although distinguished as ever, he was now portly and thinning on top. When I saw Marc across the room at a party I thought, Oh my God, how embarrassing. I felt him looking at me. I was drinking champagne and looked a million dollars but I still felt unsure of myself, so I made my excuses and left. Before too long I ran into him at another party. He looked directly at me and came up to talk. I was with debonair Welsh socialite Dai Llewellyn, who said, 'May I introduce you to my good friend Marc Burca.'

I said, 'Marc and I have already met.'

I had assumed that Marc remembered me. Instead, he was totally fazed and kept asking where and when. He telephoned me afterwards and said, 'Look, this is driving me mad. Where did we meet?' I still wouldn't put him out of his misery and arranged to meet him at a restaurant in Chelsea for lunch. 'Look,' I told him, 'think back to all the Cindys you've dated.'

'There was only one Cindy I knew. That was about 20 years ago,' he replied. 'That couldn't have been you. I mean, she looked nothing like you.'

'Ah, but it was me,' I told him, showing him a photograph of me at 21. He looked like he'd seen a ghost. In a way, I suppose he had.

Marc brought me up to date. He had founded *Boardroom* magazine in 1982, and later sold his stake for a considerable sum. His marriage had come to an end and he was looking to settle down again. At that time he had been seeing someone, but she eventually dropped him, ironically enough, because she heard I was on the scene.

In an interview with a British newspaper in November 1996, Marc said of our romance 20 years earlier, 'Cindy and I did all sorts of exciting things, but it was just a fling. I thought we both knew that. I don't think I ever did or said anything to raise her expectations. I dated other women while I went out with her but that was usual for bachelors then.

'It is true that Cindy was not as attractive as some of my other girlfriends, but she was not unattractive. Clearly I would not have gone out with her if that had been the case.

'When I saw her the second time, I thought she was stunning. I love women who aren't afraid to be feminine, who make the most of what they've got. Obviously, I remembered the Cindy I had gone out with all those years ago, but couldn't believe it was the woman I was looking at.

'I had no problem with the fact I had known her before. It was a quirk of fate. The fact is she is now incredibly beautiful and obviously I love to be with her. The years have not, of course, been so kind to me. I am the one who feels lucky to know her.

'A friend of mine likened our relationship to *My Fair Lady*. Maybe she will be my Eliza Doolittle, who can say?'

Here was the very same man who dumped me when I was 22,

who'd shattered my ego and made me feel more unattractive and uncouth than I already did.

It's surprising the power that beauty holds. And did I enjoy using that power? Of course, I did. Thanks to men like Marc, I had been forced to become my own Eliza Doolittle in a painful and expensive process that had taken years of hard work. Armed with my new looks, I had the confidence to turn him down, even though I was still fond of him. Once upon a time I was in love with Marc, but the tables had turned. We can laugh about it now – and I hope we'll stay friends. He has since remarried and they seem very happy.

After I changed my looks, Roberto also took an interest in me. He split briefly from his wife, during which time his youngest son contacted me and said his dad wanted to invite me over for dinner. I went, and it was good to see him, but there could be no turning back. Besides, he spent most of the evening complaining about his present wife. Although he was sixty and now had grey hair, he had kept himself very fit and looked great. When he asked me if I were 'free', meaning was I seeing anyone, I answered, 'Yes', meaning that freedom was mine and I intended to keep it.

We never did speak the same language. Of course, now that I no longer needed him, Roberto kept calling me up until his wife finally came back. Funny the way things work out.

We are all going down our own paths in life. When I look at people I have known over the years – Gloria, Roberto and Marc, for instance – they knew all along which path they wanted to follow, who they did or didn't want to be, and today each of them has moved further down that very same path.

My sister wanted to grow up and have a nice little girl, a nice husband and a nice house. The word she used was always 'nice'. Not fabulous, not stupendous, but nice. She now has a nice husband, a nice little girl and a nice house. She's lucky that her path took her exactly where she wanted. She wouldn't change a thing.

Although Roberto insisted that he wanted to change direction, he stuck to his path like glue. When I met him he was always complaining about his ex-wife and how life didn't treat him well. I know he didn't want to marry me because he was afraid of getting involved again – just like in the country and western song, he didn't want to 'divide his half in half again'. Yet after I left him, he repeated the same old pattern by going ahead and marrying someone else, who in turn he probably complained to about me.

What he probably didn't realise was that, as with Martyn, I didn't want to take him for anything. It's ironic how drastically my path has changed since I walked out on Roberto, yet his still remains the same.

As for Marc Burca, his path led him away from me simply because I was not pretty enough. It led him back again once I became better looking, but by then my life had already taken a completely different direction.

None of these people have changed a bit. But then, neither have I, except on the exterior.

What did *I* always want? To look pretty so people would like me, have a bit of glamour because I'm attracted to things that glitter, own as many pets as I could accommodate and to shelter from the cruel world inside my Enchanted Egg. It's not much to ask. (Oh, and a late-model Mercedes Benz.)

Another interesting thing that often happens when I go out is that, upon being introduced to a man, my American accent will often prompt him to ask how long I've been in England. When I tell him I've lived here since 1977, he will invariably ask, 'Where have you *been*?' I've never figured out how to tell them that, until fairly recently, I didn't actually exist.

There have been so many times in the past when I'd be walking down the street with a guy, and if a prettier girl walked by he'd turn and look her up and down. That really used to hurt. I was the sort of woman that men would use. Men were unfaithful to me even though I did everything for them: cooked for them, ironed their clothes, did their laundry, scrubbed their floors and acted as a step-mother to their children. Nothing I ever did for them was enough to earn their respect.

Any man who tries to treat me like a doormat will get no co-operation from me, although it's pretty much ceased to be a problem. Nowadays, instead of me being the one trying to please men, men usually try to please me. Instead of the guy I'm with looking at other women, I'm the one men turn to look at. But I know they're not really seeing me, they're staring at my outer shell, the Enchanted Egg in which I dwell. Any man who is only interested in my looks will never mean anything much to me. It stands to reason that the ones who are most attracted to the way I look now are the very same ones who would have rejected me for the way I looked before. Marc Burca is a case in point.

You can't change people who make it a habit to judge a book by its cover. But you do have the power to seek out those who look deeper and live on a higher spiritual level. It doesn't mean you have to abandon any appreciation of aesthetics. Beauty and spirituality are no more mutually exclusive than beauty and brains are.

After every night out, I empty my pockets of the evening's haul of business cards that men have pressed into my hand. (So much for Phil's prediction that no man would ever want me.) Men send me flowers, take me to fancy restaurants and pay me compliments. All I have to do in return is look the part. These are the rewards of beauty that some women have always been able to take for granted, but to me they're still new and special. But I don't kid myself as to why I'm finally on the receiving end of such attention. I see it as applause for the quality of my masquerade, much like an actor on the stage gauging his performance by the cheers from a crowd so taken in by the convincing performance that they forget there's a real person behind it.

I still find it difficult to trust men. All my life I've been the underdog in relationships and most men I've met, given the chance, will be unfaithful. I mean if Tommy Lee can be unfaithful to Pamela Anderson, what hope do the rest of us have? Men simply can't help themselves. I always get a gut feeling when men are playing around. Most women do.

Although they didn't know it, there have been times when I've checked up on boyfriends, by pushing the redial button to see who they have been calling, or turning up unexpectedly when they say they are having a quiet night alone at home. One boyfriend used to always boast that he'd had lots of girlfriends, so I waded my way through his address book, subtly changing their telephone numbers. A number 3 can be easily changed to an 8, and a 1 to a 7 or a 4. So if he ever went to dial that number again, he'd get the wrong number. He'll never be able to call any of these girls again, I thought. It also gave me a way of detecting if he had because, thinking he had dialled the wrong number, he would then write the correct number above it, I reasoned. This never actually happened, but at least I was prepared. I have thrown away a few men's 'little black books' in my time, and disposed of the odd secret porn stash. After all, what man is going to complain to his girlfriend that he seems to have misplaced those items?

Whenever I have serious doubts about boyfriends, I hire private detectives to check on them, since I got so much information about my stalker that way. I'm not particularly paranoid, but they have aroused my suspicions by lying to me. I seem to have a sixth sense about when I'm being lied to, which can be very handy as well as a mixed blessing. Since I need to know exactly where I stand with people, if these men weren't going to tell me the truth, I was determined to get the facts from another source.

I had one boyfriend under 24-hour surveillance. A two-man team was shadowing him. They consisted of a detective on a motorcycle wearing an infrared body camera, who had served with the SAS in Northern Ireland. He was backed up by another private investigator – a former policeman – in a van with blacked-out windows. At one point I received a telephone call from the man in charge of the operation. He informed me that the suspect was currently in a pub, by himself, reading the newspaper and drinking a pint of beer. But when I rang my boyfriend on his cellular phone to ask him where he was and what he was doing, he was very cagey and pretended he couldn't talk. Even when I pressed him, he wouldn't tell me the truth about where he was. The fact is, I could have told him what tie he was wearing and what newspaper he was reading, yet he still had to act mysterious. Men like to pretend they have exciting lives because they don't want to seem boring. As for the other boyfriend who was followed, I have a comprehensive surveillance report and video footage of his movements and it was equally uneventful, yet he told me a completely different version of events. And men say women are hard to fathom.

Both times the private investigators said to me, 'I have to warn you that when women hire us to track someone, their instinct is usually right. You might find out what you don't want to know.' But in both cases there was no other woman on the scene. It must have been pretty boring for the guys on surveillance, but at least I found out what was going on, even if I didn't understand it.

However, checking up on men is no way to live. Although they weren't being unfaithful, I stopped seeing both of those men shortly after having them followed. I couldn't believe a word either one of them said, and that kind of thing will drive you nuts after a while. If I ever thought it necessary to do that again, I would walk away from the relationship before it got that far. Who wants to spend their life with someone they can't trust? (And who can afford to keep private detectives on the payroll?)

I don't need a man to provide for me. I have my own career, my own home and I'm not going to have children, so if there is a man in my life it will be an honest relationship based on mutual interest and affection, not financial or emotional dependence.

Besides, I only really need a man for one thing, and that's to operate on me.

Chapter Nineteen

Everybody's Talkin'

Mixing with famous people and members of the aristocracy all started through my appearances on television shows. They would often ask for my phone number after the show and then come and see me to discuss their cosmetic surgery needs. Other times they would recognise me after seeing me on the television. Now when public figures and titled people discreetly approach me at society soirées and charity balls wanting information on cosmetic surgery, I'm flattered and thrilled. I find it incredible that these people are asking *me* for beauty advice. Every time I visit the powder room at places like Annabel's nightclub in Berkeley Square or the Hotel de Paris in Monte Carlo, I'm surrounded by celebrities and debs who tell me about the surgery they want to have and ask for my opinion. I'm always glad to speak to them, except that I am a little paranoid about staying in the ladies' room too long, in case whoever my date happens to be assumes my prolonged absence is due to a bout of constipation.

But TV appearances do not always introduce me to such a genteel breed. Like the time in 1998 when I was made to answer for my sins not, surprisingly, before a braying bunch of trailer park dwellers, but before Joan Bakewell on the BBC's *Heart Of The Matter*. Initially, I had been thrilled at my invitation to appear on a programme that has a reputation for taking a serious look at social and moral issues. I had always admired Joan Bakewell and I was looking forward to a lively debate on cosmetic surgery – so much so that I even felt guilty negotiating my fee.

My first inkling that anything might be wrong came as I walked on to the set and felt a strangely familiar, circus-like atmosphere. Oh dear, I thought. Here we go again ...

My claim to television fame is that I have had over 20 cosmetic procedures on my face and body, and the subject holds growing fascination for aging baby-boomers. In America, I've appeared on dozens of chat shows over the years – some of them good experiences and some so bad that I have been treated as little more than a freak. For this, I have only myself to blame since, as I've said before, I agreed to appear on my first such show when I was offered free tickets home to see my family in America. The hour of ritual humiliation seemed a reasonable trade-off.

Since then, I've been served up to quite a few voracious television audiences, who clearly view me as part of the entertainment. On the *Jenny Jones Show* in Chicago I had to sit next to a 280lb drag queen in a basque and tights, with huge false breasts, who called himself Queerdonna, while I was bullied by the audience on air. I make my points regardless and hope that someone out there is registering what I have to say. But I can no longer claim to be shocked by anything that happens on a television show.

One of the most ignorant arguments that is regularly put to me has to be the one that involves an able-bodied person leaping out of the audience to berate me for having cosmetic surgery to look better, when there are lots of disabled people in the world. These folks have obviously never met anyone with a disability.

I have. They used to come to my office when I saw clients personally. I've regularly received letters from them over the years. Apart from the obvious physical difference, disabled people are no different from the rest of the population, which statistically means that some of them would like to have cosmetic surgery. And many of them do. It's so very unkind for others to assume that the disabled don't care about the way they look. Perhaps those people don't consider them to be human.

Then there are those who insist that I should have given the money to charity. I explain to them that I have earned a place in society that has allowed me for the first time in my life to be able to give my time and money generously to a host of different charities, mentioning them by name. For my own amusement I always ask my critic exactly how much they give to which charities, knowing full well that their argument is strictly hypothetical. This has prompted every single one of them, without exception, to sheepishly sink back down into their seats without answering the question.

But maybe I was being a little unfair, considering that I had the advantage. In my extensive experience with charities, I've never met a volunteer or donator who has either the time or inclination to sit in a tabloid talk show audience and trash people they've never met before. How charitable would *that* be? So I knew in advance that I was on safe ground asking my detractors about their charitable activities where they were venturing into assumed territory. I've learned that you should never assume anything. They obviously hadn't.

The theory of my being addicted to cosmetic surgery is yet another badly thought-out proposition. Addiction is a serious social problem that devastates families, costs jobs and ends lives. To try and place me in that category does a serious disservice to genuine victims of addiction and those dedicated to helping them.

Some of the other arguments are so banal and illogical that I can't get a grip on the reasoning so I refrain from joining in. They seem to be speaking a different language. On one US show a rabid member of the audience jumped up and yelled at me, 'Lookism! Ageism! Sexism! You represent everything that's wrong with America today!' Suddenly I was to blame for the decline of Western civilisation. I smiled weakly and thought to myself, 'Nobody's perfect.'

My cousin Ron once asked me why they always round up every 'coyote date' in the county to appear on shows to be nasty to me. (A 'coyote date' is a Midwestern term for a woman who is so repulsivethat when you wake up the next morning with your arm around her you'd rather chew it off than wake her up.) My answer was that most other people either have lives or day jobs, or both. Some people have neither. And if they brought on a reasonably normal person, there would be no debate.

Still, I must plead guilty to the charge of cynically appearing on dumbed-down American television. To be honest, after a while I found doing those shows oddly compulsive, kind of like slowing down to look at an accident: despite knowing full well that the scenario would be gruesome, I couldn't resist. And little did they know that they were playing right into my hands. All those years of being viciously attacked in full view of the whole world are what cured me once and for all of my acute fear of criticism.

I had finally learned not to take other people's nasty remarks personally, because I realised that there is just no pleasing some people. After I'd gone through all the pain and expense of getting rid of the physical traits that people teased me about, they started attacking me for what they perceived my mind and spirit to be like. All those years of seeking the approval of others at the expense of my own feelings had been a complete waste of time. Those tabloid television shows reinforced that.

But *Heart Of The Matter* – now, surely that would be different. Finally I would get a chance to take part in a meaningful discussion. After all, this was the BBC.

I couldn't have been more wrong. Over the course of 40 minutes, I was treated like some kind of freak. During the so-called debate, I was labelled 'superficial', a 'futile narcissist in pursuit of eternal youth' and accused of putting 'pressure' on young girls.

These insults came from a panel of 'experts' that included the feminist writer and former *Late Show* presenter Sarah Dunant – who, for some unfathomable reason, wore reading glasses perched on the end of her nose – and a Catholic writer in serious need of a haircut.

Sarah Dunant felt I had, 'set women's liberation back 25 years,' and the man with the shaggy hair predictably accused me of making the disabled feel bad about themselves – although he was unable to cite any examples.

The therapist Philip Hodson had been assigned to help me fight my corner, which he proceeded to do with such eloquence that I could barely get a word in edgeways.

None of these experts, however, knew anything about the subject. Surely the whole point of such programmes as *Heart of the Matter* is to have an intelligent discussion rather than yet another knockdown, drag-out fight, contrived to grab the attention of the jaded channel-surfer.

As it turned out, I had no wish to join in the undignified shouting match to which the show was often reduced. I never do so on American television, either. The difference there is that even Jerry Springer – for all the crassness of his show – ensures that each person has his say. During *Heart of the Matter*, no one seemed interested in hearing my views. At least Jerry Springer does not for a moment expect to be taken seriously. Nor do viewers' licence fees fund his show.

Of course, my chief sin in the eyes of *Heart of the Matter* was to be politically incorrect. On the surface that may seem to be true, but I was hoping that for once someone might see the facts for what they were. Here were successful privileged, educated middle-class, so-called intellectuals telling me, a woman over 40, not naturally attractive and from the wrong side of the tracks, that I should not be eligible for a better life. Now who is politically incorrect?

Unfortunately, I wasn't the only guest on the show: also invited was a heavily tattooed, shaven-headed young man with a shockingly pierced face containing multiple studs and spikes. They didn't treat him as a freak, of course. They fawned all over him and praised him for being non-conformist, when he advised people that it was important to be 'at one with your body piercer.'

He had deliberately made himself look scary – but no one questioned the psychology of his behaviour. It was art. It was self-expression. I bet that if he had applied for a job with any of the panel members, they wouldn't have hired him. And yet, in true PC fashion, they were applauding him – perhaps because they were intimidated by him.

It was me whom they treated as some kind of criminal, though I've never hurt anyone and never urged anyone to do as I do. Yet, if I'm such a bad influence, surely they shouldn't even have me on television programmes ...

Of course, that's not really how such people see me. I am just a soft target because I dare to say that I've remade myself into a 21st-century feminine archetype. I like having a small nose. I like having unlined skin in my forties. I enjoy male attention. *Ergo*, I will never please the likes of Sarah Dunant.

Until then, I had good experiences on British television, notably on *Wogan*. For all I know, Terry Wogan may have disapproved of my cosmetic surgery – but he knows how to keep control and let his guests get their point across. People watching at home will still draw their own conclusions. Television doesn't have to be a row between opposing sides who aren't allowed to find any common ground; you can have decent discussions as long as the people taking part are informed – and don't keep interrupting one another.

Yet I'm able to see the funny side. Like when a chubby young man with greasy hair and bad acne yelled at me from a New York studio audience, 'I wouldn't go out with you, you're made of plastic. I like real women!' Or when a grotesquely overweight woman accused me of being 'fattist'. Each time I returned to America, I noticed the talk shows becoming more and more adversarial and – like the mangle of neon lights on Sunset Strip – all shouting for attention. The pursuit of ratings had reduced them to a garish collage of unintelligible noise.

I know perfectly well that I have not been invited on any of these shows because I'm a member of Mensa or for my vast encyclopedic knowledge of cosmetic surgery. There is one – and *only* one – reason that anyone is repeatedly invited to appear on television year after year. That's because they consistently attract high ratings.

While the minutes tick past, I've become quite good at keeping the odd brain cell trained on the proceedings, while devoting my thoughts to higher matters, just like I did back in grade school when the teacher was banging on about the Dick and Jane books. Most of these shows are neither challenging nor interesting: they do not tax the intellects of the viewers *or* the participants.

I'm not an angry person, and neither are most of the people who vent their spleens on talk shows. For the most part, they're playing to the camera, as I've often found out afterwards. Ironically, I'm usually the only guest who is for real. I don't have the audacity to insult the intelligence of those who are watching, or the inclination to abandon my dignity for their entertainment. So, in addition to the free trip home, I get a chance to speak directly to those who are interested in what I have to say while demonstrating the art of maintaining one's composure. What, I wonder, are the rest of them doing there besides lining the coffers of the men in suits at the top of the heap?

It saddens me that the spirit of the freak show has crossed the Atlantic, blotting out any genuine attempt to understand; in my case, the reasons why people decide to change themselves and why cosmetic surgery is becoming more and more popular.

I'm happy to talk about this to anyone, but *Heart of the Matter* clearly had other fish to fry. Incidentally, like so many talk show guests, Sarah Dunant took me aside after the show and went to great pains to apologise for her remarks.

A surgeon friend of mine who saw the show speculated that the reading glasses Ms Dunant wore throughout could have been to disguise a nose job, but we have no confirmation of that. It would, however, explain two things – why she was wearing them and her apology afterwards.

I wrote up my experiences with *Heart of the Matter* for the *Telegraph,* who published the full story of my account. It put a serious dent in the credability of the show. (Well, they'd tried to discredit *me.*) But I wasn't interested in revenge. I only wanted to tell my side of the story.

On the other hand, TV appearances have often led me to experience acts of incredible kindness. After a talk show in Amsterdam, I was presented with a huge bouquet of fresh tulips to take back to London, which lasted for two whole weeks. Then I was asked to speak at an avant-garde artists' installation in Paris that regarded me as a living piece of modern art. The next day, some of the artists I met took me for breakfast on the Rive Gauche. We sat in the sunshine, eating freshly baked pastries and sipping café au lait. It's a memory I'll always treasure.

Another time I flew to New York and the driver from the talk show on which I was to appear wasn't there to meet me at the airport. I only had British money and, as it was a Sunday and the banks were closed, I couldn't convert it to dollars. I didn't even have change to use the payphone. There I was, stranded in JFK's international flight arrival hall with my luggage, wondering what to do, when a handsome young man approached me and asked if everything was all right. I explained my dilemma. He picked up my suitcase, took me outside and waited with me for a courtesy van that takes passengers to all the major hotels, including mine. Just before I boarded the bus, he pressed a $20 bill into my hand to 'get me by' until I could change some money. I never saw the guy again.

Things like that never happened to me before I had surgery.

Chapter Twenty

Sympathy for the Devil

My life continued to be stranger than fiction. When I was growing up in Ohio I used to watch a cartoon programme called 'Fractured Fairytales'. My next adventure reminded of one of those, when my name became linked with James Hewitt. It's not every day that you meet 'The Most Hated Man in Britain' – a title he gained from the tabloids after secrets of his affair with the late Princess Diana were made public. The fact that he was condemned as a cad and a love rat made him all the more interesting.

I met James in July 1998, at a party thrown by former Rolling Stone Bill Wyman at his Sticky Fingers restaurant in London. I'd been speaking to Bill and his American wife Suzanne, who had just given birth to their third child, telling them how much I had enjoyed a recent article about them in *Hello!* magazine. The place was packed, and James and I happened to reach over simultaneously to pluck a tasty morsel from a tray of hors d'oeuvres. He introduced himself, although there was no need – having been Princess Diana's lover and the scourge of the British media, his face was instantly recognisable. He was with his best friend Rupert Mackenzie-Hill, with whom he had served in the Gulf War. We began talking and they came to sit with me and the famous British model Jilly Johnson, whose guest I was at the party.

I had met Jilly for the first time at the hairdresser's a few years before. We got chatting, and a few months later I ran into her at a party given by Marc Burca shortly after I had bumped into him again. He had given me a formal written invitation – a stiffy, as we call them – and when I went along there was Jilly Johnson.

We got on like a house on fire, exchanged telephone numbers and started calling each other up. One time when we were talking, she said, 'Must go, I've got a cab waiting.'

I said, 'I've got a cab coming soon anyway.'

We arrived at our respective destinations and, by coincidence, it was the same place. We had both been booked for a modelling job and, as we sat backstage getting our hair and make-up done, we soon found we had a lot in common. It wasn't long before we became good friends. That's how Jilly and I ended up talking to James Hewitt and Rupert McKenzie-Hill at Bill Wyman's party.

Later that evening Jilly and I were going on to a party in Soho given by the manager of the actress Caroline Aherne, best known for her roles in popular UK TV series *Mrs Merton* and *The Royle Family*. James said, 'I'm a big fan of hers,' so we invited them to come along.

As we left Sticky Fingers, a pack of paparazzi ran after us, flashing away as we jumped into the cab. One of the pictures appeared in the *Daily Star* the next day. But we weren't the only ones to make the headlines. When we got to the party, there was hardly anyone there. 'Where's Caroline?' I asked her manager, Jan. 'She's been taken to hospital,' she replied simply. We went to Tramp instead and someone brought in the first edition of next morning's papers. CAROLINE AHERNE IN SUICIDE BID, it was reported. The papers said she had been admitted to The Priory, a famous west London clinic that specialises in alcohol and drug addiction.

We ordered dinner and I was finding James more and more fascinating – after all, he will go down in history. He said he despised the way people hated him and, being an underdog myself, I understood his feelings. He told me that he had even considered undergoing plastic surgery to change his identity, so that he could go away and live anonymously, and asked me for full details of how he would go about it.

Here I was again, befriending a misfit. Or as Gloria would say, 'Always bringing home strays.' After that evening we became pals, and he began to confide in me more and more. The biggest shock is that he is a really an OK guy and a fellow animal lover. He can also be hilariously funny.

A few months earlier, I had finally been able to bring home a kitten of my own, an F2 Bengal, which is a wildcat hybrid that looks like a miniature leopard. I named him Cato. One day while he was at my apartment, James picked Cato up and sat him down on his lap. Cato said, 'Meow.' James put his right hand on Cato's underside and pushed up and down on his diaphragm. Cato went 'Meowowowowowowowow,' which annoyed Cato and made him meow even more, so before long he was going, 'Meowowowowowowowowowowowowowow.' James knows how to play a cat like the bagpipes. He told me he did that to his own cat. It was a gag he pulled on Cato every time he came over.

When James eventually moved to a flat in South Kensington, Cato and I were invited to come over. James had brought lots of artefacts from his house in Devon, including two mounted fox heads that he'd hung in his hallway at the top of the stairs. When Cato spotted those fox heads, he was totally spooked. Noises came out of that cat I've never heard before or since. He let out a bloodcurdling scream, then nearly choked himself trying to emit more hisses per second than a cat was built to do. He sounded like a sneezing machine gun. James and I laughed and laughed. After a while, Cato realised the foxes weren't alive, calmed down and eyed them with contempt.

Shortly afterwards, I began to realise that Cato was bored silly being an only cat, despite a social life that meant he appeared in the Dempster society column more often than most dukes and earls. On the advice of top British feline behaviourist Vicky Halls – she dosn't like being called a 'cat shrink' – I got a Kitty friend for Cato.

James was one of the first to come over and see my new kitten, a Bombay named Pip, who was is black with outrageously oversized ears. (Hugh Cornwell, former lead singer of the Stranglers, suggested I name him Batty because of his ears.) Although Pip loved James, he refused to fall for the bagpipe routine.

All cat joking aside, James told me that he suffers from bouts of depression and chronic ailments he didn't have before he served as a tank commander in Operation Desert Storm. Whether or not Gulf War Syndrome is ever officially recognised, James is convinced there is something to it. He is not, however, so convinced that the Americans landed on the moon, and insists that it was all a hoax.

Before James moved from Devon to Chelsea he didn't have a London base. He often travelled abroad, and would stay down the road with Rupert or at my flat the night before his flight, and head for Heathrow the next day. On one such occasion undercover photographers had been following him and were lurking outside my apartment. They snatched pictures of James and me together and the *Sunday People* ran a front-page story, 'Hewitt's Bizarre New Lover'. The intro said, 'Princess Diana's ex-lover James Hewitt is having a secret affair with a woman who has had 27 operations to improve her looks. Cindy Jackson says she is besotted with Hewitt.'

The article went on to quote me as saying to 'pals', 'He's everything I want, yet I know he still has feelings for Diana,' and 'I can see exactly why she [Diana] chose him. He makes me feel wonderful, so sensual and alive,' and 'More than anything, I want to support James and let him know the time is right to open his heart. I want to heal him.' Yet it concluded, 'Yesterday, Cindy refused to comment about her relationship with Hewitt. She said, "I have absolutely nothing to say."'

James and I howled with laughter as we took turns reading the article out loud to each other.

The paper also said that one 'friend' said, 'James just can't keep his eyes off Cindy. She's certainly an attractive woman but one of the things he loved about Diana was her natural beauty. All his (James') friends think it's strange to say the least that he's ended up with a woman who has had so much plastic surgery.'

James said to me, 'It's ironic that they think all Diana's beauty was natural, because she did have plastic surgery – she had a nose job.' That only confirmed something I already suspected. The time I saw her in Roberto's restaurant one thing I noticed about her was the size of her nose. But the shape of it went on to change – it was flattened at the top and was given a dip just before the end. The surgeon who performed the operation did a very conservative job, but if you look at pictures of the Princess over the years, you can easily spot the difference. A trick Diana used to disguise her new nose was one that many women who have plastic surgery use – she changed her hairstyle.

James told me he had spoken to Diana not long before she died. He said the rift between them was mended and that she wasn't mad at him any more. They were on speaking terms and he believed that, had she not been killed, they would have been friends again. Diana was like that, he said. One week she would freeze people out, the next week they were back in favour. He told me that he was deeply shocked when she admitted their love affair on TV. Never expecting her to announce it so publicly, he said it was like being hit by a bolt of lightning. Afterwards she admitted there was nothing left to hide.

He talked a lot about Diana, of how no one at the Palace gave her the support and help she craved, and how she was desperately in need of a friend. 'I looked after the Princess of Wales because no one else would,' he explained. Yet when they split up, she left him out in the cold to fend for himself.

James said government agents had threatened him. They told him, 'If your friendship with the Princess of Wales continues, we cannot guarantee your safety.' He felt that he'd given up everything for her, and she turned her back on him. James was certainly taken with Diana, but he told me she wasn't easy to deal with.

Being labelled the most reviled man in the western world really hurt him. That's easy enough to understand. No one likes to be badly thought of. However, there was one thing James told me that remains a mystery. It was when we were discussing our favourite names. He said that if he ever had *another* son he would like to name him Maximillan. It may have been a slip of the tongue, but I still think it was an odd thing to say.

James told me that he had planned a lifelong career in the army, but his relationship with Diana ended all that. He said that he preferred army life because at least you know where you stand with your fellow officers. Since leaving the army he had been tricked and set up many times by the press and so-called friends. He said you don't get that kind of behaviour from your own side in the service.

Maybe he was shortsighted. Perhaps he was too trusting. Or it could be that he is simply not the best judge of character. He thought that, once he told his side of the story to the world, it would clarify everything. Instead, the world didn't want the Charles and Diana fairytale to end, and he bore the full brunt of the public's outrage. He thought he told the story in the most gentlemanly manner he could, but still he was pilloried. Perhaps he shouldn't have talked, but the affair was common knowledge in many circles, and he didn't want it revealed in sleazy tabloid headlines instead.

James often seemed insecure and rooted in the past. He even bought a green Jaguar almost identical to the one Diana used to drive. Still, he is a nice enough guy and can act the perfect gentleman – whatever anyone might say to the contrary.

He's also very amusing. One time as we were driving through Berkshire *en route* to a polo match, Windsor Castle came into view in the distance. James mentioned that he had spent a lot of time there and quipped that you would have thought they would have known better than to build it right under the Heathrow flight path.

The press love to portray James as a friendless outcast, but this couldn't be further from the truth. I've seen firsthand just how popular he is. Being a man's man, he can easily hold his own in conversation with other men, and women flock around him like bees to a honey pot wherever he goes. He's always the centre of attention. At first when I would turn up at private functions with James, I thought I was being terribly controversial. Then I discovered that, far from being the social pariah the press makes him out to be, everybody wants him at their parties. For example, after I introduced James to top London socialites Andrew Neil and Nicky Haslam, both men wasted no time in inviting him to their exclusive birthday celebrations, although neither had ever met him before.

As I got to know James, I saw there was much more to him than simply being the former lover of the Princess of Wales. Since everyone was still so interested in him, I suggested he write his autobiography for the sake of history, as generations to come would value his firsthand account of the Gulf War as much as his relationship with the most famous woman in the world. I said he should call it *Love and War*. He followed my advice and the book was published a year later.

The *Sunday Telegraph*'s Mandrake column called me up after seeing pictures of James, Jilly and I together. They asked, 'What's going on with you and James Hewitt? We called Jilly and she said she's not going out with him, but you are.' The three of us being photographed together at Bill Wyman's party had caused untold confusion in newspaper offices all over the world. James joked, 'Tell them that you and Jilly share me.' So, as a joke, I did and they actually ran the story. Jilly wasn't terribly pleased, to put it mildly, but James was delighted. For him, it was a bit of positive press at last.

Unfortunately, because of my very public friendship with James, other guys stopped asking me out thinking that I was his girlfriend.

Although it may have appeared that way to some, as we all know, looks can be deceiving. James, meanwhile, had been seen out with another woman. The press started calling me to ask if I knew about it, and wanting to know who she was. At that point I thought I had better let everyone know I was a free agent and that James and I were not romantically involved, otherwise I would never get another date. So when the *Sunday People* called to ask me what was going on between James and me I told them, 'Yes, it's over. But we're friends.' I was horrified when I saw the headline: DI'S CAD DID DIRTY ON ME and a picture of me looking sad and rejected. I didn't exactly put it that way, but James's reputation precedes him and he's the guy the press love to hate. You could compare him to JR Ewing – no one wants to show another side to him. Instead he's regarded as the devil incarnate in some quarters. It's a shame to waste all that hate on a war hero who fell in love with a princess, when there are so many genuinely despicable people in the world, who are much more deserving of such vitriol: child molesters, serial killers, rapists, murderers, vivisectionists ...

Over the years Jilly has been a great friend. When I began having surgery and my new looks were my passport to the London set, she was helpful over what clothes I should wear and how I should wear my hair. I admire her taste – she has that classic, timeless style that I still hadn't figured out back then. When we shopped together, I loved her honesty. I'd find a dress I liked and would hold it up, and she would say, 'For heavens sake, put it down – it's awful.' When I first came to London she was a famous model and had her band, Blonde On Blonde with Nina Carter. Nina married Rick Wakeman, the legendary keyboard player from Yes and became a tax exile on the Isle of Man. (They're divorced now.)

I really appreciate the help and advice Jilly has given me. We've gone on vacations and done catwalk modelling together. Her legs are about a mile long and her figure is like a teenager's. Her bone structure is perfect – she's elegant and graceful. I hang around with her hoping some of that will rub off on me.

Jilly has never talked to the press about the celebrity gossip to which she has been privy over the years. However, we indulge in serious girl talk and I have learned a lot from her. Like me, she has had her share of heartbreak, and we are both older and wiser.

We've also had some great laughs doing some outrageous things. Jilly has been involved in the Prince's Trust charity for many years, and we went to a formal dinner in Sussex thrown by the charity in the summer of 1998. We hired Dave, a chauffeur with a big Mercedes, to drive us there. We were at the reception and Prince Charles came over to us. I said, 'The last time I saw you, sir, you were all wet and muddy.' It was at a polo match where he had been playing in the pouring rain on a muddy field. He laughed and Jilly said, 'Don't mind my friend, she's American.' Prince Charles said, 'Have you come all the way from America to be here tonight?' He was joking, of course.

Prince Charles is known for his Goon-like sense of humour. In fact, I'd come all the way from Chelsea, where I'd had lunch with James Hewitt the same day. Or as a friend teased, 'Lunch with James Hewitt and then dinner with Prince Charles? You must know how Diana felt.'

At dinner I sat next to the Prince's bodyguard. Although I was talking to him, his eyes were always protectively on the Prince. So I spent the whole evening in conversation with this guy whose eyes went straight past me all the time. He couldn't drink, because he was on duty, so he gave me every one of his alcoholic beverages, a different type for each course – champagne, white wine, red wine, port and champagne again – which I downed as well as my own. Back in the car, I completely passed out.

The next day I called Dave. 'That was an interesting drive home,' he said.

'What do you mean?'

'I've got some amazing pictures,' he laughed.

His best friend is Dave Bennett, a top paparazzo photographer. When I lost consciousness, Jilly made him stop the car and she climbed into the front seat. I was sprawled out in the back in my ballgown and they took pictures of me in a state of disarray. That's what you get for drinking Prince Charles's detective's booze. I expect those pictures to surface one day in some tabloid.

Another time, Jilly and I went to Castlemartin in Dublin, owned by Tony O'Reilly. It was a costume party and we had to dress Georgian-style. She decided to dress as a man in breeches and a tri-cornered hat, with her hair tied back in a ribbon. I wore a huge embroidered Empire gown complete with bustle. It looked like I was wearing a pair of curtains draped over a chest of drawers. We made a peculiar couple. (Incidentally, Tony O'Reilly is one of Ireland's richest men. He owns, among other things, Heinz. I must be the only former employee from the factory floor who has been a guest at his house. I mean his *castle*.)

Then I was faced with a dilemma when I was invited to have tea with the Queen after a service at the Holy Trinity Church on Sloane Street. I got a call from *Kilroy*, the British equivalent of the American *Phil Donahue Show*, who wanted my cat, Cato, to appear on his show about unusual pets on the same day. So I had to debate whether to meet the Queen or let my cat have his British television début.

I called Jilly. 'You can meet the Queen any time but if you want to take Cato on TV he might not get another chance for a while,' was her advice.

'I've lived in London for over 20 years but have never met the Queen,' I said.

'Oh, there will be other chances.' Jilly has met her loads of times and said that I would too. Cato got his TV début but I still haven't met the Queen.

It's a shame, because before I had been asked to do the television show, I told James Hewitt I was going to meet the Queen. He was thrilled for me.

'When you meet royalty,' he told me, demonstrating how to curtsey, 'always look them straight in the eye, put your left foot behind your right and stoop down as far as you can without falling over.'

He made me practise over and over in front of him until he was satisfied that I had it down pat. I wasn't entirely certain whether he was really concerned that I wouldn't do it right, or if he just likes being curtseyed to.

Since then, Cato's been on TV several times. He's appeared on *Men For Sale, Entertainment Tonight,* a French TV crew came over to film him and he's featured on German, Italian and American shows with me. He's famous because there are very few domestic cats who have that much wild blood and his strikingly handsome looks.

Cato has also met Shirley Bassey. I was invited to a garden party thrown by Peter Shalson and his wife Polly. They are renowned for their lavish entertaining – Elton John played at their wedding reception.

'The party's outdoors,' Peter said. 'Please bring Cato.'

I went to his mansion and there were two security guards on the door holding clipboards. I introduced us: 'Cindy Jackson and Cato.' And there was Cato's name on the guest list. Everyone at the party wanted to meet the leopard cat, including Shirley Bassey who was there in the garden by the pool.

'Oooh,' she said. 'Look at this gorgeous cat.' She speaks in a very loud voice and I was afraid that Cato might bolt or scratch her, especially as she pointed her long talons at him. Luckily they took an instant liking to each other.

Barry Humphries, aka Dame Edna Everage, approached us and asked if he could hold Cato. This is always risky because, as much as Cato loves going out, he is not keen on being passed around. Nonetheless, I handed him over, while remaining poised to take him back immediately if there was a problem. But, to my amazement, Cato put his head on the famous shoulder and cuddled up to him, while Barry gently stroked his fur and spoke softly to him.

'I love cats,' he told me. 'I communicate with them.' That was pretty obvious.

Once people learn that you are involved in charity work, you get invited everywhere. This is how I came to be invited to a charity dinner attended by Prince Michael of Kent in the Officer's Mess at Knightsbridge Barracks. I had never met him before but, as I knew he and his wife loved cats, I whipped out a picture of Cato. The Prince wanted to know all about him.

At dinner I sat next to Harry, the Commanding Officer, and told him Prince Michael was very interested in my cat. 'He's being looked after just down the road, shall I bring him in to meet His Royal Highness?' I asked.

'What a splendid idea,' Harry said.

I called my friend who was cat-sitting and asked him to bring Cato. Shortly afterwards, Cato, inside his cat carrier, was duly escorted through security. When I presented him to the Prince, Cato looked him in the eye, then climbed on to the Royal shoulder and stayed there. All the members of the Household Cavalry came over to see him. Cato took one look at all these hunky soldiers' red-jacketed shoulders and clambered across each one until he'd walked over the whole Cavalry. Then one of the soldiers placed him on an enormous mantelpiece among priceless vases and *objets d'art*. He delicately wove in and out of them, thankfully without breaking anything.

Afterwards, I heard from friends at Kensington Palace that the Kents were always asking after Cato. A few months later I went to another charity event and Princess Michael was there.

'I'm the one with the cat, Ma'am,' I told her, curtseying as James Hewitt had taught me.

She grabbed my hand and said, 'Please can I come and meet him? My husband thought he was so wonderful.'

A couple of days later I received a call from Kensington Palace.

'Her Royal Highness the Princess Michael of Kent would like to arrange a suitable time to come and visit your cat,' a secretary informed me. This seemed bizarre even by my standards, but we arranged a day and I cleaned my flat from top to bottom, not knowing if I was supposed to repaint the place or what.

I was told beforehand by friends who'd done this before, that you're not supposed to hang around and wait for the doorbell to ring. Instead, when royalty is due to visit, you're supposed to stand outside the door ready to greet them as they arrive.

So I stood at my front door and waited. Right on time, Princess Michael arrived with another princess from the Middle East, leaving their security men waiting in the car. Both princesses came in to my apartment and played with Cato and two other visiting Bengal kittens for over an hour. The cats all loved Princess Michael and she gleefully romped with them on the floor, casually dressed in black slacks and a woollen jacket. Everything went very smoothly. Cat lovers speak the same language. (I have since aquired a third cat, a rescue called Claude.)

The following year, Prince Michael entertained Cato again at the Knightsbridge Barracks, and invited me to attend Crufts, the famous dog show, along with a few other animal-loving friends, including Lady Annabel Goldsmith, the widow of billionaire James Goldsmith after whom the Mayfair nightclub Annabel's is named. The Prince is President of the Kennel Club and presents the winning trophy.

Another cat lover is Lord Archer, who I also met through charity work. I fell on the idea of auctioning a date with Jilly and myself, at an event to raise money for Children's Playing Fields, and Lord Archer was acting as auctioneer. We went under the gavel for £2,000 to the elder brother of Sarah Ferguson's ex, Peter McNally. We took him and a friend to dinner at a Mayfair restaurant.

Perhaps Jeffrey Archer noted my charitable spirit, because not long afterwards he asked me to tea at the House of Commons. He gave me a tour and I got to sit in on some of the debates. A few months later, I noticed his name on a cat breeder's advertisement and discovered he has two Bengal cats as well.

Lord Archer may have fallen from grace in the eyes of the British public, but it was really sweet of him to give me that tour. He took great pains to explain how the British government works and it was interesting to hear Members of Parliament being so rude to each other and yet sounding so polite. During debate, their eloquence at putting each other down almost made it sound like they were exchanging compliments. The magic of the English language can only be fully appreciated when hearing it articulated in such a manner.

Other luminaries I've met through my cat include pop star Gary Numan and his wife Gemma, who became firm friends after Cato and I appeared on the same British talk show as Gary and his band. They put me on their guest list whenever Gary has a London gig. I love being a Numanoid for an evening. Needless to say, I have all the Goth gear to blend right in with the rest of the audience.

There can be no arguing that looks do count. Before my surgery I was never invited anywhere special, and I never met such interesting and successful people. Back then I was invisible. Nobody wanted to know me. Suddenly I was being accepted in the most unexpected circles.

Even so, everything still seems unreal and exciting to me, and there has been a strand of ridiculousness throughout my life that seems to have grown since the day I was born. I seem to attract strange situations and find myself in unbelievable company.

My niece Adrienne unknowingly summed up that phenomenon nicely with a tennis analogy. When discussing our respective abilities on the court I asked her, 'Why is it that when you're playing against someone really good you play a better game and when you're playing an inferior player you play a lot worse?'

Her reply was, 'Because when somebody hits you the ball weird, you hit it back weird.'

In an instant, I realised what my problem had been. I was only returning weird balls that had been hit to me weird in the first place. Maybe it wasn't my fault after all.

I wonder if that could explain what happened as a result of my meeting the actor Burt Kwouk, who played Cato in *The Pink Panther* movies. My cat Cato is named after him.

Burt is friendly with Terry Major-Ball, the brother of John Major who was Britain's Prime Minister at the time. Burt, Terry Major-Ball and I used to go out together a lot. (Picture it: A *Pink Panther* star, the British Prime Minister's older brother and *me*.)

One night when Burt came to pick me up I was wearing a long, strapless pink dress that swept the floor.

Burt took one look at me and said, 'You're not wearing that! Every time we go out and you have a dress without a back, I end up giving you my jacket because you're cold. What happens if *I* get cold? Wear something different.'

'Like what?' I asked.

He marched into my bedroom and flung open the doors to my wardrobe. I watched the normally inscrutable Chinese actor take a step back, reeling at the Barbie-like collection of incongruent costumes. (I had amassed an unlikely selection of outfits that allow me to pass unchallenged in almost any social situation you care to mention.) However, it was only a moment before he regained his composure.

Burt reached in and rifled though my cache of costumes.

'Here, put this on!' he said triumphantly, pulling out a short silver dress and jacket that I had bought for photo sessions and had never been seen outside a photography studio.

'And hurry up, we're late!' he barked as he left the room.

Because the pink dress was tight and long, I was wearing tights but no knickers. Otherwise they would have shown through the dress and given me a VPL. I quickly swapped dresses and we went off to the party, still wearing no underwear.

Terry Major-Ball was there and he asked me to dance. To my horror, as we danced, my dress rode up to expose my backside. To make matters worse, a photographer from the *Sun* took a picture of the embarrassing scene. Later that week my butt appeared in a series of pictures spread across two pages in the paper.

'You're the only person I know whose ass shines out of the *Sun*,' Burt quipped.

Chapter Twenty-one

Two Worlds Collided

In the Spring of 2002 I received an invitation from Liz Brewer that would take me in yet another unexpected direction. Unlike the invitations I normally receive from Liz, this was not to attend an opulent ball or classy cocktail party. Instead, I was being invited to a gig at the Borderline club, a small grungey basement venue in the West End with a bar and live music. Her university student daughter, Tally, had recently joined a rock band as the lead singer and they were booked to play there.

As I sent off my RSVP in the affirmative, I tried without success to picture Lizzie at a gig at the Borderline. The incongruity stretched even *my* imagination.

On the appointed evening, a small gathering of people normally seen wearing black tie in the pages of *Hello!* gathered at Liz's elegant home in Belgravia dressed in jeans and leather jackets. After a round of champagne and smoked salmon sandwiches, we all headed off to the gig.

I hadn't been to the Borderline in at least 10 years but it still looked pretty much the same. Tally's band went down a storm. She's a very talented singer and it was great set. After a couple of pints of beer (on top of the champagne at Liz's), I needed the ladies room. Covering the toilet wall were flyers with dates and bands for forthcoming gigs. One of bands that would be playing the following month caught my eye. It was my old pals, the Vibrators. I couldn't believe they were still together after all these years. I tore one of the flyers off the wall and shoved it into my fake Prada handbag.

When I got home that evening I pulled the out the flyer and noted the date of the Vibrators gig. I'd been toying with the idea of putting the band back together for a while. Maybe it's my imagination, but since I had cosmetic surgery I swear I can even sing better. And far from feeling like I was too old, I felt like the time was right. All the best live acts are over forty now: Bryan Adams, U2, the Stones, and even Madonna, to name but a few. Tony Feedback and I had had dinner a few weeks before. He now runs his own company and drives a Bentley. We talked about doing something again musically but nothing came of it.

As the date of the gig approached, I could scarcely contain my excitement. It had been a very long time since I'd seen the Vibrators play. They were always such a brilliant live act. It would be great to see the guys again – and to find out if Eddie was up for playing drums in a new band up with me.

On the way to the gig I began to get a little nervous. I wondered if they'd be glad to see me – or if they'd even recognise me. When I got to the Borderline I went straight to the bar for some Dutch courage.

I spotted Eddie a few feet away. He didn't look much different. I walked up behind him and tapped him on the shoulder. This was an old friend I hadn't seen in at least 10 years. Yet he simply turned around and calmly said, 'Oh, hiya.' Eddie was still as laid back as ever.

'I'm putting the band back together. Are you in?' I asked him.

'All right, then,' was his reply. Eddie always was a man of few words.

Now all I needed was a guitarist, bass player and a couple of backing singers.

'Do you know any bass players?' I asked Eddie.

'Robbie,' he said, pointing to a tall guy with lots of tattoos wearing a Tweety Pie t-shirt, over by the stage. He was the 'new' Vibrators bass player, having been with them for four years. That would mean I had the Vibrators rhythm section.

'Who should we get on guitar?' I continued. This was easier than I thought it would be.

'Knox might do it,' he replied. Knox, the Vibrators guitarist, had played guest spots with my band nearly twenty years ago.

But that would mean I would have the entire Vibrators line up, since they were now a three-piece band. I wasn't sure how they'd feel about that. Then I saw Knox coming our way. I smiled and waved at him but he ignored me and went over to talk to some other people he knew. That made me feel terrible. Although we went back a long way, I guessed that he didn't agree with what I had done or maybe he never really liked me anyway.

I continued talking to Eddie, still feeling deflated but pretending otherwise. Eventually Knox came over to us. Eddie said, 'Cindy's here.'

Knox looked at me and gasped, 'Oh my God, I didn't recognise you!' and gave me a big hug.

I breathed a sigh of relief and we picked up pretty much where we left off all those years before. And he agreed to play guitar in the new band, which we decided to call the Dollz.

Before long it was time for the Vibrators to take the stage. And they *rocked*.

I was still on the lookout for a pair of backing singers. A few days after the Vibrators gig I spent an evening with Juliette McCrimmon, who I hadn't seen since she was 14. We'd lost touch after I moved away but she had recently contacted me through my website. Now in her mid-twenties, she was all grown up and running a theatrical agency. After we'd finished catching up on the intervening years, I started to tell her about the band. But I was soon interrupted. 'I want to be a backing singer!' Juliette declared.

Why didn't *I* think of that? I asked Juliette to bring a friend so there would be two of them. She brought Isabel and that's how the band was put together. All thanks to Liz Brewer.

Chapter Twenty-two

18 Til I Die

Before the surgery, no matter what I did differently, I always got the same reaction. But when I changed my looks, the world instantly changed its attitude towards me. Looking back, my solution seems almost too easy. It was simply a question of manipulating some skin, bone and cartilage.

Yet there are some things you can never change. After spending a good deal of my life trying to fit in, I've come to the conclusion that I was never meant to fit in at all. Finally, I'm comfortable with that. If the rest of the world isn't, well, that's their problem.

Despite all the changes of address, the different lifestyles I've lived and the complete transformation of my appearance, I've been the very same person all along. Fortunately, I was never made to feel bad about who I am inside. But then again, few looked beyond my appearance, or else they might well have passed judgement on my character while they were at it.

Some of the choices I made were by no means easy. Having taken anything but the path of least resistance, I'm the first to admit that there were many times I thought of giving up. It was only my dreams of what the future could hold that kept me going. In return, I brought those dreams to life.

But where did those dreams come from? I have no idea. I only know that they've always been with me, showing me what my life *could* be like. It was the existence I left behind that always felt unreal and uncomfortable. Who knows where I'll eventually end up? I have no fear of either change or the unknown. After all, they're the only two things in life we can count on so we might as well embrace them.

We all carry inside us an infinite number of alternative destinies. The destiny you shape for yourself is determined by the choices you're making this very minute. The future is hurtling towards us every second of the day. I realised a long time ago that if I didn't like the path I was on, it was up to me to do something about it, otherwise I'd only be further down that same path in years to come. What's the excuse for letting life decide where it takes you, if it's possible to steer it in the direction you want it to go?

That's why I think it's so important to explore the possibilities our dreams show us. And never to dismiss anything that strikes a chord with our souls, no matter how insignificant it may seem at the time – they may be marker symbols along your path. (Looking at my life now, how else could my early Barbie doll and Ben Casey fixations be explained?)

Most of all, we shouldn't forget what was important to us when we were children, a time when we were simply younger versions of the people we are today – a time when our dreams were still our own. A time before we learned to suppress our dreams in order to try and live out the dreams of our parents, our lovers, our society.

That's probably why, when anyone asks members of my family

what they think about all the surgery I've had, their usual answer is something to the effect of: 'It's just typical of something Cindy would do.' No one who knows me well thinks it's out of character.

Whenever I'm asked how I feel about having a face and body that 'aren't really mine', I always reply, 'They *are* mine and I have the receipts to prove it.'

Having spent almost four decades watching life from the sidelines, I gained quite an education, graduating from the School of Hard Knocks with a degree in Murphy's Law. There were valuable lessons in human nature all around me, and I became a keen student. Unnoticed, I observed a lot of life from the cheap seats. Although I've now become the subject of scrutiny, I haven't stopped observing, and I know a lot of things for certain:

- *Cruel words can cut just as deeply as knives, and leave wounds that bleed for a lifetime; you never know when you're creating a memory.*
- *Beauty can open doors, but it takes compassion to open hearts; looks can be deceiving so don't be deceived by them.*
- *Being young is overrated; with each decade we lose some things while gaining others; youth has its advantages but so does maturity – as we get older we shouldn't neglect to collect the gifts and prizes we've earned along the way.*
- *Despite women's lib, sexism is alive and well; men are allowed to be handsome and intelligent while women are still expected to choose one or the other.*
- *The media is not to blame for the proliferation of perfect body images; marketing men don't care about the politics of beauty, they just know it sells.*
- *While beauty pageants are now considered politically incorrect, they're still here, in the form of supermodels and fashion shows featured almost daily on television news and even the front pages of the broadsheets.*
- *When you look at a person, you should look at their character,*

not their face, clothes or circumstances. Those things can – and will – change over time, but their character won't.

What people are really seeing when they look at my surgically enhanced face, in addition to some nifty scalpel work, is a reflection of human values. Some are uncomfortable with the fact that I was willing to go through a lot of pain and expense to achieve something that some women just happen to be born with.

After being told repeatedly, in no uncertain terms, exactly what was wrong with my looks, I responded to the criticism by completely transforming my appearance and re-emerging as a reflection of what is scientifically shown to be the image that humans prefer to see. I admit to being a little disappointed that I had to go to such extreme lengths to gain acceptance. The world would not acknowledge me until my scars were on the *outside*. Maybe the wounds we always thought were invisible eventually come to light in one form or another.

Or maybe I'm merely playing yet another role. Most people are afraid of not being accepted for who they are and I was no exception. It was, after all, my intense desire to fit in and be recognised by my peers that forced me to live such a chameleon-like existence. I learned the power of masquerade back in 1975 from Mr Goodier. Every day when we open our wardrobes and decide what to put on, we are the masters of the illusions we create.

Just like the Barbie board game named *We Girls Can Do Anything*, all we need are the appropriate outfits and accessories to create the right images for the game of life. Shakespeare summed it up when he said, 'All the world's a stage.' And I've proved that I can play whatever role is required. But why did I feel compelled to do that?

There is always the possibility none of us actually has free will, which would be convenient, because it exonerates us from blame for anything. Take the scientific studies of 'nature' versus 'nurture'.

Apparently we're all products of the combination of our ancestors' genetic codes, handed down through the generations and the environment in which we live. You never hear about 'nature versus nurture' versus 'your own stuff'. (I would expand on that, but time is limited – I have some gilding projects under way on the kitchen table ...)

According to zoologist Richard Dawkins, author of *The Selfish Gene*, the ultimate goal of life is the immortality of one's information, which can be achieved in two ways. One is genetic, which is the passing on of one's DNA via your children. The other is memetic, or the process of passing on your ideas. If that's the case, when I've joked that I don't mind not having had children, because I'm mother to the world's cosmetic surgery patients, there are scientists who might agree.

Considering that I've always been stronger mentally than physically and emotionally, perhaps it *was* my destiny to pass on my ideas rather than my genes. Richard Dawkins believes the memetic legacy to be equally valid. (One practitioner, after examining my medical history, remarked, 'Looks like you've got a Ferrari mind in a Volkswagen body.')

There's no longer any reason to let others make me feel bad about myself, and I guess there never really was. It's just that I was born without some gifts – besides good looks – that others take for granted, such as a thick skin and the ability to rationalise personal criticism.

While regretting what might have been is futile, I can't help wondering what I would have become had others not slapped me down every step of the way and kept me from opportunities that were often given freely to those who weren't even interested in them. I'll never know what else I could have achieved with a little encouragement, which would have cost nothing. Instead, I proved what I could do with a little money.

I also proved that *anyone* can change their looks with cosmetic surgery. Perhaps that's part of my karma – to give courage to the legion of other sensitive souls who've been inspired to use cosmetic surgery to gain power. If so, maybe one of them will go on to achieve something great, for which I'll have been indirectly responsible.

Although there may be those who now criticise me for the amount of surgery I've had instead of the way I look, I've now come to realise that some people will always find something to gripe about, no matter what you do. I don't argue with them. Life's too short.

You've really got to ignore those who condemn the things you do that work for you and enable you to survive. So many friends I've known over the years never found the right tools and are no longer with us. I could have so easily been one of them.

Besides, you never really know the agenda of those who are attempting to undermine you. They may be trying to make themselves look better by comparison, or they may even be planning to take your place. At any rate, they're their own worst enemies, not yours. Take my word for it, I've watched enough of my own detractors eventually fade into obscurity – that's because nobody can get ahead of you while they're busy stabbing you in the back. Nor can they go up in the world while they're nipping at your ankles.

Since I took away the stick I was being hit with, I've learned that some people will just pick up a different stick and keep on hitting, because they *like* hitting people. They wake up spoiling for a fight every morning. I do my best to stay out of their way. You can't help them – they don't *want* your help. Instead, these toxic people want to spread their poison. (Remember that if someone has a habit of falling out with everyone, it *will* be you one day.) Once again, it's all about choices. With billions of people in the world to choose from, why even give the time of day to petty, mean spirited characters?

Now, I try to fill my life and mind with all things positive – people, activities and situations. I've seen that negative attracts more negative and positive attracts more positive. Why not just see the good in life and let the bad pass right on by and land on someone who's looking for it? After all, you don't invite every person into your home who comes knocking.

At last I've found my own niche in life. I have a job that I was literally cut out for, a lifestyle that suits me and, most importantly, people are kinder to me. Sometimes I feel like I'm the luckiest woman in the world. I have a professional career researching cosmetic surgery, a creative outlet helping others re-design their faces, and I'm in a rock band. Movie stars send me first class airline tickets to come and discuss their cosmetic surgery plans. What's more, with the correct surgical maintenence, I'll always look much younger than I really am. Even though it took me a long time, I have few regrets and wouldn't change anything I did to get here. After all, if you alter the journey, you alter the destination.

Although I get to mix with some interesting and stimulating people, a door has been opened to me that is more significant than on any stately home. Having cosmetic surgery led me to start seeing a spiritual healer. Despite what sceptics may say (I was one myself), when I saw how much quicker my face healed after healing sessions compared to before, I needed no further proof of its powers. After more than two years of receiving regular healing with amazing results, Una Wilson, my Gaia Master, asked me if I wanted to become a healer. I was humbled and honoured to be invited to join the healing community. This is what led me to eventually qualify as a professional spiritual healer.

As Carolyn Myss explains in her book *Anatomy of the Spirit*, everything that has happened in our lives is recorded by the energy field that surrounds each of us. It's very damaging to carry negative energy from past experiences around with you. With an ailing spirit you can have neither beauty nor health because it causes the face to grimace and the physical body to break down. We must all learn to forgive, forget and look positively towards the future.

Mind, body and spirit walk together. When one lags behind, the other two are held back. Over-emphasise one at the expense of the others. With the current surge in popularity of self-help books, the continuing accent on health and beauty and increasing spiritual awareness, it's easier, and more important than ever, to ensure that the equilibrium is maintained.

Having learned to conquer my fears by meeting them head on, I've managed to see off a good many of them. I'm no longer afraid of criticism, of speaking in public or of being on my own the world. One stubborn fear, however, remained until fairly recently, and that was the daddy of them all.

I was invited to a lunch party in the south of France at a fabulous villa owned by a well-known society figure. Ivana Trump, the Graffs and the editor of French Vogue magazine were among the illustrious guests. Waiters in black tie served exquisite food on precious china; fine wines were presented in glittering crystal glasses that reflected the summer sunlight in a thousand shimmering rainbows. Outside, a clear, sparkling swimming pool glistened like a flawless diamond set in magnificent gardens, as a string quartet serenaded guests sipping vintage champagne. It was a truly magical afternoon. (Despite the fact that I was there as an invited guest, on occasions such as these I always have the nagging fear that someone is going to realise that it's *me*, and ask me to leave. Sometimes I feel just like a Trojan Horse.)

Afterwards, I had arranged to return to Nice Airport by helicopter to catch my flight back to London. I was looking forward to getting home, as I had big plans for the evening that involved putting on some old jeans and going to a down and dirty London rock'n'roll club. I couldn't wait to drink cheap beer and listen to loud music with some of my old bohemian friends.

I dropped off my rented Mercedes at the heliport, and looked for Michel, my pilot. Since it was only the two of us who would be making the journey, once again I found myself assigned to the co-pilot's seat. My heart was in my mouth as the engine revved faster and faster until we rose into the air. Suddenly we darted upwards and sideways at the same time, leaving both my stomach and the heliport behind. I looked down at my feet and saw the ground rapidly disappearing beneath them. The clear bubble window that encased the cockpit enabled a view that left nothing to the imagination.

I'd become very good at hiding my fear of flying, even from myself. So good, in fact, that I can actually appear to be enjoying the experience. This was as a result of often finding myself seated next to children on commercial flights. Not wanting to frighten them, I learned to disguise my terror and put on a brave face for their sakes. Eventually I realised that, to paraphrase Rick's dialogue with Sam in the movie *Casablanca*, if I could do it for them, I could do it for me.

That may be why, a few minutes after becoming airborne over Monaco Bay, the pilot yelled above the engine noise: 'Voulez-vous piloter l'helicoptere?' He was asking me if I would like to fly the aircraft.

Suddenly, I felt like I was six years old again. My Guardian Angel smiled and nodded. This was something I knew I had to do.

In the story of Peter Pan, when grown-up Wendy was talking to her daughter about how time flies, the little girl asked her mother why she herself could no longer fly. Wendy answered, 'When people grow up, they forget the way.'

Some of us are fortunate enough to find it again. And, although I'd grown up, I hadn't forgotten how to fly. Like Peter said, 'You just think lovely wonderful thoughts and they lift you up in the air.'

I listened to the pilot's instructions and, this time, instead of a terrified child's hands desperately gripping the controls in a blind panic, I saw a grown woman's hands confidently take the controls. 'Where did those come from?' I wondered, as we soared above the azure water with the Pink Palace in the distance.

The Beginning